The Winning Edge

THE
WINNING
EDGE

Naval Technology in Action, 1939–1945

Kenneth Poolman

SUTTON PUBLISHING LIMITED

Originally published in 1997 by the Naval Institute Press, 118 Maryland Avenue, Annapolis, MD 21402-5035

Published simultaneously in Great Britain by
Sutton Publishing Limited • Phoenix Mill
Thrupp • Stroud • Gloucestershire • GL5 2BU

British Library Cataloguing-in-Publication Data
A catalogue record of this book is available from the British Library

ISBN 0 7509 1588 9

ALAN SUTTON™ and SUTTON™ are the
trademarks of Sutton Publishing Limited

Printed in the United States of America on acid-free paper

Distance is swept by the smooth
Rotations of power, its staring
Feelers multiplying our eyes for us,
Marking objects' range and bearing.

Linked to them, guns rehearse
Calculated obedience; echoes of light
Trigger the shadowing needle, determine
The arrest of night.

Control is remote; feelings, like hands,
Gloved by space. Responsibility is shared, too.
And destroying the enemy by radar
We never see what we do.

Sub-Lt. Alan Ross, RNVR (Radar)

Contents

Acknowledgments

I wish to thank: the Naval Historical Branch, Ministry of Defense, London; Operational Archives, Naval Historical Branch, United States Navy, and the National Archives, Washington, DC, for generous access over the years to the official records that have been my main sources of information; the Museum of Science and Technology, Chicago; the Public Records Office, London; the Imperial War Museum, London; the Fleet Air Arm Museum, Yeovilton, Somerset, England; and the National Maritime Museum, Greenwich, England.

Of the books listed in the Select Bibliography, *The Battle of the River Plate* (Pope); *Dönitz, The Last Führer* (Padfield); *Midway* (Fuchida and Okumiya); *Rendezvous at Midway* (Frank and Harrison); *Undersea Victory* (Holmes); and *United States Fleet Carriers of World War II* (Humble) were particularly helpful.

Introduction

From the first aggressive move, war is a process of action and reaction, punch and counterpunch, in a contest of strategy, tactics, morale—and weaponry.

When he invaded Poland in September 1939, Adolf Hitler was confident that his *Blitzkrieg* of tanks and aircraft would overcome all resistance in Europe, including that of Britain. That he possessed only a small navy did not deter him as much as it did his naval commander in chief; there would be time to build the planned superfleet. . .

Defeat of the Luftwaffe by the Royal Air Force in the Battle of Britain, however, frustrated the invasion of England, and Hitler was forced to fall back on the submarine, which had almost won the Great War for Germany. Once again it was brought to bear, aided by surface raiders, in a savage campaign to deny Britain vital war materials, fuel, and food.

Under devastating pressure, the Allied navies deployed new weapons like asdic (sonar) and RDF (radar), convoy-protection aircraft carriers, high-frequency direction finding, forward-firing mortars, and rocket projectiles.

In turn, U-boats acquired surface weapons—acoustic torpedoes, Schnorkel tubes to breathe under water, radio-controlled missiles, supersonic undersea detectors. It became a boffins' war. Sailors on both sides were only as good as their weapons, which were tested in many desperate battles, developed and improved in many sleepless back rooms.

In the Pacific, American radar fought the superb Japanese Long Lance torpedoes in bloody night actions; U.S. Navy submarines overcame faulty torpedoes to decimate enemy shipping; and carrier air power, controlled on new high-frequency radio and multichannels, dominated surface actions.

In all theaters, special new amphibious craft put troops ashore, covered by carrier aircraft. Sensitive listening stations relayed enemy messages to cryptographers who broke "unbreakable" codes.

This book is an attempt to describe in lay terms the development of the most important of the weapons that dominated naval warfare from 1939 to 1945, and their employment in action.

The Winning Edge

Secret Fleet

Its young men decimated and its treasury empty, Britain welcomed the Washington Naval Treaty of 1921, which obligated it to scrap 583,000 tons of warships, while the United States had to scrap 846,000 and Japan, 449,000 tons. The agreement limited the size of battleships to 35,000 tons, aircraft carriers to 27,000, and cruisers to 10,000. Britain retained ten battleships and three battlecruisers and reduced the size of two super-battleships under construction.

Germany had surrendered almost its entire High Seas Fleet in 1918 and had been restricted by the Treaty of Versailles to a force of squadron size. None of its new ships were to displace more than 10,000 tons, and submarines, which had almost won the Great War for Germany, had been banned altogether.

Almost immediately, however, Germany began to circumvent the treaty.

A secret U-boat department was created under an unofficial Befehlshaber der U-boote (commander of U-boats). In 1922 three German shipbuilders formed the Ingenieurskantoor voor Scheepsbouw (IvS) in Holland. This company designed three types of new submarines—for Baltic, North Sea, and Atlantic operations. Practical U-boat training began with a 500-ton Finnish boat designed by IvS and built by German technicians, with the trainees disguised as civilian tourists.

Completed in 1933, the year Hitler became chancellor of Germany, ostensibly under the terms of the Versailles Treaty, was the *Deutschland*, the first of three Panzerschiffe (armored ships). The new Kriegsmarine claimed that by using electric welding and diesel propulsion, both new in warship construction, Germany had conformed to the

1

treaty's 10,000-ton limit for cruisers—even with an armament of six of Krupp's new 11-inch guns, eight 5.9-inch guns, and six 4.1-inch high-angle guns. There were also torpedo tubes and two seaplanes.

In practical terms, the new technology had enabled the ship's architects to combine with the greater gun power a high and very economical speed as well as great range—prime assets for a commerce raider. The new main armament would fire a big 670-pound shell. Range finders, in a country renowned for its optics, would be Zeiss's finest.

No ship with all these features on a hull 609 feet long could really keep within 10,000 tons of displacement. The true figure grew to 11,700, and then, on commissioning, topped the 12,000-ton mark. The Kriegsmarine smiled when the naval world called the new vessel, with her 11-inch guns, a pocket battleship. It was a good joke. Two more such vessels, the *Admiral Graf Spee* and *Admiral Scheer,* were laid down.

A Panzerschiff was equipped with the finest of warship wireless communication systems. Of paramount importance were the special radio receivers, which monitored all frequencies and homed in on any message being transmitted. If it was in code, the ship's elite code section, B-Dienst, went to work on it. If they could not decode it, the message was passed on to Seekriegsleitung (Sea Warfare Command) in Berlin. SKL boasted that their special computer could unlock any code in twenty minutes.

"The Panzerschiff," crowed Grand Adm. Erich Raeder, German naval commander in chief, "can out-fight any vessel it cannot out-

The *Admiral Graf Spee*. The seaplane shown is a Heinkel He 60, predecessor of the ship's wartime Arado Ar 196A-1. (Maritime Photo Library)

run." She would certainly be a daunting opponent for any British cruiser she would be likely to meet.

With his plan for world domination, Hitler knew that confrontation with Britain and the United States was eventually inevitable and would require a very powerful fleet, to be constructed over the next ten years. Meanwhile, to appease Britain and buy time, Germany offered to limit its increase in naval construction to 35 percent of Royal Navy tonnage in battleships, carriers, and cruisers. The British government accepted the offer, mainly to avoid a possible overreaction in building if it was rejected, and in 1936 the Anglo-German Naval Treaty was signed.

For Germany this meant five capital ships. Since the three Panzerschiffe were commonly known as pocket battleships, Germany allowed it to be assumed that with the addition of the two new battlecruisers *Scharnhorst* and *Gneisenau*, the quota was complete. Hitler told Admiral Raeder that the ships must be described for the *Jane's Fighting Ships* entry as "improved 10,000-tonners,"[1] not the 25,000-tonners on the drawing board (eventually reaching 32,000 tons). Armed with 11-inch guns initially, they were to be fitted with 15-inch guns when these became available. Secondary armament was composed of 5.9-inch guns with a battery of fourteen 4.1-inch to be controlled by high-angle directors, showing an awareness of the threat of air attack well ahead of other navies.

Raeder requested, and the chancellor agreed, that the eight battleships secretly planned for the eventual struggle against Britain should be given 35-cm (13.65-inch) guns to match the 14-inch type to be introduced by the Royal Navy in the five new battleships of its 1937 Emergency Program. This had been introduced after increasingly aggressive behavior by Germany, and it also included seven cruisers with the new 5.25-inch high-angle main armament; sixteen destroyers; and the new aircraft carrier *Ark Royal*, with plans for the new *Illustrious*-class carriers. In Germany two new 45,000-tonners, the *Bismarck* and *Tirpitz*, were armed with 15-inch guns.

Germany was also allowed by treaty two aircraft carriers and twenty-one cruisers. These would include a new *Hipper* class of five 8-inch cruisers. Nominally of 10,000 tons, when completed they exceeded the limit by some 3,000 tons and incorporated the finest materials and technology, having exceptionally high steam pressure. Sixty-four destroyers completed the shopping list of surface warships. Materials and yard space were ordered for an initial fifteen U-boats; all available German yards would be full for the next few years.

Soundings

During World War I, the capacity had been developed for cross bearings plotted in different receiving ships to locate the position of a surface ship transmitting wireless signals. Allied experiments went on through the war to produce an equivalent that could precisely locate submarines under water.

For almost the whole of the earlier war, the hydrophone, based on an underwater microphone that picked up the noise made by a vessel's machinery, was the most effective apparatus in surface ships hunting submarines and in submarines tracking them. But there were snags. A hydrophone would only work properly if the operating ship made no noise. This meant stopping the ship and all her machinery. And even when a target was picked up, the hydrophone indicated only direction, not range. In turn, the target submarine could render the hunting hydrophone ineffective by shutting down all machinery and adopting "silent routine," ideally on the bottom.

Echo sounding—bouncing a sound impulse off the seabed to calculate depth—had long been in use. A device based on the same principle seemed logical, but a far more sophisticated version would be needed.

In 1917 the Allied Anti-Submarine Detection and Investigation Committee (ASDIC) was formed. Its first effort was a rotating hydrophone that projected from a ship's bottom. British scientists experimented with Maurice Langevin's transmitting oscillator, lowered over a ship's side. It worked on the piezoelectric principle, registering an echo from a submarine's hull and then timing it to calculate its range. The apparatus itself became known as asdic.

Germany had been forbidden by treaty to build submarines, but British asdic experiments continued. In 1921 a set aboard HMS *Antrim* obtained echoes from a shutdown submarine at over 2,000 yards, with the ship making just over 2 knots.

The operational form of the asdic oscillator was a sandwich of steel plates and quartz crystals projecting through the bottom of the ship and rotated in azimuth. To transmit, alternating current was applied to the oscillator, causing it to vibrate and emit a very powerful supersonic note, controlled by the operator to give a short ping that traveled to a target with the speed of sound in water and was reflected back to the oscillator, amplified in the operator's headphones using a valve heterodyne receiver. Echoes returned by the seabed, fish, tide rips, and ships' wakes were sometimes recognizable by quality and size, and a moving submarine by the Doppler effect (causing echoes from a moving target to return with a higher or lower note than the transmitter's, according to whether the target was moving toward or away). But rough weather could quench echoes, and whales could yield Doppler.

A school for operators was set up at Portland, Dorset, England. Asdic test sets were fitted in some patrol vessels, and by 1924 much progress had been made, particularly in the Type 114. This featured a streamlined steel dome around the oscillator, allowing it to be operated effectively at 14 knots. By 1927 seven Royal Navy submarines had asdic; next, heavy cruisers *Cornwall* and *Devonshire* and the sloop *Blackwater*. A 40-percent success rate was claimed, and hydrophones were abandoned in the surface ships of the Royal Navy. In 1938 the new light cruiser *Southampton* was given the new long-range Type 132 set with double oscillators, one for each beam. By 1939 more than a hundred British destroyers had asdic, as did some forty-five sloops and old destroyers for convoy escort, and twenty commandeered trawlers. Meanwhile a big stock of sets accumulated in store, ready for the remaining destroyers if war broke out.

So confident, even smug, was the Admiralty regarding asdic, that the sixty U-boats reported by intelligence to be nearing completion in Germany worried it less than the probability of surface raider action, especially by the pocket battleships. Asdic-fitted destroyers of a fleet screen were now considered in Whitehall to have a 70-percent chance of success against submarines attempting to get through to the big ships, with a 50-percent chance of a kill. Winston Churchill, after being shown the Asdic Training School at Portland, referred to "the system of groping for submarines below the surface . . . which has, as I feel convinced, relieved us of one of our great dangers."[1]

In 1931 the U.S. Navy's Underwater Sound Group had produced the QB echo-ranging set. Their sonar (sound navigation and ranging) sets, with magnetostriction transducers plus a rubber streamlined dome, were effective at 6 knots, compared to 15 knots with British asdic. In September 1939 it was decided to fit sonar in all destroyers, though the fifty old "cans" transferred to the Royal Navy in the autumn of 1940 had none. Simultaneously with the destroyer deal an exchange of information took place, and the U.S. Navy quickly adopted the British streamlined steel dome and chemical range recorder.

The detection of enemy submarines by the Royal Navy was not matched by its means of destroying them. In 1939 the Royal Navy's standard depth charge was the Mark VII, essentially the same as the Type D of the Great War, with a 300-pound high explosive (often TNT) charge. There was no satisfactory airborne equivalent, the old antisubmarine bombs being of little use. Similarly, the standard mine was the contact Type XVI, with a 320-pound or 500-pound charge, but many of those in stock were Great War H11s or Mark XIVs.

With the submarine's own weapons, production in Britain had not kept abreast of development.

In the mid-1920s Britain developed the Brotherhood burner cycle torpedo engine, a four-cylinder motor burning kerosene in air, with the hot gas fed into the cylinders. Fuel was 50 percent alcohol and air to 50 percent oxygen. This engine drove a 21-inch torpedo with a 750-pound explosive charge at 40 knots for 5,500 yards, giving Britain the lead in torpedoes until Japan developed its 24-inch pure oxygen Long Lance missile.

In September 1939 there were about 7,100 torpedoes in Britain, but only 3,000 of these were of types still in production—at a slow rate of 80 per week. The Duplex torpedo, set off by a ship's magnetic field, was tried successfully on the old destroyer *Bruce* in November 1939, and it went into production. Several promising projects, such as a short-range 21-inch torpedo that was expected to reach 60 knots, 90 percent complete at the outbreak of war, were put aside in the belief that the war would be a short one.

Rotations **3** of Power

Radar was born shortly after World War I. In Britain Dr. Robert Watson-Watt designed a simple wireless direction finder to detect the general positions of thunderstorms, and this research produced the first cathode-ray tube, available in 1922. In the United States, echoes from a steamer on the Potomac River were noted during an experiment by the U.S. Naval Aircraft Radio Laboratory, and proposals were put forward for the detection by radio waves of enemy ships and aircraft.

These experiments drew the attention of the German navy's Communications Research Institute, which in 1933 began to experiment with short waves to try to develop a range finder. The result was a continuous-wave set working on 50 centimeters (19.5 inches) that, with 50-watt power, detected a 500-ton ship at just over seven miles. In 1934 the GEMA Company was formed to develop the promising new technology.

Meanwhile, Watson-Watt told Britain's Committee for the Scientific Survey of Air Defense that a passing aircraft must reflect energy from any powerful transmitter. The Air Ministry commissioned him to develop his thesis, loaning him an aircraft to investigate the possibility of an aircraft warning system. On trials the aircraft reflected echoes as it flew near the British Broadcasting Corporation transmitter at Daventry, and money was found for development.

About the same time, the U.S. Naval Aircraft Radio Laboratory began to experiment with a pulse system and picked up an aircraft at a range of 1 mile.

Watson-Watt was having difficulty producing a large-enough echo without using impossibly big antennae. The 1-kilowatt transmitter with pulse width of 200 microseconds was at least one-hundredth of the size required. Then he switched to thermionic silica valves of the type used by the Royal Navy for their highest-powered transmitters, with antennae incorporating two copper lavatory system spheres. He crossed his fingers, pushed the anode voltage up, and, on a 50-meter wavelength (164 feet) got echoes from continental Europe bounced off the ionosphere, and later a clear echo from a flying boat 17 miles offshore. This was increased to 40 miles, then 80 miles.

In 1936 the German set Seetaktische Gerät (tactical sea instrument), working on 80 centimeters (31.2 inches), was sent to sea for trials in the pocket battleship *Graf Spee*, the light cruiser *Konigsberg*, and the torpedo boat *G-10*. The *Spee*'s Seetakt was a gunnery set mounted forward of the main armament director. Seetakt was principally a range finder, but with good directional properties that could give warnings of ships approaching. In its final development it could give a bearing to within 0.2 degrees, and, although its power was only 7 kilowatts, it could pick up a battleship at 11 miles, a destroyer at 8.5 miles, and a motor torpedo boat at 3 miles, though it was unable to register the fall of shot. By the summer of 1939 the Dete-Gerät set was in use in the *Graf Spee*, doubling the range, and there were plans for fitting it in U-boats.

Meanwhile, the British radio direction finding (RDF), as it was somewhat misleadingly called for a long time, was achieving a maximum range of 100 miles. In the United States, a Naval Aircraft Radio Laboratory set, called radar, was effective at 25 miles.

A chain of nineteen RDF stations was built along the whole of the east coast of Britain; these stations would be of invaluable help to Royal Air Force (RAF) fighter air defense. While Watson-Watt's land-based RDF was climbing to success, the Royal Navy, which had contributed vital components and expertise to the Watson-Watt experiment, was using this experience on its own behalf. An air defense RDF for a ship had radically different requirements from the land-based version. If a ship's aerials were to be directional, a shorter wavelength was necessary; also, they had to be protected from the shocks and stresses of gunfire.

The Royal Navy Signal School produced a set working on 1.5 meters (4.92 feet), which was sent to sea in the minesweeper HMS *Saltburn* and was a failure, as it was impossible to get enough power on that short wavelength. This was increased to 7 meters (22.96 feet), which was as far as it could be stretched, as beyond that the aerial would have been too big. It was tested aboard ship in March 1937 and picked up ships and aircraft at a reasonable range, using separate transmitter and receiver aerials, both turned manually. The display screen was the A-scope, a cathode-ray tube with the horizontal trace graded for range,

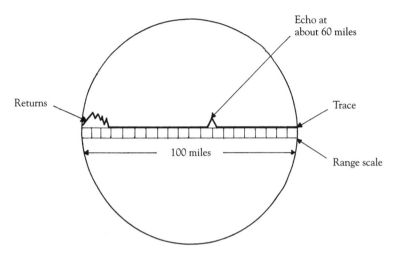

A-scope RDF display. (J. Poolman)

left to right, the echoes appearing as vertical kinks in the green line of the trace so familiar to World War II radar operators. Range given was fairly accurate. Bearing, which was read off a separate aerial direction indicator, was less so, and at first there was no indication of height.

This Type 79 RDF was fitted in the battleship HMS *Rodney* in August 1938 and in the new *Southampton*-class light cruiser *Sheffield* that November. The latter's operators were soon picking up aircraft flying at a height of 10,000 feet at a range of 50 miles. The more powerful Type 79Z, with a 70-kilowatt transmitter, which could pick up aircraft flying at 20,000 feet from 90 miles, was fitted to the old light cruiser *Curlew,* under conversion to an anti-aircraft cruiser, in August 1939. The 79Z then went into production, with an initial order for forty sets.

In 1937 the U.S. Navy sent an experimental electronic-ranging set to sea in the destroyer *Leary* with the antenna secured to a 5-inch gun mounting. Development then gained momentum, and early in 1938 a set of 6 kilowatts, working on a wavelength of 1.5 meters (4.92 feet) detected an aircraft at 100 miles.

In December 1938 an American XAF radar set was fitted in the battleship USS *New York.* This too worked on a frequency of 1.5 meters and had a 17-foot-square rotating "mattress" antenna. On exercises in the Caribbean the XAF was a resounding success in detecting aircraft and ships, as well as in navigating and spotting the fall of shot for the big ships. More XAF sets, now called the CXAM, were ordered.

In September 1936 the commander in chief, RAF Coastal Command, had asked the boffins for airborne RDF to hunt ships. Slow but steady progress was made. Valves were changed to step up power; new cathode-ray tubes, usually from American Western Electric or

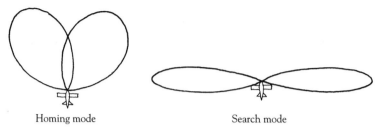

Homing mode   Search mode

Coastal Command A1 Air Interception Type ASV RDF, 1938. (J. Poolman)

RCA, were tried. The Cork lightship, off the coast of County Cork, Southeastern Ireland, a very small target at a range of just over 4 miles, was picked up. From this a set for coastal defense was developed that could pick up a 2,000-ton coaster at 17,000 yards, and even shell splashes. It could be used to direct coastal guns, giving an accurate range and bearing using beam switching.

For RAF Coastal Command airborne RDF, two modes of operation were developed: the homing mode, with forward aim and echoes to left or right obtained by means of overlapping beams; and the search mode, consisting of a narrow beam rotating sideways. With its longer beams, the latter was better in that a bigger area could be covered by its sweep. In practice an aircraft would use the search mode, then turn 90 degrees and use the homer.

A year after development had begun, a 1.5-meter (4.92 feet) set using only 50 watts was produced, and early in 1938 was flying in a twin-engine Coastal Command Avro Anson in exercises over the North Sea. Trials were also carried out using the Butter Boat, the vessel bringing farm produce from Esbjerg, Denmark, which followed a regular twenty-four-hour schedule, arriving at Harwich late in the afternoon and leaving again at nightfall. The RDF beam always picked it up in mid-afternoon and sometimes reached far into the Heligoland Bight to meet it.

The Anson used HMS *Courageous* as a target on 9–10 May 1938 as the carrier steamed in the central English Channel. The aircraft flew from west to east past the ship and produced several echoes of the carrier at a range of 5 miles, and behind her in the distance a clear map of the Isle of Wight, the Solent, and the surrounding coastline. This was the first-ever sideways-looking radar picture. From these trials was developed the air-to-surface vessel (ASV) Mark I, which radiated a beam from ahead to twenty degrees either side of the aircraft, could pick up a small ship at 4 miles and a large one at 20 miles; the coastline at 30 miles.

Covered Wagons

The aircraft carrier was not a brand-new weapon, but it had reached a maturing form, and as such had never been tested in war. Six of the Royal Navy's seven carriers were aging vessels, with their origins in the dawn of naval aviation during the Great War, but their pedigree was sound and their collective experience in trials and exercises significant. The Royal Naval Air Service had had almost five years' experience of war, then a final seven months as a branch of the new Royal Air Force.

At first, ignoring the pioneer takeoff from and landing aboard U.S. Navy warships in 1910–11 by Eugene Ely and similar flights by the Royal Navy's Lt. Charles Samson in 1911–12, only seaplanes were used. On 12 August 1915 the converted mail steamer *Ben-my-Chree* sent off a Short 184 seaplane in the Aegean Sea, which hit a moored 5,000-ton Turkish ship in the Sea of Marmora with a 14-inch torpedo, a first attack of its kind.[1] The *Ben-my-Chree*'s seaplanes also pioneered ground support for troops in Asia Minor. Another Short reconnoitered for the battle fleet at Jutland.

On 3 November 1915 a Bristol Scout made the first shipborne ascent by a wheeled fighter on war service, from the deck above the forward hangar of the packet boat *Vindex*. In 1916 the old Cunard liner *Campania* was fitted with a 200-foot flying-off deck, to operate ten seaplanes on disposable trolleys. An improvement on her was HMS *Furious*, built, with her sisters *Courageous* and *Glorious*, as a light battlecruiser with two 17-inch guns for an aborted operation in the Baltic. The *Furious* was refitted with two 18-inch guns, then the forward gun was replaced by a flying deck. On it a Sopwith Pup fighter made the first landing of an aircraft aboard a ship under way.

11

The problem of arresting an aircraft on this sort of short runway had been surmounted by Eugene Ely when he landed on an upward-sloping platform aboard the USS *Pennsylvania* and was restrained by the twelfth of twenty-two parallel transverse wires, their ends weighted with sandbags to avoid too violent a shock. On the *Furious*, the Pup was halted by men grabbing rope toggles on the undersurfaces of the plane. The *Furious* was subsequently fitted with a hangar aft, surmounted by a flying-on deck. Landing aircraft were fitted with skids incorporating hooks designed to snag fore-and-aft wires on the deck, with a rope-net barrier abaft the funnel for planes missing them. It was a dangerous-enough maneuver, and when the *Furious* was under way, heavy turbulence was set up aft by the bridge structure and huge funnel. Nine early approaches ended in crashes. After this experience the new *Argus,* converted from the hull of a 15,775-ton liner, was given the first unbroken flight deck, with funnel ducts discharging astern.

On 19 July 1918 seven navalized Sopwith Camel fighter-bombers armed with 50-pound bombs left the *Furious* to attack the Zeppelin hangars at Tondern. They destroyed *L-54* and *L-60*.

On Armistice Day 1918 all construction decelerated. The makeshift seaplanes were sold, work slowed to idling on the 22,600-ton carrier *Eagle,* converted from a battleship, and on the 10,950-ton custom-built carrier *Hermes.* The *Furious* joined the reserve fleet. Japan laid down its first carrier, the small, 7,470-ton *Hosho.* In 1922 the U.S. Navy commissioned a converted 5,500-ton collier as the carrier *Langley,* the "Covered Wagon," a nickname also attached, coincidentally, to the British *Furious.*

In that year the Washington Naval Treaty limited carrier tonnage to a total of 135,000, sweetened with an option, partly to aid dockyard employment in Britain and the United States, for the three major naval powers to convert into carriers two of the super-battlecruisers each was building. Japan and the United States, with only one small carrier apiece, took up the option. In Britain four intended battlecruisers were scrapped, and the *Furious*'s two sister light battlecruisers *Courageous* and *Glorious* were selected for conversion.

In 1925 the *Furious* was taken out of reserve for refit. Separate flying decks, bridge, mast, and funnel, were all removed, and one continuous, high, flush flight deck running three-quarters of the ship's length was fitted. Smoke was exhausted through the leeward of two sets of vents fitted to port and starboard under the flight deck. A new central bridge could be raised to flight-deck level on an elevator. Six fighters were stowed behind doors in the forward end of the upper hangar. In an emergency they were revved up against a restraining wire, released, and flown off down a sloping 60-foot runway.

The possible results of air attack on warships were hard to antici-pate. The Great War had ended before aircraft had had any really deci-sive effect on the conflict at sea. The success of airborne torpedoes in the Dardanelles had been achieved against defenseless moored ships. In 1921, led by air-power zealot Brig. Gen. William "Billy" Mitchell, American army Martin bombers scored successes against warship tar-gets.[2] On 13 July they sank the old destroyer *Krupp,* on 21 July the old German battleship *Ostfriesland,* and on 26 September the old American battleship *Alabama.*

In 1923 Seversky and Sperry developed their bombsight, and on 31 August army Martins used it to hit the battleship USS *New Jersey* from 10,000 feet and to sink the battleship *Virginia* in twenty-six minutes. These operations and attacks by the British Fleet Air Arm on the demilitarized dreadnought *Centurion* in the 1920s and 1930s, though successful as far as they went, could not reproduce action conditions. They did not face the determined opposition of a ship's antiaircraft guns and of carrier-based fighters. Neither did the 1930s British fleet exercises, in which a combined striking force of aircraft from the carri-ers *Furious, Courageous,* and *Glorious* scored twenty-one torpedo hits out of a possible thirty-two; nor did the mock squadron attack on four *Southampton*-class cruisers, in which half the "mouldies" found their target. Similarly, during exercises in the Mediterranean, the *Glorious*'s strike force of fourteen torpedo/spotter/reconnaissance (TSR) aircraft scored nine hits; and in another exercise, an aircraft from the *Coura-geous* flying in a gale off the Scottish coast hit a 5-foot-by-5-foot wooden target from 6,000 feet.

The value of aircraft for reconnaissance and spotting for surface gunfire had been clearly demonstrated. However, their power to sink or cripple warships had not been. "Except in the Japanese Navy," states British historian Captain John Creswell, "it was assumed that to try to build and maintain carriers and their aircraft in sufficient num-bers to dominate a fleet composed mainly of battleships, even suppos-ing that tactical experience showed such dominance to be possible, would be an uneconomical expenditure of effort.[3]

However, advances continued to be made in Britain, in the United States, and Japan in flight-deck operations, torpedo and dive-bombing, and the use of fighters in attack and defense. Aboard HMS *Glorious* in the Mediterranean, the tough and aggressive Capt. Lumley St. George Lyster, himself a gunner by training, continued to use his biplane Fairey Swordfish TSRs to perfect torpedo attack.

The *Furious, Courageous,* and *Glorious,* conversions from failed Great War monitor-cruisers, suffered from having no compensating weight for the huge 17-inch and 18-inch guns they had originally been designed to carry. At speed the whole after part of the ships whipped or waggled so much that it was impossible to stand upright on the quarterdeck. Aircraft landing on the *Courageous* or *Glorious* had to cope with disturbance set up by their large bridge and funnel island super-structures.

The British Admiralty, after experience with the small *Hermes,* thought that a bigger ship would make a steadier operating platform. The terms of the Washington Treaty left them 20,000 tons. They decided to use this on one new carrier.

They asked for a flight deck of 900 feet. Within the tonnage limita-tions, the constructors could offer 800 feet with an overhang on an unarmored hull made light by using the new technique of welding. The ship would have a capacity for seventy-two aircraft in two super-imposed hangars, and a speed of 30 knots. On 13 April 1937 the *Ark Royal* was launched. Some of her officers considered her construction less than solid, especially her welded plating, and potentially vulnera-ble to punishment. This was the view of her engineer officer, Comdr. Anthony Oliver. He considered her specially designed, narrow bridge island did not greatly affect air over the flight deck, but the funnel gases at first caused bad disturbance. An extra eight feet added to the funnel seemed to solve the problem. The *Ark* was stable and handled well, with a short angle of heel when she turned, so her planes were secure on deck.[4]

On 31 December 1936 the Washington Naval Treaty had formally expired. A fortnight after the launch of the *Ark Royal,* Britain laid down the first of the *Illustrious*-class carriers.

These ships were innovative. Whereas in the new carriers planned by other navies the armored "strength deck" was, conventionally, the floor of the hangar, in the *Illustrious* it was the hangar roof, the whole hangar forming a solid box with a 3-inch armored lid and sides of 4.5-inch specially treated concreted armor plate. This steel-clad closed hangar was intended to stop 500-pound bombs. But there was a penalty: the structure did not permit two hangars, as in the *Ark Royal,* and allowed only half the number of planes.

Wolf at the Door

The Kriegsmarine building program ground slowly on, years behind schedule thanks to failing steel quotas, many technical difficulties, and lack of funding. Hitler promised to improve the situation, and his objectives for an all-powerful navy increased. Admiral Raeder became fearful that war would begin before this could be achieved.

His fear deepened when Hitler seized Austria in March 1938, and again when a move on Czechoslovakia became imminent. But in September the British, French, and Italian prime ministers, Neville Chamberlain, Édouard Daladier, and Benito Mussolini, met with Hitler in Munich, Germany, and agreed to Hitler's demands that Czechoslovakia's Sudetenland, with its large German population, be ceded to Germany. Polish and Hungarian territorial demands on Czechoslovakia were also met. Britain, France, Italy, and Germany would thereafter support Czechoslovakia against further aggression. On the steps of the plane returning him from Munich, Chamberlain informed the crowd that this agreement meant "peace for our time."

In the Kriegsmarine the mood swung to the temporarily euphoric. The Führer had done it again, buying time for the navy of Armageddon. In January 1939 Raeder placed his Z-Plan on the agenda. This called for 13 even bigger battleships, 33 cruisers, 4 aircraft carriers, a fleet of destroyers, and 250 U-boats, all to be completed by 1947. The extent of this grand delusion can be gauged by the statistic that such a fleet would have absorbed more than Germany's total oil consumption for 1938.

On 22 July Raeder told assembled officers of Führer der U-boote (FdU) Karl Dönitz's two flotillas at Kiel that the chancellor had assured him there would be no war with England "in the near future."[1] But on

12 August Hitler signed a non-aggression pact with Russia, hitherto his hated Bolshevik enemy and the most likely target—the reason for the presence of 14 U-boats in the Baltic. Germany would now be free to turn its full attention to Britain and France.

On 24 August, acting on orders from Berlin, Dönitz sent his 15 operational oceangoing Type VII boats on what he himself considered an unnecessarily roundabout and cautious route around the Faeroe Islands into the Atlantic, with 3 more boats preparing to follow. A flotilla of the smaller 250-ton "canoes" was already in the North Sea. With the 14 Baltic boats, these comprised almost the whole U-boat force of 56, very far short of Raeder's dream of 250. And there were no reserves. Almost simultaneously with the dispatch of the Faeroes submarines, the Panzerschiffe *Deutschland* and *Graf Spee* sailed, the former for the North, the latter for the South Atlantic.

On 1 September Germany invaded Poland. At 0900 on the third, it was given two hours to call off the attack. At 1115 Chamberlain informed the British people that they were again at war with Germany. The Admiralty signaled by radio: "Total Germany."

The Home Fleet immediately instituted blockade. Coastal Command aircraft began their search of the sea for enemy shipping, and submarines took up their stations along those stretches of the patrol lines that were beyond the range of the Ansons. The cruisers *Southampton* and *Glasgow* and eight destroyers from the river Humber cruised off the Norwegian coast.

RAF Bomber Command, not yet permitted to bomb targets ashore, did, on only the second day of the war, try to assist in keeping German warships off the trade routes. A force of fourteen Vickers Wellington medium bombers and fifteen Bristol Blenheim light bombers attacked warships in Wilhelmshaven Roads and at the entrance to the Kiel Canal. But the Heligoland Bight was covered by a network of 2.4-meter (7.9 feet) radar stations with a range of 50 miles. The bombers were easily detected as they approached their targets, and were met by heavy antiaircraft fire, seven machines being lost. The *Admiral Scheer* was hit by four bombs, but none of them exploded.

Admiral Sir Charles Forbes, with the main body of the home fleet, patrolled the North Atlantic looking in particular for the liner *Bremen,* winner of the Blue Riband award for the fastest crossing of the Atlantic, on passage home from New York. They were too late. A signal that the German fleet was at sea sent them steaming back east at flank speed, but it was a false alarm. They patrolled the Norwegian coast and Icelandic waters, but by 12 September they were back in Scapa Flow, empty-handed.

Convoy was adopted in all waters in which submarine attacks could be expected. Ships sailing on their own were guided along tracks outside the regular shipping lanes. Fifty British cargo liners, previously selected, were commandeered as armed merchant cruisers to assist the seventy-six regular cruisers in trade protection.[2]

The densest shipping area was at the mouth of the English Channel and south and southwest of Ireland. It was here that the comparatively few U-boats worked in the early months of the war, though it was a long way from German ports. The boats were forced to take the long northern passage, the Channel being impassible for them. In October, when trying to take the shortcut, three U-boats were sunk by the minefield laid across the Straits of Dover.

The Führer der U-boote was feeling his way. In September and October 1939, with the convoy system getting into its stride, Allied losses were at the rate of about 150,000 tons a month, and for the next five months, until the war began in earnest with the invasion of Norway, they fell to 85,000 tons.

The lack of antisubmarine aircraft was as serious as the shortage of surface escorts. Coastal Command had few available and their crews had had little training, though the sheer presence of *any* aircraft could make a U-boat dive and thus limit its speed for overtaking a convoy. To bridge the gap, the aircraft carriers were used.

The *Ark Royal* was thus engaged on 14 September, 150 miles west of the Hebrides, when the *U-39* attacked with torpedoes. The carrier escaped, thanks to a vigilant lookout. The destroyer *Faulkner* got a ping on her asdic and sank the U-boat with depth charges. Three days later, however, the *Courageous* was torpedoed and sunk.

While the *Ark* was dueling with the *U-39*, 200 miles away to the southwest three of her Skuas dived on another U-boat firing on a merchantman. Two of them went so low that their bombs shattered their after fuselages, killing the air gunners.

The result of these losses was to throw the carrier back on the negative policy with which she was being operated, with her aircraft lying in the hangars drained of fuel for fear of fire, and the ship limping along behind the *Nelson* and *Rodney* at 18 knots.

On 25 September a signal came in reporting the submarine *Spearfish* damaged in the Skagerrak and unable to dive. Admiral Forbes immediately sent the 2d Cruiser Squadron to her rescue. The battlecruisers and the 18th Cruiser Squadron were ordered to act as a covering force, with the battleships as deeper support.

It was a disposition of force similar to the arrangement that had brought on Jutland. Perhaps the Germans would fall into the trap again.

But the Nazis, short on ships, were long on air power. A flight of Dornier Do 18D flying boats from one of the four Staffeln (squadrons) of the Kustenflieger (coastal groups) took off on a search.

Apparently as ignorant of the value of RDF as of the power of aircraft, and with the fear, groundless at this stage of the war, that his transmissions could be detected by the enemy, Admiral Forbes was reluctant to use the *Rodney*'s and *Sheffield*'s pioneer Type 79 RDF sets. When they were eventually switched on, their inexperienced operators picked up the hostiles. The Dorniers sighted the ships, flew low to try to avoid the radar beams, and struggled to maintain contact in the prevailing misty, cloudy weather.

Because of his tardiness in operating his RDF, the commander in chief had missed the opportunity of scrambling his aircraft to intercept the enemy, though he did not in fact believe that they could operate in the bad weather. For some time the Dorniers were allowed to circle the fleet unopposed, flitting in and out of the ground wave on the RDF screens like poltergeists. Finally, a flight of Skuas was scrambled from the *Ark* to intercept.

The Blackburn Skua fighter and dive-bomber had been heralded as the Fleet Air Arm's breakthrough into modern aircraft technology. It was indeed the Navy's first combat monoplane, first all-metal aircraft, with the new dive brakes and a powerful armament for the time of four Browning machine guns in the wings and one Lewis in the rear cockpit. It certainly looked the part, with its big radial engine and "glasshouse." But it was underpowered and slow (maximum speed 225 MPH), and in a design revision the engine had been moved too far forward, upsetting its balance. After his first flight in Number L2873, Lt. B. S. McEwan, who had been used to the much-lighter Hawker Nimrod biplane fighters, said, "She's a bit of an old tank!"[3]

The Skuas circled the ships in touch with the *Ark Royal,* which had neither RDF nor aircraft voice communication, only via the lead Skua's clumsy Morse key. Someone sighted a dark, mottled shape flying low on the water. They dived toward it. It was a Dornier, cleverly camouflaged in blue, green, and gray.

They attacked one after the other, each pilot raking the flying boat with his four Brownings, then the rear crewman with his Lewis, the Dornier firing back all the time. After each Skua had made two attacks, they saw the Dornier pancake, propellers of the distinctive tandem Junkers Jumo 5 diesels still turning. A final burst from L2873's Lewis stopped them. The "old tank" had bagged the first enemy aircraft of the war to be shot down by any of the Allied forces.

The jubilant pilots were at lunch in the wardroom when the Luftwaffe arrived to follow up the Dorniers' sighting reports. Out of the low cloud flew Gefreiter (lance corporal) Karl Francke's Junkers Ju 88A-I, one of a four-aircraft detachment from I Gruppe of Kampfgeschwader 30, operating from the airfield at Westerland on the island of Sylt, the northernmost of the German North Frisian Islands, off the coast of Schleswig-Holstein. This was at the time the nearest Luftwaffe base for operations against Allied shipping in the North Sea, and it put the 350 miles to the Firth of Forth and the 400 miles to Scapa Flow well within range (620–1,055 miles) of the 88s.

Capt. Arthur Power gave a sharp helm order. Francke's aircraft was carrying one of its optional mixes of two 1,000-pound bombs and ten 110-pounders in its after bay. One 1,000-pounder practically shaved the *Ark*'s thin hull. In a wall of white water her whole side bulged in and out again. She rolled and shuddered, her bows reeled, then she settled and listed to starboard, then came upright and resumed course. Later in the day German aircraft mistook the British 2d Cruiser Squadron for the whole fleet, failed to find the *Ark Royal*, and reported her sunk. Throughout the following weeks, Goebbels's propaganda ministry repeatedly asked, "Where is the *Ark Royal*?" The BBC as often denied the alleged sinking. Francke was awarded the Iron Cross.

With only ten U-boats at a time at sea in the densest-packed areas, and with the notable success of asdic, the Royal Navy at first held its own. Sixteen U-boats trying to attack convoys were sunk in the first six months of the war.

Few as they were in the opening months, U-boats were also used to sow the new magnetic mines, with which it was hoped to block the approaches to British ports. These mines, used first by the British off the Belgian coast in 1918, were activated by a ship's magnetic field. The British Admiralty and Air Ministry had had the same idea as the Germans, who had beaten them to it. Magnetic mining by destroyers and submarines in the British coastal routes had been going on through the autumn, and several ships had been sunk with no indication of the cause.

In November these operations were intensified and extended to the narrow channels of the Thames estuary. Aircraft joined in the attack, dropping the first parachute magnetic mines on 21 November and continuing to lay them nightly, out of range of fighters. Soon the Downs and Southend Roads were choked with paralyzed shipping. The Port of London was almost at a standstill, with the west-coast ports next on the Luftwaffe's list. HMS *Nelson*, the light cruiser *Belfast*, and the cruiser and minelayer *Adventure* were all seriously damaged. The destroyers *Blanche, Gypsy,* and *Grenville* were sunk, as were 129 merchantmen totaling 430,054 tons. The outlook was bleak.

The Royal Navy had a large force of conventional minesweepers, but they were only equipped to sweep moored mines. What was needed was a device that would explode a magnetic mine without damaging the sweeper—and this could not be tackled until it was known which of several possible types of firing gear the German mine used. This threatened to be a long and painful process of trial and error. A magnetic sweep was successfully tested against a British magnetic mine but would not work against the German type.

Then the British got lucky. An airborne magnetic mine was discovered on Shoeburyness Sands, and Lt. Comdr. John Ouvry and his staff of the navy mine and torpedo depot HMS *Vernon* bravely removed the firing mechanism. They quickly discovered that it was fired by a "dip needle" when there was a vertical change of magnetism, which could be activated by ships built in the northern hemisphere. This was very different from the British equivalent, which featured a long coil that fired the mine when there was a certain rate of change of the magnetism in the horizontal plane. Countermeasures could now be undertaken.

Mines were rendered harmless to ships by degaussing. A coil carrying a small electric current was wound around the ship, neutralizing her vertical magnetism, and ships were wiped, as a piece of iron can be magnetized or demagnetized by stroking it with a permanent magnet. For the destruction of the mines, an electric coil on a skid was towed by a drifter, with the magnetic field of the skid exploding any mine it passed over. The skid was destroyed each time, which meant a delay in replacing it, but this invention did succeed in clearing enough channels for shipping to flow again. Other less-reliable forms of sweep were a low-flying aircraft carrying a big coil, and a small ship carrying a huge electromagnet in its bows to explode a mine ahead of her.

The best method was the LL sweep, an electric cable streamed astern of the minesweeper and fed with a heavy electric current to explode a mine well clear of the ship. The LL went into action in March 1940, towed by trawlers. It was immediately successful, though the sweeper had to pass over the mine first and had to be very thoroughly degaussed. The Germans continued to lay the mines until almost the end of the war, with some successes. They introduced an acoustic firing device as well but did not introduce their masterpiece, the "oyster" mine, actuated by a ship's pressure wave and thus very difficult to sweep, until it was too late to affect the course of the war.

Panzer Ship

Unlike the magnetic mine, the raiding cruiser posed a familiar threat to the Admiralty. During World War I the British had had considerable experience fighting both the surface raider and the U-boat. The light cruiser *Emden* had been the most effective raider, tying down many British, French, and Japanese warships in the course of successful attacks on trade in the Indian Ocean, where she sank sixteen British steamers and three Allied warships.

On 21 August 1939 the *Admiral Graf Spee* left Wilhelmshaven. On the twenty-fourth, the day her consort *Deutschland* left port for her station in the North Atlantic, the *Spee* was steaming between Iceland and the Faeroes, apparently undetected thus far, outward bound for the South Atlantic. The *Spee*'s ultrasensitive wireless monitors, her Dete-Gerät radar's moving finger, and the revolving arms of her powerful range finders were on constant watch, though the Dete-Gerät was showing signs of the trouble that would plague it for the whole voyage. Vibration from the ship's diesels were causing frequent breaks in its power-cable connections.

Crossing sea-lanes by night with the ship darkened, Kapitän zur See Hans Langsdorff refueled the *Spee* from her supply tanker *Altmark*. Waiting west of Ascension Island for the signal to commence attacks on Allied shipping, Langsdorff launched his Arado seaplane.[1] Its crew sighted smoke and alerted the ship, but the *Spee*'s operator watched the stranger fade off his radar screen. HMS *Cumberland* had missed by 30 miles the raider she would soon be hunting.[2]

At last, on 26 September, the Seekriegsleitung (sea warfare command), or SKL, in Berlin, broadcast: "Commence active participation in the trade war." To sow confusion, the ship's name on the stern was painted out and the name *Admiral Scheer* substituted. The crew were issued with new cap bands bearing the same name.

The British steamer *Clement*, with a cargo of kerosene, was the *Spee's* first victim, sunk on 30 September off Pernambuco but able to transmit her position first, confirming the Admiralty's suspicion that there was a pocket battleship loose in the Atlantic. Eight hunting groups of ships were formed to track it down, including the *Ark Royal* and *Renown* as Force K, and as Force G, the heavy cruisers *Exeter* and *Cumberland* and the light cruisers *Ajax* and *Achilles*, already in the South Atlantic, based in Port Stanley in the Falklands.

The *Spee* next bagged SS *Newton Beach* and its cargo of maize, but she also managed to scramble off an attack-by-surface-raider distress signal (RRR), with the position. Langsdorff then switched east to the Freetown–Cape Town route, and on 7 October stopped the SS *Ashlea*, removing two tons of cargo of sugar before sinking her. The bigger, 8,196-ton *Huntsman*, captured on the tenth, was not sunk but retained as a prison ship, and a German operator laid a false trail by transmitting an attack-by-U-boat signal (SSS) from its wireless office.

Next the *Spee's* eavesdropping monitors picked up an enemy signal, broken down by the ship's special B-Dienst decoding section, that HMS *Achilles* was in Rio. The *Spee*, with Dete-Gerät out of action again, steamed west, back to the Pernambuco area, where on 23 October the Arado found her the SS *Trevanion*, carrying 8,000 tons of chemical concentrates.

The British Admiralty was baffled. They had disposed their forces on the evidence of one German raider at large in the Atlantic, but on the day of the *Newton Beach* sinking the SS *Stonegate* was sunk by a pocket battleship 3,000 miles away to the north. On 21 October the crew of the Norwegian steamer *Lorentz W. Hansen* were landed at Kirkwall, Orkney, and reported their ship sunk by a pocket battleship on the fourteenth. From their description she appeared, correctly, to have been the *Deutschland*. Now the two raiders had vanished again.

Then, on 14 November the crew of the 706-ton tanker *Africa Shell* landed on the Natal coast of West Africa to report their ship sunk nearby by the *Admiral Scheer*, though the British naval attaché in Buenos Aires insisted that she was the *Graf Spee*. All was confusion. Were there now three pocket battleships at large on the sea-lanes?

Having created alarm in the Indian Ocean and caused the diversion of more forces there, Langsdorff turned back for the South Atlantic. There he refueled from the *Altmark*, having eluded the *Ark Royal's* Swordfish in bad weather, and set his crew to rig a dummy funnel and turret forward to make the *Graf Spee* look like the *Renown*. On 2 December the Dete-Gerät ranged on the 10,086-ton *Doric Star*, bound for the United Kingdom with meat and dairy produce from New

Zealand. She got off an RRR and position before she was sunk. Heading for the River Plate traffic lanes, the *Spee* sank the refrigerated steamer *Tairoa* on 3 December and added the wheat carrier *Streonshalh* to her bag on the seventh, before turning southwest for the Plate and its rich meat and grain traffic. SKL reported HMS *Achilles* in Montevideo but gave Langsdorff two tempting targets, the liners *Highland Monarch* and *Andalusia Star.*

Just before dawn on 13 December, the Panzerschiff was cruising off the Uruguayan coast. Her staunch Arado had picked this time to break down with a cracked cylinder block, and the *Spee* had not sighted either of the liners.

From the positions given in RRRs from the *Doric Star, Tairoa,* and *Streonshalh,* Commodore Henry Harwood at Port Stanley had concluded that the raider was heading for the Plate's fertile pickings, which she had not tapped before, and estimated that she would reach there by 13 December. Unless, of course, her devious captain wanted to give that impression, with something quite different in mind. Reluctantly leaving the *Cumberland* behind for an urgent self-refit, Harwood took his flagship *Ajax* to join the *Achilles* and *Exeter.* Early in the morning of the thirteenth, he was cruising off the Plate.

At 0552 a lookout in the *Graf Spee* sighted two masts. The Dete-Gerät, for once on song, and the range finder gave the range as 17 miles. At 0600 the cruiser *Exeter* was identified, with two smaller ships to starboard of her. Langsdorff thought they were destroyers, the three probably an escort group for a convoy. He would dispose of the 8-inch cruiser and her pack, then fall on the convoy. . .

Five minutes later an officer said to him, "They're not destroyers, sir, they're British *Leander*-class light cruisers."[3]

Langsdorff computed the odds. A Panzerschiff, they had always been told, could outfight any ship she could not outrun. His tired diesels could give him no better than 26 knots, and the British ships were good for 30. He could not outrun them. But with his 11-inch rifles he could outfight them. Knock out the *Exeter,* their heavyweight, and the 6-inch light cruisers could not hurt him inside the *Spee's* thick armor, he reasoned. And if they came within his range, he would disable or sink them, too.

At 0610 the *Ajax,* then the *Achilles,* then the *Exeter,* sighted smoke on the horizon. The latter signaled to the *Ajax*: "I think it is a pocket battleship."[4] Harwood knew his part in the drama about to unfold. His squadron was well rehearsed. If the enemy had the weight, he had the numbers and the speed. He had guessed right. The raider was here, in sight. His job was to hang on to her, come what might, hoping for a lucky salvo, a well-layed torpedo—until the *Renown* came up with her 15-inch, to repeat the victory in these very waters in 1914, when Vice

Adm. Frederick Sturdee's battlecruisers had put down Vice Adm. Graf von Spee's ships.

Going to full speed, the British ships hoisted their battle ensigns on mastheads, yardarms and gaffs. Eleven miles away the *Graf Spee* was doing the same. Both senior officers wirelessed their enemy-sighting reports. Then, as prearranged, the *Exeter* turned to port and steered for the enemy at full speed as the light cruisers continued in loose formation together.

At 0617 the *Graf Spee* opened fire on the *Exeter*, using base-fused shells at first for ease of spotting, later switching to impact shells for hard hitting. A near miss flung steel splinters over the *Exeter*'s decks and through the thin, unarmored sides, killing and maiming, cutting leads and gun-ready lamp circuits, starting fires. The third salvo hit the forecastle, abaft B turret. The *Exeter* opened fire, range 18,700 yards, and near-missed. The *Spee* turned one turret on the *Ajax*. At the wrong end of its salvo, Harwood was nevertheless pleased: he was splitting the enemy's fire. The *Spee* turned parallel to the *Ajax* and *Achilles*, which turned toward it. The *Achilles* opened fire, the *Ajax* followed, range just over 19,000 yards. A salvo from the *Spee* straddled the *Ajax*, which jinked to starboard, then back. Langsdorff, fearing torpedo attack, turned north and fired on the *Achilles*, then switched back to the *Exeter*. With his eighth salvo he hit the cruiser's B turret, killing its crew and nearly everyone on the bridge and wrecking the wheelhouse. The *Exeter* turned away, making smoke to cover herself. Some twenty minutes had passed since the *Spee* had commenced firing.

Now the Panzerschiff swung to port, making smoke with the chlorosulphuric apparatus aft, smoke floats and funnel. The *Ajax* closed the range again and launched her Seafox seaplane, which had to brave the blast from X and Y turrets. The *Ajax* and *Achilles* were now operating the continuous-firing tactic. After thirteen broadsides, another salvo from the *Spee* fell alongside the *Achilles*. Heavy splinters sliced through the 1-inch-thick armor of the director control tower and the bridge, causing heavy casualties and cutting wireless commu-

Table 1

Comparative Firepower

Ship	Caliber of gun	Weight of shell	Muzzle velocity	Range
Graf Spee	11 in.	661 lb.	2,896 ft./sec.	39,904 yds.
Exeter	8 in.	256 lb.	2,805 ft./sec.	32,631 yds.
Ajax and *Achilles*	6 in.	112 lb.	2,758 ft./sec.	25,480 yds.

Source: Ministry of Defence

nication with the *Ajax*. The *Achilles*'s after control took over and she fired twelve ragged salvoes.

But the *Exeter* was hitting back. Two salvos hit the *Spee* near her funnel, and the German turned northwest at high speed. Two more hits forward on the *Exeter* tore a jagged hole just above the waterline and another in the forecastle, scattering splinters. The bow began to flood, but the *Exeter* fired her starboard torpedo tubes. The *Spee* swung to port parallel to the torpedoes' course, and combed their tracks. The *Exeter* swung to starboard to unmask her port torpedo tubes and fired three tin fish. Then two more 11-inch shells hit her, knocking out the right gun of A turret and putting the turret out of action. Fires raged internally. Another shell tore a huge hole above the 4-inch magazine and cut many electrical leads. The *Exeter* was punch-drunk now, after forty minutes' heavy punishment, with a 10-degree list and her bows down three feet and all wireless telegraphy communications destroyed, though Y turret was still firing.

To ease the *Exeter*'s torment, the *Ajax* and *Achilles* brought all guns to bear upon the enemy, with the desired effect: the *Spee* turned on them. The *Ajax* turned to starboard to fire her port torpedo tubes, and from 9,000 yards got off four "mouldies," but they all broke surface and the *Spee* combed them.

At 0729 the *Exeter*'s remaining Y turret ceased fire, all electrical power lost as water gushed through splinter holes in her side.

The battle was now between the *Spee* and the 6-inch lightweights, at a range of only 4 miles. An 11-inch salvo hit the *Ajax*, knocking out her director control tower and the two after turrets. The Seafox signaled: "Torpedoes approaching," then added: "They will pass astern." A and B turrets were hitting the enemy frequently, but his 5.5-inch armor deflected them. Harwood said, "We might just as well be bombarding her with a lot of bloody snowballs."[5] The ammunition hoist failed in B turret, leaving only A turret in action.

His ships punished enough for now, Harwood took the *Ajax* and *Achilles* off eastward to make what repairs they could and snatch a quick breakfast. The Seafox alighted alongside the *Ajax* and was hoisted inboard. Harwood was worried about the *Exeter*, which had not answered his urgent signals. How badly was she damaged? Had she sunk?

The Seafox found her, 18 miles to the southwest. Pilot Edgar Lewin had "never seen such a shambles."[6] At a heavy list, the blackened ruins of the bridge and forward turrets and the dead barrels angled grotesquely at the sky. As the ship rolled, her mainmast worked perceptibly. With every knot, the jagged holes in her side sucked in more water. Men could be seen trying to rig jury wireless aerials. Returning to the *Ajax*, the plane signaled: "*Exeter* severely damaged."[7] Forty minutes later, jury aerials finally in place, the stricken cruiser signaled: "All guns out of action." Harwood ordered the *Exeter* to make for Port Stanley. Then he turned west with the *Ajax* and *Achilles* and began shadowing the enemy, who was heading northwest at high speed.

He wondered why the German, apparently almost unscathed, was not making an effort to finish off the *Exeter*. But he was underestimating the damage he had inflicted on the *Spee*. Seventeen hits, mostly by 6-inch shells, had cut vital electrical leads and wrecked ammunition hoists, several 4-inch guns and one 5.9, the antiaircraft command post, telephone communications, the night control station, the big range finder, almost all the searchlights, the faithful Arado, and Dete-Gerät's radar eye. Shells had punched a 6-foot by 4-foot hole near the waterline and showered splinters through engine-room hatches. Thirty-seven officers and men had been killed and fifty-seven wounded, including Langsdorff, who told his officers that they must run into port, the ship not now being seaworthy for the North Atlantic. He headed for the Plate.

At irregular intervals the *Spee* reversed course, and Harwood braced himself to deal with a breakout. But these were only valedictory signs of defiance. At 0500 on 14 December, the *Graf Spee* anchored in Montevideo roads. Three days later, Sunday 17 December, Langsdorff was as sure as he would ever be that more cruisers awaited him outside the estuary, with the *Ark Royal* and *Renown* in the offing. The *Spee* raised steam and headed westward across the estuary, toward Buenos Aires and the setting sun. Stopping once to disembark some of the crew, the *Spee* carried on until she slid onto a mudbank and dropped anchor. There the last few men aboard set scuttling charges, and at 1954 the ship blew up. As a grim finale, in his spartan room at the naval arsenal in Buenos Aires shortly after midnight on the nineteenth, Captain Langsdorff, the devil of conscience on his back and accusations of dishonor in his ears, shot himself.

In three months the *Graf Spee* had sunk nine ships, not a large total compared with her World War I model, the *Emden*. But she had also diverted thirty-four major Allied warships with attendant destroyers and several submarines, leaving gaps to be filled on stations from the North Atlantic to the China Sea.

The *Deutschland* had much less success. She spent just two weeks cruising on the northern edge of the Atlantic routes, encountering three ships: the British *Stonegate*, the Norwegian *Lorentz W. Hansen,* and the American *City of Flint*. The *Deutschland* sank the first two and attempted to sail the third to Germany through the Denmark Strait with a prize crew, but the Norwegians took her over when she was in their territorial waters. In mid-November, the *Deutschland* made her way home north of Iceland through the Denmark Strait. The effect on the crew of this half-hearted foray was deepened when Hitler had the ship's name changed to *Lützow,* fearing psychological repercussions should the "Germany" be sunk.

Seven secretly armed German raiders were active on the trade routes. The *Atlantis, Orion, Widder, Thor, Kormoran, Komet,* and *Pinguin* destroyed or captured a number of loaded Allied merchantmen and disrupted British cruiser arrangements in all three great oceans. They carried, closely hidden behind movable panels, folding deckhouses, and false bulwarks, 5.9-inch guns, 21-inch torpedo tubes, numerous quick-firing cannon, and mines. They rigged dummy ventilators and cargo king posts; they stored paint and material for false structures with which to alter their appearance when their cover had been blown.

The most successful of these secret raiders was the 3,862-ton Schiff 10 *Thor,* ex-fruit carrier *Santa Cruz* of the Oldenburg-Portugiesische Line. Leaving Germany on 6 June 1940 with an Arado 196 seaplane in her hold, the fast *Thor* smartly captured six Allied merchantmen, then fell in with the armed merchant cruiser HMS *Alcantara.* In the ensuing hot fight *Alcantara* came off worst, with bad holes in her hull, communications cut, bridge and range finder badly damaged. The *Thor* was driven off, listing. On 5 December, repaired, repainted, and disguised as a freighter, the raider met armed merchant cruiser *Carnarvon Castle.* The *Thor* set the big ex–Union Castle liner on fire and was able to retire at will to repair her own damage. On 4 April 1941, the *Thor's* old 5.9s outgunned and sank the armed merchant cruiser *Voltaire,* on passage from Trinidad to Freetown.[8]

Air Power, Norway

As they watched their new fleet being built up throughout the 1930s, German naval officers mused about a possible future war against Britain. Norway would have to be taken, they said, so that they could have free access to the Atlantic.

But when war came much sooner than he had anticipated, Admiral Raeder, commander in chief of the German Navy, thought that he lacked the ships to seize the country. In fact, with a great respect for the Royal Navy and little faith in the cooperation of the Luftwaffe (whose head, former World War I fighter ace Hermann Göring, was known contemptuously in the Kriegsmarine as the Fat Man), Raeder considered that the vital iron ore traffic that in winter took the route down the Norwegian coast from Sweden via Narvik would be more endangered with Norway in German hands than with a neutral Norway.

But as the months passed of what the American press in particular was calling the Phony War, Hitler grew increasingly worried that Norway might invite a British occupation. This would cut the Narvik route and perhaps result in the hostility of Sweden. He persuaded Raeder that risks must be taken and Norway captured before Britain could get there. In the early months of 1940 plans for this were formed, in preparation for a move in April.

In mid-March, B-Dienst intercepted signals and detected a concentration of British submarines off the southwest coast of Norway and in the Skagerrak. Eight U-boats were sent to prevent the British boats from reporting imminent moves in the area. The *Scharnhorst* and *Gneisenau* were dispatched on a feint to the north to distract the Royal Navy, which on 8 April was in the area to lay the first British minefields.

High seas, darkness, and heavy weather, bringing bad visibility, were handicapping the operation, which was covered by the battle-cruiser HMS *Renown* and the Second Destroyer Flotilla, led by Capt. Bernard Warburton-Lee in the *Hardy*. The German battlecruisers appeared out of a snowstorm. The *Hardy* saw them first and at 0410 engaged them. Then the *Renown*'s 15-inch guns went into action. Using their Dete-Gerät and superior speed, the German pair fled, out-pacing the heavier vessel, which was making 30 knots. But both sides had suffered hits: the *Gneisenau* on the after turret, *Renown* on the halfdeck.

On 10 April the submarine HMS *Thistle* was torpedoed and sunk by the *U-4*. The sub had apparently not noticed the buildup in northern German ports, but increased signal traffic eventually gave the game away.

A demand for occupation by German troops was already in the hands of the Danish and Norwegian governments. With resistance hopeless, Denmark submitted. The Norwegian government resisted strongly, despite the activities of Vidkun Quisling's Fascist Nasjonal Samling (National Socialist) party.[1]

A fleet of transports protected by German cruisers invaded Oslo Fjord. Timed to coincide with this, troops ferried in warships and sup-ported by naval gunfire took Kristiansand South, Bergen, Trondheim, and Narvik, while Stavanger was occupied by airborne troops.

In Oslo Fjord, Norwegian coastal batteries sank the cruiser *Blücher* but were soon overpowered. With the assistance of airborne assaults on neighboring airfields, the capital was soon in German hands. King Haakon VII and his government escaped to London and formed a gov-ernment in exile on 5 May 1940. In Norway, M. Terboven was ap-pointed commissar of the German Reich, supported by Quisling.

Watching at periscope depth off Kristiansand South was Lt. Commdr. C. H. Hutchinson in HMS *Truant*, which had been one of the twenty-one British submarines in home waters on the outbreak of war. The *Truant* was a T-class oceangoing saddle-tank boat that represented a peak of technical efficiency in submarine design. Designated a patrol submarine, she had been built with a strong emphasis on simplicity of construction and maintenance, equipped with a powerful arma-ment of eight bow torpedo tubes, six of them reloadable from inside the pressure hull, and two external tubes in the casing at the base of the conning tower. Typically, the *Truant* was equipped with asdic but not with RDF, which would not be fitted in British submarines until 1941.

Taking a snap shot from 4,500 yards, Hutchinson hit and sank the 6,000-ton light cruiser *Karlsruhe* and was then hunted for four and a half hours. Shaken by depth-charge near misses, swept by fierce currents into an almost landlocked fjord in the darkness, her compass shattered and with no stars to guide her, the sturdy boat survived nevertheless, and Hutchinson managed to con her out to the open sea.

In the same area the Free Polish submarine *Orzel* sank the 5,261-ton transport *Rio de Janeiro*, and the British submarine *Sunfish* the 7,129-ton *Amasis*. The *Trident* sank the 8,100-ton tanker *Poseidonia* off the Skaw, inside the Skagerrak.

To hold what they captured the Germans relied on land-based air power, in which they were so strong. Air power would decide the issue for the first time in history. The Luftwaffe established itself in Denmark and in southern Norway around Oslo and at Stavanger, ready to oppose any counterstroke by the Allies.

The Royal Navy struck in the north. Narvik, the ore port, was held only by the landing parties brought there in ten large destroyers, which had remained but intended to leave after refueling. Narvik was out of range of the Luftwaffe in Norway for the time being. Given discretion to take action there, Warburton-Lee wasted no time in taking the five ships of his Second Destroyer Flotilla, fresh from action with the *Renown* against the *Scharnhorst* and *Gneisenau*, right into Narvik harbor. There he engaged the German destroyers, which he thought numbered only six, at point-blank range.

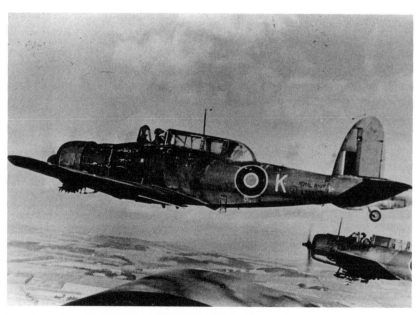

Blackburn Skua dive-bomber of the Royal Navy. The aircraft in the background is a Lend-Lease Vultee Vengeance. (B. Seymour)

But the British were outnumbered two to one and outgunned. Nevertheless, they disabled three of the larger, more modern enemy ships before the Germans could man their guns. Warburton-Lee lost his ship, HMS *Hardy*, HMS *Hunter*, and his own life in the withdrawal.

Next day saw the first British aircraft over Norway. At Hatston in the Orkneys, Numbers 800, 801, and 803 Skua Squadrons of the Fleet Air Arm had been acting as the air defense of Scapa Flow. There was no carrier immediately available. The *Ark Royal* was in the Mediterranean, the *Glorious* in the Indian Ocean hunting raiders, and the *Hermes* and *Eagle* in the Far East. Although the brand-new fleet carrier *Illustrious* had been forewarned and was to head for Norwegian waters without working up, and the old *Furious* was puffing her way toward Scapa, the Norwegian situation would not wait. The Skua units at Hatston were briefed for a dawn attack on shipping in Bergen harbor, the biggest target within their range, though they would be flying to the very extreme of their fuel endurance.

Not long after the adoption of aircraft as weapons of war, it became clear that placing a bomb accurately on a concentrated military target stood a much greater chance of success if the aircraft delivered the bomb from a dive as near the vertical as possible rather than in level flight. This improved the aim and velocity and greatly reduced the curvature of the falling missile and the time it took to fall. The target also had less time to take avoiding action, and the incalculable effect of crosswinds and air currents on the bomb's flight path were weakened. The greater the angle of attack, the greater the degree of accuracy.

HMS *Furious* off Norway in company with HMS *Renown*. (D. J. Cole)

The early dive-bombers tended to break up and their pilots to black out, but Lt. Harry Brown sank a munition barge by this method in 1917, and the Royal Flying Corps conducted thorough trials. The strategic use of bombers, however, supplanted the tactical use between the wars, and dive-bombing lost favor except in the Royal Navy's Fleet Air Arm and the U.S. Army Air Corps. Air Corps DH4s dive-bombed on the Mexican border; U.S. Marines used the method in the Nicaraguan intervention; and trials in fleet exercises converted the U.S. Navy. The Japanese Navy developed its Aichi design in China.

In the Spanish Civil War, the Luftwaffe experimented on Spanish civilians with the Junkers Ju 87, the Stuka. A Stuka pilot had a range of technology in his hands far in advance of anything that was even on other drawing boards. The Royal Navy had been asking in vain for more than a decade for the development of a computerized dive-bombing sight. Not until 1942 would the American Norden company, which had produced the famous Norden bombsight for level bombers, answer the U.S. Navy's request for a dive sight. A British design stalled for lack of funding.

A Stuka pilot decided on the dive angle and height of pullout appropriate to the target; then he set the time interval on a time-distributor device and the height of pullout on a contacting altimeter. Above the target he trimmed for dive angle, usually 70 degrees, closed the throttle and cooling gills, lowered the dive brakes (which operated an elevator tab controlling the trim), then winged over into the initial shallow dive, adjusting his Revi gunsight according to headwind strength before beginning his main bombing dive, with the plane preset nose-heavy.

The bomb was released during pullout at a time set on an automatic bomb distributor and calculated as a function of height of release and dive angle. Just before release the contacting altimeter reversed the trimming sequence, the aircraft became tail-heavy and pulled itself out of the dive, and the bomb was automatically released even if the pilot had temporarily blacked out, with the arms of the typical dive-bomber's "bomb crutch" beneath the fuselage swinging the missile forward and clear of the propeller arc. By the outbreak of war, the BZA-1 dive-bomb sight had been introduced in the Stuka and the Junkers Ju 88. This was essentially a computer fully integrated with the flight controls. After it had been fed all relevant data, constantly checked, it controlled the attack. In the autumn of 1939 the sophistication of this equipment in a captured Ju 88 reduced British boffins to shamed astonishment. Allied pilots continued to use their front gunsight or some projection on the engine cowling to provide a basic sighting line—or they relied on just plain eye-sighting, making an adjustment for wind. A danger here, at least for beginners, was that preoccupation with sighting tended to make pilots forget their rapidly diminishing altitude.

Purely as a bombing instrument, the Stuka, with its dated unretractable undercarriage, was excellent. But at the end of its dive it was relatively helpless and vulnerable. In addition, this fine-tuned instrument had, up until the Norwegian campaign, never really been used in its proper precision role. Guernica and Warsaw were not fit targets for *Vorsprung durch Technik* ("advanced technology").

In the States, the Army Air Corps had abandoned its early enthusiasm for dive-bombing in favor of the twin-engine attack bomber. Only in the summer of 1940, with the obvious achievements of the Stuka in Europe, did it wake up and demand dive-bombers, turning at first to models the U.S. Navy had developed, such as the excellent Douglas Dauntless 200 SBD-2 and the less-than-excellent Curtiss Helldiver SB2D-1. Eventually, after a plague of technical problems with Curtiss, Brewster, and Vultee types, the Air Corps went sour on the dive-bomber. But then it discovered that a Mustang fighter, fitted with hydraulic, slatted double-dive brakes and shackles for two 500-pound bombs, was superb for the job.[2]

In Britain the Royal Air Force, which for almost the whole interwar period had run the Fleet Air Arm, was devoted to the strategic-bomber concept. But dogged pressure from the Admiralty finally produced the custom-built Blackburn Skua, an excellent dive-bomber compromised by typical Admiralty insistence on a twin role as a fighter, for which it was too slow and cumbersome in modern terms. As such it had a falsely promising start when Skuas from the *Ark Royal* scored the first enemy aircraft kill at sea, against a Dornier flying boat. It was in Norway that morning of 11 April 1940 that they performed their true function. Petty officer pilot Eric Monk recalled,

> GOING OUT TO THE AIRCRAFT, I HAD MIXED FEELINGS AND WONDERED IF MY KITE WOULD FAIL TO START. IT WAS THEN THAT I FOUND OUT THAT ONCE I WAS STRAPPED INTO MY FAMILIAR L2934 IT WAS JUST ANOTHER FLIGHT, NO MORE WORRIES. ALL WAS READY, BOMB ON, SAFETY-PIN FOR MY BOMB IN MY POCKET IN CASE IT WAS NOT DROPPED, COLT .45 IN MY FLYING OVERALL POCKET ALONGSIDE THE COMPASS, AND L2934 STARTED UP FIRST CARTRIDGE. WARM UP THE ENGINE, CHECK BOOST AND REVS, THROTTLE BACK TO CHECK THE MAGNETOS AND CHECK THAT THE TANKS ARE FULL. LIEUTENANT [EDWARD] FINCH-NOYES MOVED OUT, FOLLOWED BY LIEUTENANT [K. V.] SPURWAY, AND I FOLLOWED ON BEHIND. IT WAS A FINE MORNING AS WE CLIMBED UP TO 16,000 FEET, HEATER ON, AND DOING 140 KNOTS . . .[3]

Leaning out their fuel mix as much as possible to increase range, they jogged the 250 miles northeast over the sea for the Frisians and Bergen. None of the crews had ever flown with a 500-pound bomb on the ejector arm, or at such long range. At briefing they had been told, "If you have less than 60 gallons of fuel after the attack, fly on to Sweden, destroy your Skua, and try to get back."[4]

"Eventually," says Monk, "the coast came into sight, the sun was up, the sky blue, the hills topped with snow, lower down the pine trees and then the waters of the fjord . . ."[5]

He was the "tail-end Charlie" of the sixteen aircraft, and as he stall-turned to enter his dive, shell bursts covered Bergen like a black lace curtain.

> THE *KÖNIGSBERG* HAD BEEN DAMAGED BY THE NORWEGIAN
> COAST BATTERIES BUT THERE WERE STILL QUITE A LOT OF
> SHELL BURSTS ON THE WAY DOWN. STEADY ON THE TARGET,
> OFFSET TURRET, RELEASE, DOWN TO SEA LEVEL, WEAVING
> AWAY DOWN THE FJORD, 80 GALLONS INDICATED IN THE
> TANKS, THEN OUT TO SEA INTO FORMATION FOR THE TWO-
> HOUR FLOG BACK TO HATSTON. WE CHECKED FOR SIGNS OF
> OIL OR FUEL LEAKING ON ANY OF THE AIRCRAFT IN THE SUB-
> FLIGHT, AND KEPT A CONSTANT CHECK ON MY OIL PRESSURE.
> THE LEADER'S OBSERVER "ZOBBED" (MORSE CODE BY HAND
> SIGNALS): "REPORT FUEL REMAINING." REPLY: "75."[6]

After two hours' gritty slog back across the "German Ocean," the Skuas all landed at Hatston with almost empty tanks, the crews with some fatigue—which disappeared when they were told they had sunk the *Königsberg*. She was the first major warship to be sunk by dive-bombing, and the Stuka squadrons in Norway now took a thoughtful look at the potentialities.

The raids continued for some time, until the *Ark Royal* and *Glorious* arrived to give the beached Skuas a hitch.

Meanwhile, the half-cooked situation at Narvik had to be put right. Three days after Warburton-Lee's aggressive attack, the old but reconstructed battleship *Warspite* led eight Tribal and one K-class fleet destroyers into the fjord. Pilot PO Ben Rice, in the *Warspite*'s Swordfish seaplane L9767, nicknamed Lorna, scouted ahead in the drizzly weather with two 250-pound high-explosive, two 100-pound antisubmarine, and eight 40-pound antipersonnel bombs on the plane's racks.

Kapitänleutnant Otto Schulz's new Type IXB 1,178-ton (submerged) *U-64* had been on trials and was surfaced in a side fjord when Lorna's observer, Lieutenant Commander Brown, sighted her.[7] Rice dived and released his two submarine bombs at 200 feet. One of these hit the *U-64* and sank her, the first U-boat to be sunk from the air in World War II. The surface forces followed this up by sinking all eight enemy destroyers in Narvik and the adjacent fjords.

In the Skagerrak on 10 April, the submarine *Triton* sank the 5,219-ton transport *Friedenau*, the 3,648-ton *Wighest*, and the 354-ton *Rau 6*; the *Sunfish* sank the 2,593-ton *Antares*. Next day the *Spearfish* badly damaged the *Lützow* (ex-*Deutschland*) putting her out of action for several months. But the Luftwaffe presence prevented any surface interference. Under its umbrella, an army unit from Oslo relieved the landing party at Trondheim.

The Allies were trying to raise an expeditionary force, but with all organized units sent to hold the position in France, only 12,000 men could be mustered for an ad hoc force that the cruiser HMS *Glasgow* put ashore at Namsos to the northeast and Aandalsness to the southwest of Trondheim. The idea was to make a pincer movement on the port in concert with a direct assault from the sea that was planned for 25 April, in hopes that the Aandalsness force could also slow down the German advance from Oslo.

The Royal Navy, with the record of the debacle at Gallipoli in the history books, still had no organized amphibious units to help an army landing—combined operations were in the distant future—but the makeshift commandos were scrambled ashore. Then the Stukas appeared, filling the sky, and the soldiers looked for their own aircraft in vain.

It was not for want of trying. The RAF operated some Gladiator fighters from a frozen lake southeast of Aandalsness, in imitation of the Luftwaffe, which was making extensive use of other "icedromes." But the British machines had all been bombed and destroyed as they stood parked on the ice.

The three carriers that operated at different times offshore represented the utmost air strength the Navy could bring to bear at this period, and it was seriously inadequate. The first vessel on the scene was the *Furious*. Because she was an old ship, it was assumed that she could not operate modern fighters, and the three Skua squadrons were reserved for the *Ark Royal*. Yet the former light battlecruiser was to fly Seafires—navalized Spitfires—in the not-too-distant future, thanks to a demonstration in the Norwegian campaign yet to come. For now, the *Furious* brought just the two Swordfish Squadrons 816 and 818 to the battle. These pitched in early with a torpedo attack on shipping in Trondheim harbor. Two hits were claimed on a destroyer, but most of the "kippers" blew up sandbanks.

The old ship and her aircrews almost burned themselves out with the pressure of operations. Swordfish in the fjords made head-on attacks on Me 109s, hoping to be mistaken for Gladiator fighters—themselves obsolete. None too soon the *Ark* and *Glorious* relieved the *Furious*, but even their four squadrons of Skuas, with a few Rocs (the ineffective rear-turret version of the Skua), and four Swordfish squadrons could not hope to keep the Luftwaffe at bay.

"With our strictly limited number of aircraft," writes then–PO Eric Monk, who won two Distinguished Service Medals and a commission for his work in the campaign, "inferior in quality to the 109s and 110s we met, and not fast enough to catch Heinkels or Ju 87s, it was a difficult task. Not the least of our problems was to find the *Ark* some hundred miles out to sea after a two-hour patrol, plus the fact that our ammunition only lasted about twenty seconds of firing time."[8]

Stavanger airfield was the main Luftwaffe base. The RAF bombed it almost every night, and the heavy cruiser *Suffolk* gave it a night bombardment, during which she and her escort were themselves also heavily bombed. The *Suffolk* and the battleship *Resolution* were both damaged by Stuka ace Werner Baumbach.

The antiaircraft cruisers *Curlew, Carlisle,* and *Curacoa* were three of the only six Allied ships on hand that were fitted with radar. The *Curlew* was equipped with the Type 79, and the *Curacoa* with an improved 79—Type 279—featuring a range-finding device with which it could control the fire of the ship's antiaircraft armament as a barrage. The *Carlisle* had been given the Type 280, a naval version of the GL Mark I developed for the army for antiaircraft gun control. The 280 was a 3.5-mm set of great value for air warning as well as fuze prediction, but it could not be adapted completely to naval antiaircraft control. The three cruisers were sent into the fjords, where high ground seriously interfered with the radar signals. There the Stukas found them and, benefitting from the British Skuas' destruction of the *Königsberg* by dive-bombing, sank the *Curlew* and badly damaged the *Curacoa*. None of the carriers had RDF, and thus they were unable to give proper fighter direction. The RAF had little strategic mobility, though it had set up three airfields, at Skaanland, Bardufoss, and Laksely, helped by the crew of HMS *Glasgow's* peripatetic Walrus amphibian.

Everywhere on land the small Allied force was pushed back, with the Luftwaffe denying it the offensive, and it became clear that the situation was hopeless. Even if the planned assault on Trondheim from the sea had been attempted and had initially succeeded, and the advance of the German army from the southward had been delayed, it would have been impossible to withstand the strength of enemy air power. Narvik was captured and held while it was still beyond German bomber range, but by early June all Allied forces had left Norway.

Two fruitful developments in this last phase of the campaign, however, brighten the stark picture of failure. In the first, new assault craft, afterward known as LCAs (landing craft, assault) were used for the first time in the taking of Narvik, with success.

The second was a breakthrough for British naval aviation. The carrier *Glorious* stood by to evacuate air parties from Narvik. It was assumed that the ten surviving RAF Gladiators stood a good chance of making it aboard the carrier's deck, even without arrester hooks. When it came, however, to the seven Hurricanes of Number 46 Squadron RAF, which had been working from the Narvik airstrip, their commanding officer was told that they could not be crated for shipment, and, with a landing speed of 70 MPH and no deck hooks, could not be flown aboard. But, encouraged by ex-*Glorious* captain, now Admiral Lyster, who was ashore there at the time, he insisted on making the attempt.

Letting some air out of his tires for a better grip on the deck, he enlisted the help of the cruiser *Glasgow*'s Walrus pilot (the cruiser having left her amphibian aircraft behind) Sub-Lt. J. A. Ievers, who gave the RAF pilots some elementary deck-landing instructions. Then, on the early evening of 7 June, the Hurricane commanding officer landed his aircraft with no trouble, his wheel brakes halting him with plenty of deck to spare. When the turn of the remaining six came six hours later, the Walrus flew around the *Glorious*, its crew monitoring each Hurricane as it came in to land. All six landed safely, as did the ten Gladiators. When Ievers himself lowered the wheels of the "Shagbat" amphibian, he was waved off and signaled that the carrier was full. He diverted to the *Ark Royal* some 30 miles away, which was actually to save his and his aircraft crew's lives.

This successful landing of fast modern fighters on a carrier's deck, which had been dismissed by Royal Navy (RN) "salt horse" non-aviators as impossibly dangerous, reinforced the views of Lumley Lyster, who, as rear admiral, aircraft carriers, had asserted, "Give me a Hurricane or a Spitfire and I'll hook 'em on my air stations and fly 'em aboard any time you want!"[9] After Norway he got his way.

Never again did the Fleet Air Arm have to make do with aircraft that were inferior to the latest land-based machines. Within a few months Sea Hurricanes were operating from its carriers, then, fitted with deck-landing hooks, Spitfires, and finally the fully navalized Seafires. These came in company with Lend-Lease fighters from the United States—the Martlets (Wildcats), Hellcats, and Corsairs, and the modern TBF Avengers, which superseded, though by no means completely replaced, the Swordfish. With these machines, RN carriers sank U-boats and supported landings in all the worldwide theaters of war.

With this in mind, the finale to the Norwegian campaign is bitterly ironic. Having embarked her strangers, the *Glorious* continued on south independently, except for two destroyers in company, independent of the other forces because of her low fuel endurance. The *Glorious* had five Swordfish aboard in addition to her mixed bag of fighters, but they had been at full stretch for days, and no reconnaissance patrols were flown. Capt. G. D'Oyly-Hughes, a gallant submariner in World War I, must have thought that to fly off the Hurricanes or Gladiators would be tempting providence, but in any case the *Scharnhorst* and *Gneisenau*, the Terrible Twins of the Scandinavian scene, caught the *Glorious* before she could launch any aircraft. Their Seetakt radar-guided guns hit her at 14 miles' range and swiftly destroyed the carrier and all her aircraft.

On the beaches of Dunkirk the British Expeditionary Force, driven into the sea by combined air and panzer blitzkrieg, was suffering heavy strafing by the Luftwaffe and long-range artillery. E-boats infiltrated the rescue vessels and sank a destroyer. At dawn on what the Royal Navy traditionally celebrated as the *Glorious* First of June (commemorating an old victory), three destroyers were sunk by waves of Stukas.

The RAF in England did what it could, handicapped by the distance from its airfields and RDF stations, but there were no carriers offshore to hold off the Stukas. Nine destroyers were lost in the evacuation and many more would need dockyard repair—twenty-three from the Dunkirk operation alone.

8
Bismarck and the 284

On 5 November the pocket battleship *Scheer* attacked a convoy in the North Atlantic, but after a doomed defense by the armed merchant cruiser HMS *Jervis Bay* only five of the scattering vessels were sunk. The *Scheer* then combed the South Atlantic and Indian Ocean, sinking eight more ships and sending in two prizes in a further four months' marauding, not a great achievement.

Next to sortie was the 8-inch cruiser *Hipper*, which left Germany in December 1940, eluded the Northern Patrol in bad weather, and made for the Sierra Leone and South American routes. On Christmas Day she sighted a military supply convoy near the Azores, bound for Suez via the Cape. The cruisers *Berwick* and *Bonaventure* were in attendance and drove the raider off but were unable to maintain contact with her, as neither ship had RDF. On a second cruise, the *Hipper* sank seven of an unescorted Sierra Leone convoy of nineteen ships, but afterward found only one more victim in all.

Meanwhile, the *Scharnhorst* and *Gneisenau* eluded a patrolling armed merchant cruiser by use of their radar, and on 8 February 1941 they intercepted a convoy from Halifax, Nova Scotia, only to find the battleship *Ramillies* playing watchdog. On 22 February they sank five ships from an outward-bound convoy that had not dispersed sufficiently. On 7 March they sighted a Sierra Leone convoy with HMS *Malaya* in attendance. They directed three U-boats to the convoy, which lost five ships.[1] On 15 March they ran across another gaggle of insufficiently dispersed merchantmen and sank or captured sixteen of them, which could have been more but for the appearance of the battleship *Rodney*.[2]

Their next cruise was to be in company with the *Bismarck* and the new 8-inch heavy cruiser *Prinz Eugen*, a formidable combination. But the *Gneisenau* was damaged by a Coastal Command torpedo and her consort by RAF bombs, and the *Bismarck* and *Eugen* sailed without them.

On the evening of 23 May, 8-inch cruisers HMS *Suffolk* and *Norfolk* were patrolling the Denmark Straits between Iceland and Greenland. Both had RDF, the *Suffolk* a Type 279 (an improved Type 79, with a range-finding device with which she could fire antiaircraft guns in barrage) and a Type 284, the first form of 50-cm (19.5-inch) radar for surface gunnery control. This set was really only a range finder, with a maximum range of 20,000 yards. The *Norfolk* had a type 286, a version of the ASV Mark II with fixed aerials covering an arc on both sides of the ship from fine on the bow to just abaft the beam, giving only very rough bearings.

The *Suffolk*, patrolling the ice edge, was the first to sight the *Bismarck* and *Prinz Eugen*, but neither of her radars was responsible. Able Seaman Alfred Newall sighted them at 1922 at a range of 7 miles, dangerously close to the *Bismarck*'s 15-inch rifles, but the cruiser turned back into the prevailing mist when Able Seaman "Tich" Tinkler picked up the battleship on his 284 gunnery-ranging RDF without being seen by the Germans.

The *Norfolk*, patrolling about 15 miles abeam of the *Suffolk*, also contacted them by eye (at 2032) before getting an echo on her cathode-ray screen. The *Norfolk* was closer than the *Suffolk* and the *Bismarck* opened fire, but the cruiser managed to disengage.

For the next ten hours the two cruisers shadowed the Germans on their RDF, reporting their progress to Vice Adm. Lancelot Holland, who was steaming up with the battlecruiser *Hood* and the new 14-inch battleship *Prince of Wales* and six destroyers. They also reported to the commander in chief of the Home Fleet, who hoped that this force would turn them back.

In spite of the bad visibility during that anxious night, Holland in the *Hood* imposed a rigid radio and radar silence on his squadron. But at two o'clock in the morning of 24 May the cruisers lost touch with the enemy, and the admiral asked the *Prince of Wales* to use her Type 284 RDF to search an arc for the *Bismarck*. When told that this radar would not bear, he refused permission to use the battleship's 281 set, which could pick up an aircraft at 20,000 feet from 100 miles, though its surface range on a battleship was only of the order of some 11 miles, with range-finding capability about 30 yards. Holland considered it not worth the risk of betraying their position.

At 0535 on 24 May Holland sighted the *Bismarck* at 17 miles' range, much farther away than his radar, either the 284 or the 281, could have reported. The *Hood* opened fire first, at 26,500 yards—just over

13 miles—followed almost at once by the *Prince of Wales* and both German ships. The first, short, stage of the battle was between the two 15-inch vessels, the *Hood* and *Bismarck*, the old and the new.

The *Prince of Wales* got no results from her 284 or her 281. The first salvo fell 1,000 yards short and it took six salvos to cross the target. But the *Bismarck's* first salvo fell just ahead of the *Hood*, and her third hit the great battlecruiser, penetrating a magazine. At 0615 the *Norfolk* signaled the Admiralty: "*Hood* blown up."

At the battle of Jutland in 1916, well-aimed German shells had probed the light armor of Adm. David Beatty's battlecruisers and found its weakness, and three ships had blown up with cataclysmic magazine explosions. The *Hood*, the biggest ship in the Royal Navy (40,000 tons standard displacement) and a model of symmetry and grace, was supposed to have embodied all the lessons of Jutland. Extra armor plate had been added in the early days of the war, but in fact the ship was inadequately protected. The *Bismarck's* radar-guided 15-inch projectiles had gone through the 3-inch armor over the after magazine, and the mighty ship was gone, leaving just three survivors. The loss was a great shock to the Navy and to the British public, to whom the *Hood* was the only Navy vessel really known. Because of frequent newspaper publicity, the *Hood* was the Navy to the public. As for effect on the morale of men in other British ships . . . "How our hearts sank and how the news made us more edgy, but even so more determined to avenge *Hood*," recalls Bill Earp, a gunner in the *Suffolk* who had had friends on board the doomed vessel.[3]

Now the contest was between the battlewagons, the *Bismarck* and *Prince of Wales*, with the new *King George V* and the carrier *Victorious* summoned, as well as the heavyweight *Rodney*. The *Bismarck's* Dete-Gerät radar, which had achieved ranges of 18.5 miles on a large ship, 9 miles on a cruiser, was principally a range finder but had good directional properties as well, and could also be used for warning of the approach of ships. Although the radar could not spot the fall of shot, the *Bismarck* used it to make already superb gunnery even more accurate.

Table 2
Comparative Firepower

Ship	Caliber of gun	Weight of shell	Muzzle velocity	Range
Bismarck	15 in.	1,764 lb.	2,690 ft./sec.	37,992 yds.
Prince of Wales	14 in.	1,590 lb.	2,483 ft./sec.	38,560 yds.
Rodney	16 in.	2,048 lb.	2,614 ft./sec.	39,780 yds.

Source: Ministry of Defence

The *Prince of Wales*'s new equipment had not been thoroughly tested, her radar had not functioned well as a range finder, and she had begun to suffer breakdowns in her turrets. These were of a new, unproven design and had only been in use for a few weeks.

The *Bismarck*'s radar-guided shells were hitting the *Prince of Wales* now. The British ship signaled to Whitehall: "Bridge out of action. Y turret out of action." The battleship turned away under smoke. But she had hit the *Bismarck* twice, and a Coastal Command aircraft reported the German to be trailing oil and steaming at a reduced speed. By now the British radar had picked up the two raiders again, and the *Norfolk, Suffolk,* and *Prince of Wales* continued to shadow the *Bismarck* and the *Prinz Eugen.*

In the afternoon the *Bismarck* turned toward her pursuers and opened fire in order to screen the *Prinz Eugen* as the latter broke away under orders from Adm. Gunther Lutjens in the *Bismarck* to locate one of their supply ships, then to engage in cruiser warfare independently.

The *Prince of Wales* replied with a few salvos but scored no hits, and the *Bismarck* turned back on to her southerly course. At 2056 the German ship signaled Group West Command: "Impossible shake off enemy owing to radar. Proceeding directly to Brest owing to fuel situation."

Meanwhile the commander in chief, Home Fleet, Adm. Sir John Tovey, in the new battleship *King George V,* sister ship of *Prince of Wales,* was steaming to intercept. He detached the new fleet carrier *Victorious,* which launched her Swordfish aircraft, though they were not properly worked up with the carrier, to try to slow the *Bismarck* down.

Just after midnight on 25 May, one Swordfish, fitted with ASV Mark II, found the enemy and scored one hit, which left the *Bismarck* trailing oil. Darkness set in, and the *Suffolk,* the only ship whose RDF was now effective, continued to shadow the German from the port quarter. Despite the darkness, the cruiser also continued to zigzag, in order to minimize the risk from U-boats. At the end of the port zigzag leg, radar contact with the quarry was temporarily broken and then regained again regularly, as the cruiser swung back. About 0300 the *Bismarck,* using her own radar intelligently, took advantage of this— when the *Suffolk* swung back, the echo was gone from Able Seaman Tinkler's A-Scope.

Meanwhile Lutjens was circling around to the west, then he turned northward and back eastward behind the British squadron. The *Suffolk* was sent to the west to search, but of course could not find her, nor could any of the hunting ships. Five fruitless hours later Group West signaled the *Bismarck*: "Last enemy contact report 0213. We have impression contact has been lost."

"Never lose touch" was an old naval maxim, and the *Suffolk,* for the sake of the small additional safety that was all zigzagging could achieve, had ignored it. Now operations had virtually to begin all over again, except that more ships had had time to join in the chase, with the *Bismarck* short of the oil she was leaking. British direction-finding stations had picked up the exchange of signals between the *Bismarck* and Group West, and though British cryptographers could not break the code, the position indicated that the German ship was making for France.

Admiral Tovey could not imagine Admiral Lutjens taking the risk of stopping to refuel knowing the British Home Fleet must now be on his trail, though the commander in chief, Home Fleet, did take the precaution of sending the *Suffolk* off to search for the enemy supply ships *Belchen* and *Lothringen*. Then at 1030 a Coastal Command Catalina flying boat signaled: "One battleship in sight."

The *Bismarck* fired on the Catalina, which was already having difficulties with thick clouds, and the aircraft lost touch. But it was now definitely established that the enemy was steering for France. Tovey in the *King George V* was coming down from the north, with the *Rodney*, which had been on her way to the States for refit, steering to join her. From Gibraltar, Adm. Sir James Somerville's Force H, with the *Renown, Ark Royal*, and the 6-inch *Sheffield*, was approaching at high speed.

The latter was sent on ahead to supplement the shadowing aircraft. These included Swordfish from the *Ark Royal*, and one of them regained contact with the *Bismarck*. The pursuers were closing in, but there was still no guarantee that they would catch the enemy. Tovey's two ships could not hope to intercept and were in any case becoming aware of a fuel shortage from all their high-speed steaming. The *Renown*, with its light armor, was no match for the German. Everything depended on slowing the *Bismarck* down, with hope resting mainly on the *Ark Royal*'s "Stringbag" Swordfish torpedo planes, though there was a reserve force in four powerful Tribal-class destroyers and a Polish destroyer, under Capt. Phillip Vian in the *Cossack*, now approaching at high speed.

At 1115 an *Ark Royal* Swordfish using ASV (air-to-surface) radar signaled: "One battleship in sight."

Torpedo Swordfish attacked, but at 1746 the search machine's operator reported: "Eleven torpedoes fired at *Sheffield*." Thankfully he was able to qualify this with: "No hits." One Swordfish torpedo did actually hit the *Sheffield*, but the tin fish was a dud.

At 1954 the *Bismarck* was attacked by a second striking force from the *Ark Royal*, and at 2015 it reported to Group West: "Ship no longer maneuverable. Torpedo hit aft." A damaged rudder was sending her around in circles. The destroyers *Cossack, Zulu,* and *Maori* attacked her at night with torpedoes, claiming two hits. At dawn the *King George V* and *Rodney* arrived, and before long the *Bismarck*'s guns were silenced, though the ship had to be finished off by torpedoes from the cruiser *Dorsetshire*.

In the next few days five supply ships were rounded up, leaving the *Prinz Eugen* unable to continue her raiding cruise. Within a week she had returned to Brest with a blank score sheet. The *Bismarck* sortie, the most serious German attempt to attack the Atlantic trade routes with heavy ships, was over.

The *Bismarck* battle was the first naval engagement in which radar had played a vital part. ASV Mark II, in its Type 286 version, was a failure as an aid to gunnery but a great success in shadowing, as was the older Type 79 in the *Sheffield*, which had provided Force H with air warning for nearly a year. Dete-Gerät was partly responsible for the remarkable accuracy of the German gunners against the *Hood*, and it was better than the British Type 284, though not of great use for surface warning.

The performance of Swordfish torpedo aircraft was disappointing. The *Victorious*'s crews had been insufficiently worked up, and there had been torpedo failures. Several of the *Ark Royal*'s aerial kippers had exploded soon after entering the water as a result of faults in their new magnetic pistols. The old contact type was reinstated until the bugs could be eliminated.

Wolf Pack

The weapon was the U-boat Type VII, called the Sea Wolf, based on an IvS boat of the late 1920s that displaced 500 tons surfaced, 800 tons submerged. A 625/915-tonner was ready by 1936, and a second batch of 10 enlarged VIIB boats was built in 1938–39. These were propelled by a twin-shaft diesel/electric power system giving a surface speed of 17 knots, 8 knots submerged. They could remain submerged for eighteen hours at a cruising speed of 4 knots. The VIIBs were followed by the 863-ton Type VIIC, 593 of which were built between 1940 and the end of the war. These boats were fitted with four 21-inch torpedo tubes forward and one aft, and they carried fourteen torpedoes. The gun armament varied, especially after boats transmitting the Bay of Biscay on the surface began to encounter serious opposition from RAF Coastal Command aircraft. A typical VIIC boat might have been allocated a 1.45-inch gun on the forecastle casing forward and two twin 0.8-inch antiaircraft guns. These modern U-boats had the advantages over their World War I predecessors of wireless, new torpedo-firing methods and electric torpedoes, which left no telltale bubbles.

As for asdic, BdU Dönitz (Befehlshaber der U-boote, or flag officer, submarines) wanted the Royal Navy left to hide behind its miracle aura. He had experienced real sea warfare, and he knew that no weapon was perfect. Just in case, however, his boffins were experimenting with possible non-reflecting materials and torpedoes that would home in on an escort vessel.

Dönitz's plan was to use his boats in packs of six to ten, instead of operating singly. Each pack was to spread out across the probable line of approach of a convoy, with long-range Focke-Wulf Condor aircraft of Oberst (Col.) Edgar Petersen's 1 Staffel (squadron) of 1 Gruppe (wing), Kampfgeschwader 40 (bomber group) at Bordeaux scouting for convoys beyond the Azores to 20 degrees west and up to the coast of Iceland.

The Focke-Wulf 200C Condor bomber and reconnaissance aircraft was based on an airliner that had proven successful immediately before the war. It had been adapted to its maritime role because of delays in the Heinkel He 177 program.

In June 1936 chief of air staff Albert Kesselring severely cut back the German heavy-bomber program as unnecessary. Only low-key work on the advanced, experimental He 177 Greif (Griffon) was maintained, despite repeated requests by the Kriegsmarine to speed up its development as a long-range machine to cooperate with U-boats.

In the spring of 1939, the Luftwaffe operations staff woke up to the fact that none of its combat bomber units had any experience operating over the sea. This was only part of the general neglect of naval aviation in Germany. There was only the Kriegsmarine's See-Luftstreitkrafte (naval air arm), a Luftwaffe unit under operational command of the navy. This was a force of four mixed Gruppen (wings), each with three Staffeln (squadrons) of flying boats and floatplanes. The flying boats could reconnoiter as far as the Shetlands but could not carry bombs or torpedoes. The floatplanes could carry 1,100 pounds of bombs or one torpedo, but their maximum operational range was only 250 miles. This force was clearly inadequate to support the numerically inferior Kriegsmarine against the Royal Navy.

Focke-Wulf Condor 200C-1. (Luftwaffe)

Hastily a course of instruction in maritime operations for bomber crews was set up under Hauptmann (captain) Edgar Petersen, a veteran of long-range navigation. Still FdU Dönitz (later promoted to BdU) demanded a new, long-range, bomber and reconnaissance machine. But the He 177 was only in prototype, and the He 111s, Do 17s, and new Junkers 88s lacked the range. Development of the Greif was speeded up, and on 6 July 1939 an order of twelve was increased to twenty.

But production was a long way off, delayed by Erhard Milch, Göring's deputy, and World War I ace Generalluftzeugmeister (chief of armament and supply) Ernst Udet, who wanted to build the latest technical innovations into the Greif. Among these was the replacement of the original four engines, which had given good results, with new installations. A pair of Daimler Benz motors coupled together and driving one common propeller was fitted on each wing. At one stage Udet wanted the aircraft fitted with dive brakes, and the Technische Amt (technical branch) demanded 60-degree diving angles. Designer Siegfried Gunther tried to oblige, but the necessary strengthening of the big bomber's airframe to absorb the stresses of dive-bombing meant more time lost. The second prototype crashed on diving trials, killing test pilot Hans Ricker.

The new engines overheated, and aircraft He 177A-01 was destroyed by fire. The new system of surface evaporation was a failure, and bigger, more orthodox radiators were fitted. These added to the airframe drag, reducing speed and range. Extra fuel cells in the wings necessitated more structural strengthening, with weight increases and a further reduction in performance. More weight and drag were added by the manned turrets introduced when the revolutionary remote-controlled barbettes failed. The general increase in weight decreed research into a heavier, more complicated undercarriage. . . .

The time when the Greif might be operating beyond the British Isles to attack shipping seemed a long way off. The Junkers 290, a commercial derivative of the canceled Ju 89, might have been adaptable, but there were only two specimens available, and no production line had been set up.

Then Hauptmann Petersen, appointed navigation officer to the 10. Flieger Division when it was formed on 1 August 1939, thought he had found a solution in the four-engine Focke-Wulf Condor passenger transport, at least until the Greif was ready. He took plans of the aircraft to his chief of staff, Oberstleutnant (lieutenant-colonel) Martin Harlinghausen, himself an antishipping expert, who was enthusiastic.

In 1938 there had been a series of spectacular long-distance flights at speeds of up to 224 MPH, securing orders from Denmark, Brazil, and Japan. But on the outbreak of war, all foreign deliveries were can-

celed and machines under construction converted to military transports. Petersen and Harlinghausen checked on loads with fuel and
bombs, chose positions for machine guns, and concluded that fuel for
about fifteen hours could be carried, with 2,205 pounds of bombs at a
speed of 167.67 MPH, allowing a radius of about 931.5 miles, which
could be increased with extra tankage.

They took their scheme to the chief of air staff, who gave it his support and ordered Petersen to form a special antishipping unit. The six
B-series Condors of the original Japanese order, one of which was
actually a maritime reconnaissance version for the Japanese navy, and
six standard transports were taken over for conversion into Fw 200C-
0s. Both of the original sponsors were well aware that from an operational point of view, the aircraft suffered from potential weaknesses in
structure and a vulnerable location of fuel lines near the outer skin of
the lower fuselage. But the need for them was urgent. They were
given some local strengthening, and the single main wheels were
replaced by twin-wheel units to allow for the greater weight of the
military aircraft. The former passenger cabin was packed with extra
fuel tanks. Harlinghausen called the converted machines Hilfskreut-
zeren (auxiliary cruisers).

On 1 October Petersen established 1 Staffel of 1 Gruppe of the new
Kampfgeschwader 40 at Bremen, and exercises began over the North
Sea.

The Fw 200C-0's single 7.9-mm machine gun firing through a belly
hatch was replaced in the C-1 by both a 20-mm cannon and a 7.9-mm
machine gun in a belly gondola. The upper forward-firing 7.9-mm
was now housed in a fixed cupola instead of a hydraulically operated
turret. Another 7.9-mm machine gun faced aft.

A basic Condor crew of five comprised pilot; copilot; a navigator
who quadrupled as bombardier, radio operator, and gunner; an engineer who doubled as a gunner; and a rear gunner.

Bomb loads depended on targets and distances. Four 551-pound
bombs were carried under the wings and an optional fifth in the belly
gondola, though this was sometimes a cement bomb used to check the
accuracy of the rather primitive Revi bombsight or the even more
basic ring-and-bead type. A mix of two 1,100-pound and two 550-
pound bombs was also used, sometimes supplemented by twelve 110-
pound bombs.

Condors on their familiarization flights had often seen the little 255-
ton trawler *Volante* in the Icelandic fishing grounds, and her crew had
often waved. On 12 July the *Volante* became the Bordeaux Condors'
first victim, swamped by near misses 10 miles off the Whaleback, her
stripped Lewis machine gun and single rifle silent. On 15 July, 900
miles farther south, the Panamanian *Frossoula* was sunk with a valu-

Two near misses by a Focke-Wulf Condor. (Luftwaffe)

able cargo of potash fertilizer; the small, 853-ton Portuguese *Alpha* also went down. Trawlers were hit and damaged. Other ships were sunk or crippled in August. On the tenth, the 929-ton Swedish *Varia* was sunk off southern Eire, another in a bag of eighty-five ships in six months. On 25 August the 3,821-ton British Steamer *Goathland* was steaming 200 miles west-southwest of Cape Clear, County Cork, with a cargo of Spanish iron ore when she was attacked by a Condor and hit by three bombs. Her call sign, GBZX, and her SOS were picked up, but she sank an hour after the attack, her crew safe.

In clear weather the Rudeltaktik (pack attack) would not depend on aircraft. In each convoy there was always at least one vessel (careless, or burning bad coal) writing the convoy's signature on the sky with smoke, and convoys could then often be sighted 20 miles away. A pack could be spread 20 miles apart on a line across the trade routes—in positions often decided by radio intelligence—with a good chance of sighting any convoy crossing that line by day. Dönitz accepted that the pack system necessitated a free use of radio, allowing British direction-finding (DF) stations to plot transmissions (though with the high frequencies used, the bearings were not very accurate). He hoped his back-room people could come up with better transmitting equipment.

With the pack spread out, the first boat to sight a target would report it to U-boat headquarters at Lorient, which would direct other boats to positions ahead of the convoy, surface speed 16 or 17 knots against a convoy's 8 or 9 knots. The original sighter shadowed the convoy as the touch keeper. In the early days the U-boat also homed in on her consorts by radio.

Old tactics would then have been to dive when the convoy was sighted and attack from below with torpedoes. But this greatly limited the submarines' mobility. To make use of their superior surface speed—and to render the enemy's asdic useless—Dönitz, following doctrine he had evolved before the war, ordered his boats to attack on the surface at night, with torpedoes or even gunfire.

Joachim Schepke was a graduate of the small *U-19*—a "canoe"—which, with only five torpedoes, had survived depth-charge damage to sink four ships. On 25 August 1940, Schepke approached Convoy HX 65 (homeward-bound) in his new *U-100*, on the surface in darkness, and sank three ships.[1] Three days later, it was outward-bound ON204's turn. Even should he be spotted in the darkness, Schepke had little fear of the convoy's escort of one corvette and one armed trawler to protect twenty-one ships. Just before midnight, the *U-100* fired a "fan" of torpedoes, in accordance with FdU's rules, when the convoy was 175 miles off Bloody Foreland, Northern Ireland. The first missile hit the British SS *Hartsmere* on the starboard side under the bridge. One minute later another tin fish struck the commodore's ship SS *Dalblair* amidships, and she sank in ten minutes.

On 1 September, FdU moved his headquarters from the barracks at Wilhelmshaven to a spacious house on the Boulevard Suchet, Paris, and began to issue detailed instructions on the application of Rudeltaktik to the night attack. When a pack had closed it was to wait for darkness. Then boats were to use their diesels, which gave a speed in excess of the enemy's, to attack in unison on the surface.

On the night of 7–8 September, Göring switched his bombers from English fighter airfields to night attacks on London. The Battle of Britain was over, the Battle of the Atlantic was about to begin. That night a quartet of U-boats, acting on information from the German radio-intercept service, ambushed the fifty-three ships of the slow, homeward-bound convoy SC2. Kuhnke in *U-28* was the first to sight the convoy, and he became the touch keeper. In very heavy weather he held on and guided Kapitänleutnant (senior lieutenant) Gunther Prien, the "Bull of Scapa," in his *U-47* and Otto Kretschmer in the *U-99*, the "lucky" boat with the two golden horseshoes on her conning tower, to the attack.[2] A Sunderland flying boat of RAF Coastal Command kept them down for a time, but a coordinated attack sank five ships.

Still at sea on 25 September, at the end of his patrol and looking forward to a soft bed and schnapps at the base in Lorient, Prien had one torpedo left when he was diverted far out into the Atlantic on a weather patrol. En route he sighted the forty-one ships of fast, inward-bound HX 72. He wirelessed headquarters, then hugged the convoy, the ether burning with homing signals. Next morning Kretschmer, Schepke, and Heinrich Bleichrodt in the *U-48* joined him; that evening the four closed in for the kill on the surface, maneuvering to put the bulky silhouettes of the merchantmen against the bright moonlight. The sea was calm, though occasional heavy rain showers spattered the bridge, necessitating oilskins.

HX 72 had a minimal, inexperienced escort of four ships, led by the sloop *Lowestoft*. At about 1020 the red light signaling that a ship had been torpedoed soared into the night from the center of the convoy. The *Lowestoft* illuminated the port flank with star shell—but the ocean was bare—then steamed to the rear with the corvette *Heartsease*. Just then a ship was torpedoed front-center, and another in the rear. The convoy began to break up, and the See Wolfen fell upon the scattering ships. The escorts fired more star shell, but the U-boats were faster and grateful for extra light on their targets. Only once in seven hours of attrition did an escort's asdic get a ping and start a depth-charge attack. In that time eleven ships were sunk, and 100,000 tons of supplies from the United States were lost.

In October Hitler postponed Operation Sealion, the invasion of Britain, and the Luftwaffe began bombing British ports and factories by night, with U-boats and surface raiders stepping up their campaign of destruction. Dönitz moved to Kernavel, near Lorient. From his operations room he could see his boats returning from patrol in time for him to meet them at the quayside.

No action better illustrates the early application of Dönitz's doctrine than the bloody convoy battle of 16–17 October 1940 for Convoy SC 7.

Bleichrodt's *U-48* sighted this slow convoy bringing supplies, mainly timber, from Nova Scotia to the Clyde just before midnight on the sixteenth, about 500 miles northwest of Ireland, escorted by three old sloops. He maneuvered his boat to within just over a mile of the convoy undetected by asdic, then contacted Lorient. Thus far he had followed the rules of Rudeltaktik, but he then gave in to temptation and fired a fan of three torpedoes on his own account at the mass of ships. The French tanker *Languedoc* exploded and the British merchantman *Scoresby* listed violently, tipping her deck cargo of pit props into the sea before sinking within minutes.

With dawn fast approaching, Bleichrodt distanced himself from the convoy, but shortly after daylight a Coastal Command Sunderland caught him on the surface.[3] As he crash-dived, the big flying boat's bombs exploded close aboard the boat. Lights and dials shattered, water sprayed in through hatches and periscope gaskets. The sloop *Scarborough* hunted the *U-48*, made an asdic contact, depth-charged, and lost it again. But Bleichrodt had been prevented from continuing his sighting reports.

When his signals ceased, the five boats detailed to attack the convoy—Gunther Endrass's *U-46*, Otto Kretschmer's *U-99*, Schepke's *U-100*, Fauenheim's *U-101*, and Fritz Moehle's *U-123*—were left with too big an area to search. They were ordered to reverse course, head east at full speed, and form a north-south barrier east of Rockall, well ahead of the enemy's last known position as reported by *U-48*. Meanwhile, Liebe's *U-38* and Kuhnke's *U-28* were alerted in case the convoy entered their parish. At dusk Liebe sighted SC 7, stalked the convoy until dark, torpedoed the freighter *Carsbreck*, and then resumed his original patrol.

After that the wolf pack began its surface attack. At 2015 Endrass fired a salvo of three torpedoes at the unguarded port bow of the convoy, sinking the Swedish freighter *Convellaria*. The sloop *Leith* and the corvette *Heartsease* joined the escorts, making four—still ludicrously insufficient for a convoy of thirty-four ships. Most of the boats followed doctrine and fired fans from outside the convoy. Kretschmer had become so skillful that in many cases he was able to sink a ship with the expenditure of only one torpedo. He made individual attacks whenever a target presented itself. In and about the convoy the U-boats prowled like wraiths, trimmed down with casings just awash, conned by the sore eyes of their young commanders among the looming vessels, whose bow waves and white wakes often slapped their conning towers in passing, propellers thumping. In the center of the convoy Kretschmer coolly picked off his targets, with torpedoes from other boats exploding all the time.

When dawn came the remains of the convoy limped toward the Clyde, leaving a wake of burning wood and oil and dead, dying, and shocked men with blackened faces desperately clinging to bits of flotsam. The convoy had lost twenty ships of its original thirty-four—seven to Kretschmer, four to Moehle, and the remainder to Endrass, Fauenheim, and Schepke—with priceless cargoes of steel, ammunition, timber, oil, petrol, and aircraft destroyed. The U-boat service began to refer to this brilliant and bloody action with some awe as the Night of the Long Knives.

Attrition by Condor, which Winston Churchill was calling the Scourge of the Atlantic, continued, though ships attacked were now often fighting back more effectively. On 6 September the little, 314-ton *Iwate* drove off three attacks with her Lewis. The defensive arming of merchantmen with old guns had been speeded up. On 30 September a Condor made a perfect attack on the 11,063-ton *Sussex,* carrying New Zealand dairy produce. The first bomb went down the funnel, and the second started a fire very near a cordite store. The Condor signaled by lamp for the *Sussex* to stop, but the ship ignored it. The Condor then sprayed the decks with cannon and machine-gun fire, the *Sussex* replying with her 3-inch gun and a few rounds from her 1902-vintage 6-inch. The fire in her hold was gaining, but the ship's resistance was enough to drive the Condor off. Wheelhouse wrecked, the *Sussex* navigated home by lifeboat compass.

Two stragglers from Convoy HG 44 were bombed. The *Baron Vernon* drove off her attacker with her 12-pounder and 4-inch, but the *Latymer*'s fire-gutted hull had to be destroyed because it was a danger to navigation.

The Condors' score of merchantmen sunk mounted. At the end of October came a star victory for Kampfgeschwader 40, which also featured at long last the sort of cooperation between Condor and U-boat that BdU had almost given up as a pipe dream.

Relations between the Luftwaffe and Kriegsmarine were notoriously bad, made worse by a personal antagonism between Göring and Dönitz. Time and again the BdU complained that his boats were not getting the assistance needed from the airmen. Then Kampfgeschwader 40 would grudgingly release one machine to work with the boats for a while, though so far there had been no instance of a Condor directing a U-boat to a convoy, and if any aircraft sighted a straggler it usually made an immediate attack on its own account.

This was exactly what happened in the first phase of an attack on 26 October. At 0400 the Condor of Oberleutnant Bernhard Jope lifted off the runway at Bordeaux for armed reconnaissance over the Atlantic to the north and northwest of Ireland, heading out over the sea in the pitch dark. Five hours later, a few minutes after nine o'clock, they were butting through heavy cloud and rain about 70 miles northwest of Donegal Bay when three huge funnels became visible through the grayness of the drizzle below.

The 42,500-ton Canadian Pacific liner *Empress of Britain* was on the last leg of her voyage from the Middle East, carrying servicemen and their families. This prestigious and beautiful ship had a top speed of 24 knots and was therefore making the passage unescorted.

The big Condor dived, flew over the ship from stern to bow at 500 feet, and dropped a bomb that hit the *Empress* abreast of the center funnel. The upperworks amidships began to blaze fiercely and give off clouds of choking, blinding, black smoke, which, as she was then steaming into wind, obscured the vision of the ship's after 3-inch anti-aircraft gunner. The Condor made two more runs. The after steering position was hit and the 3-inch wrecked. A dense pall of smoke rose up and fire consumed the exotic public rooms, glowing out of portholes and hatches. The great ship listed to starboard. Jope was sure she was doomed, and he set course for Bordeaux.

Thanks to heroic efforts, most of the people aboard this floating holocaust were taken off by the few boats that it had been possible to get into the water. They were transferred to destroyers and armed trawlers. The *Empress,* still smoking fore and aft, was still afloat on an even keel, and the tugs *Seaman* and *Thames* were ordered to salvage it.

KG40 thought Jope's attack report important enough to pass on to U-boat headquarters at Lorient. German intelligence and further air reconnaissance established the identity and approximate position of the Condor's victim. In the afternoon the 500-ton *U-32*, which had left Lorient for her operational area northwest of Ireland the day before, picked up a radio signal from base informing all U-boats in the area that the English liner *Empress of Britain,* in use as a troop transport, had received bomb damage from a German aircraft about 300 miles west of Malin Head. The boat was commanded by Oberleutnant-zur-See Hans Jenisch, an experienced submarine skipper with over 100,000 tons of Allied shipping in the bag.

The reported position, which was inexact, lay off the *U-32*'s course to her patrol area, and the *U-31* was likely to be closer to the ship, so Jenisch did not act on the report. But when a second message came through the next day, saying that the *Empress* lay burning and crippled in the same position, Jenisch altered course. He steered 60 miles to the east of the reported position, in case the liner was managing to make any way toward home, if she had not sunk in the meantime.

Toward noon the next day, with visibility good, he sighted the trucks of the *Empress*'s masts, dead ahead. Other masts could be seen, including those of escorting destroyers, and aircraft were sighted overhead. The *Empress* was under tow, escorted by the destroyers *Broke* and *Sardonyx*.

The presence of a Sunderland forced the *U-32* to dive and kept her below all day. With dusk approaching, Jenisch surfaced. But he could no longer make out the target, and he submerged again to use his hydrophones. At a distance of 20 miles he picked up propeller noises, surfaced, and headed toward the position at a good speed. Toward midnight the *Empress* was sighted, steaming at about 4 knots with her destroyer screen off her port and starboard bows.

Jenisch followed the ships patiently on the surface for about two hours, assessing their course, speed, and escort pattern. The destroyers were maintaining a zigzag. There came the perfect moment, when they moved outward from the *Empress* and opened up a gap into which the U-boat could slide for a point-blank attack. Jenisch seized the opportunity, maneuvered the boat into position to port of the liner, and dived to fire two torpedoes from a range of between 550 and 600 yards, one aimed at the ship's foremast, one at her mainmast. Then he turned away.

The first torpedo detonated prematurely. Jenisch turned the *U-32* toward the target again and aimed a third torpedo at her middle funnel. The liner was huge in the periscope's eye. The premature explosion of the first torpedo had obviously alerted the skeleton crew aboard the *Empress*, and lights moved about her scarred and blackened decks, sirens hooting. The forecastle was still on fire.

One after the other the two torpedoes found their marks, rocking the *U-32* with the explosions. One hit amidships and a boiler exploded. A white mushroom cloud rose high over the ship, which listed rapidly to port. The *U-32* was so close that in the periscope the huge shape seemed to be falling on top of her.

The tugs cast off their lines, and the destroyers probed for the attacker with their searchlights in the likely firing position off the *Empress*'s port bow. The *U-32* withdrew swiftly, trimmed low, down the wake of the liner. Jenisch watched the destroyers circling the toppling giant, firing at shadows on the sea. A flying boat swept very low over the submarine's conning tower without seeing it.

The *Empress*'s list increased, and after about ten minutes the liner sank. As a statistic, she was just one of sixty-three ships sunk by

U-boats in October, totaling 352,407 tons, the highest monthly loss of the war to date. This sinking was part of the Happy Time, as the U-boat service called the four months after the occupation of the Biscay ports.

Jenisch set off westward and reported the sinking to Dönitz. Two days later the *U-32* was sunk by the destroyer HMS *Harvester,* after an attack on a convoy straggler. Jenisch and most of his crew were taken prisoner.

Mother of Invention

In August 1940 Condors sank fifteen ships totaling 53,283 tons, and they damaged many more. When they extended their range by using Stavanger as a pit stop, their score rose. In November they sank eighteen ships totaling 66,438 tons. In January 1941, in the worst of winter weather, they sank fifteen ships (63,175 tons), while U-boats scored twenty-one ships (126,782 tons). In February the Condors' total rose to twenty-two ships (84,515 tons), the U-boats' to thirty-nine (196,783 tons).

Countermeasures were taken in hand.

RAF Coastal Command Whitley reconnaissance bombers were fitted out with air-to-surface-vessel (ASV) RDF. New Wellington reconnaissance, Beaufort torpedo reconnaissance, and long-range fighter squadrons were formed, and reinforced Beaufighter and Blenheim fighter squadrons were moved to Northern Ireland airfields. RAF bombing of the Condors' Bordeaux airfield began.

A program was set up to fit all oceangoing merchant ships with an antiaircraft gun, two Lewis machine guns, and one Hotchkiss in addition to a 6-inch or 4-inch antisubmarine gun. Coasters and short-sea traders over 500 tons were to have a 12-pounder and two machine guns, smaller vessels one machine gun. Oerlikon and Bofors were fitted if available. Kites and barrage balloons were flown as deterrents.

Other, more bizarre, devices were adopted. The Holman projector or "spud" (potato) gun was a stopgap weapon given to some ships in lieu of a high-angle antiaircraft gun. This was a smoothbore gun for throwing Mills grenades at low-flying aircraft using steam, compressed air, or cordite propellant. Another ingenious invention was the Harvey multiple 2-inch trough rocket projector, firing a fourteen-rocket salvo vertically. More effective was the unrotated projectile or parachute-and-cable rocket installation invented by Lord Cherwell, Churchill's scientific adviser. This fired projectiles containing parachutes that trailed explosive devices on wires. Two recorded instances of the UP's success were both during a Stuka raid on shipping in Dover harbor on 29 July 1940. Two Ju 87s tried to pass through gaps in the balloon barrage, became entangled in UP wires, and exploded.

Neither carriers nor catapult-equipped cruisers were available for convoy defense, but the old World War I seaplane-carrier *Pegasus* had an outmoded cordite-operated catapult used to train floatplane pilots. Equipped with three Fairey Fulmar naval fighters, the *Pegasus* was sent to sea with Gibraltar convoy OG 47 on 3 December 1939. She had no RDF and no proper wireless for communicating with her aircraft. Her aging triple-expansion engines could provide no more than 9 knots maximum, and defensive armament consisted of ten machine guns. Once launched, a Fulmar pilot could not be recovered by the ship and had to make land, ditch in the sea, or bail out.

Another stopgap measure was a reversion to the Q-ship of World War I, a heavily armed vessel masquerading as a merchantman. The merchantman *Crispin* went to sea with a hidden armament of one 6-inch low-angle gun for U-boats, a 12-pounder high-angle gun, four Oerlikon quick-firing cannon, and four single-barrel 2-pounder pom-poms for Focke-Wulfs. Her tactic was to drop out of a convoy and imitate a straggler. The *Crispin* did this with six convoys, but after some bad experiences with overtly armed merchantmen, U-boats were not keen to provoke a gun duel. On her sixth convoy, OB 280, the *Crispin* was sunk by torpedo.

In September 1940 Capt. M. S. Slattery, the Royal Navy's director of air material, proposed in a memorandum to the Fifth Sea Lord, responsible for naval aviation, "the fitting of catapults to suitable merchant ships." Accordingly, the liner *Springbank*, already under conversion to an auxiliary antiaircraft ship, and the three refrigerated fruit/passenger-carrying ships *Ariguani, Maplin,* and *Patia* were equipped. The 5,155-ton *Springbank* was given the heavy cruiser *Kent's* old cordite catapult, to carry a Fulmar fighter. In the *Ariguani* (6,746 tons, a coal burner built in 1926), *Maplin* (5,824 tons, built in 1932), and *Patia* (5,000 tons, built in 1922), a 6-inch gun on the forecastle was replaced by a rocket-powered catapult that was more powerful than the *Springbank's* cordite model.

These three vessels were designated fighter-catapult ships, to operate solely as warships, independently of convoys and without cargo. The *Ariguani*, typically, was armed with one 6-inch gun, one 12-pounder high-angle, two pom-poms, four rocket projectors, and two Holman projectors. There was a good workshop and crew room in a deckhouse on the well deck aft of and below the forecastle and under the after end of the catapult, with a large bench and ample racking. This space also accommodated a spare set of ailerons and elevators, fabric dope, Rolls Royce engine flight tool kits (for the Fulmar Mark I's Merlin VIII engine), gun-cleaning and other essential tools and spares. There were spark plugs and magnetos, Glycol coolant, special aircraft covers for weather protection, and flameless heaters for the cold.

The Fairey Fulmar was an excellent airplane, with clean lines, good maneuverability and takeoff, a moderate climb rate of 1,105 feet per minute, and long endurance. But a fighter's essential requirement of speed was fatally reduced by the weight of the observer and the rear cockpit. A "clean" Mark I's maximum speed at 9,000 feet was 246 MPH; 20 MPH lower at sea level, where many combats took place. Its speed was about equal to that of the Fw Condor. With a full load it could not catch the Fw, and too often this was indeed the result. Its armament of eight Browning machine guns was powerful but prone to let it down.

On 16 September 1941 the new Fulmar Mark II N4065 was launched from the *Springbank*. Its uprated engine, a Merlin XXX, gave it a good 10 knots more than the VIII, and Petty Officer Shaw over-hauled the shadowing Condor. But a very promising quarter attack was blighted by an almost-complete gun stoppage. On 17 September the *Springbank* was torpedoed and drifted helplessly until the nine-teenth, when it had to be sunk by a corvette's depth charges and 4-inch fire. A month later the *Ariguani* too was torpedoed but was towed to Gibraltar, to be returned to trade on 27 December.

HMS *Maplin*, the last of the fighter-catapult ships to be completed and the first to be equipped with a Hurricane, was commissioned on 22 April 1941. The Sea Hurricane Mark IA had only a marginal superi-ority over the Fw 200 at sea level. A new, clean machine had a top speed of 315 MPH against a Condor's 240, but those selected by the RAF for naval use were often expired veterans with low performance.

Inspection on delivery uncovered a mass of defects: threadless drain plugs; worn-out coolant pumps; twisted trim tabs; immovable levers; airspeed indicators reading yesterday's news; time-expired air com-pressors, generators, and magnetos; defective instruments; bolts, nuts, clips, seals, bonding strips, and locking wires missing; cables frayed; piping bent; and rust everywhere, especially on engine parts. The machines came in from conversion in this sort of condition, though spools and strengthening were in position and sound. One machine had been operational since October 1939 in two different RAF squadrons, had been shot down once and crashed twice. It was unusual to be able to check these details in logbooks, most of which were missing.

By May 1941 the U-boats were working as far out as 40 degrees west and as far south as the Sierra Leone area. But by this time there were also more antisubmarine craft available to the Allies, including fifty old destroyers loaned by the United States. In June the first all-the-way escorts were introduced on the Halifax route; in July on the Sierra Leone route. Shipborne radar and Snowflake illuminating rockets helped small escort groups to fight off night attacks. About the same time the Americans started to patrol the convoy routes part of the way across, establishing bases in Iceland. Aircraft with ASV began to attack U-boats at night, and the number sunk by aircraft rose.

On 17 June the *Maplin* met her first convoy, HX 131, between Greenland and Iceland. The ship escorted it through the Focke-Wulf danger zone and then transferred to HX 133, which had been roughly treated by weather and U-boats. "We expected low-level Focke-Wulf attacks," recalled Ron Spencer, then third officer of SS *British Progress.* "None transpired. We attributed this to the presence of HMS *Maplin.*"[1]

Early on 18 July the ship was with OB 346 west of Donegal Bay when escorts sighted a Condor. Lt. Richard Everett was launched in Sea Hurricane W9227 and tried to head off the Fw as it made for SS *Pilar de Larrinaga* in a "turnip" beam attack from starboard, dropping a bomb that hit the ship's saloon. Everett was about to press his firing button when the Condor's port wing broke off under fire from the ship. He flew 300 miles and landed in Ireland, still considerably frustrated.

On 3 August he was able to make amends. The *Maplin* was on her way to pick up a convoy when she sighted a Condor low on the horizon, 10 miles astern. Six minutes later the *Maplin's* Sea Hurricane IA was launched, with Everett at the controls. In the face of a hot fire from two cannon and three machine guns, with oil from the Condor covering his windscreen, he set the big machine alight with five-second bursts, ditched, and was picked up.

At Mr. Churchill's prompting, the catapult-ship idea was enlarged to include catapult aircraft merchant (CAM) ships, equipped with Hurricanes operated by RAF Fighter Command and carrying cargo.[2] Captain Slattery had also proposed "the fitting of the simplest possible flight deck and landing equipment" to merchant ships, which, as originally suggested, would continue to carry their normal cargo. This resulted in the merchant aircraft carriers (MACs), but first the Admiralty converted the captured 5,537-ton German cargo liner *Hannover* into an auxiliary aircraft carrier. Work had begun on 17 January 1941.[3]

A similar experiment was under way in the United States. In March 1939 Capt. John S. McCain, commanding the fleet carrier *Ranger,* had urged the secretary of the navy to build small carriers for use where a fleet carrier would be inappropriate. Rear Adm. William Halsey, com-

CAM ship with Hawker Sea Hurricane Mark 1A. (Shell U.K.)

mander, Aircraft Battle Force, was thinking along the same lines. At the age of fifty-two, he had won his gold wings as a carrier pilot to make him eligible to command a carrier. He watched the Royal Navy struggle through twelve months of war, and he also urged the conversion of some suitable merchantmen into auxiliary carriers. When the chief of naval staff Adm. Ernest King mentioned the concept to the president, Franklin Delano Roosevelt, the latter was enthusiastic and contributed the idea of equipping such ships with autogyros.

On 6 March 1941 the 13,499-ton SS *Mormacmail* was commandeered for conversion to a carrier. Meanwhile, in Britain, the Blyth Shipbuilding Company had been turning a German banana boat into an auxiliary aircraft carrier half the size of the *Ark Royal*.

After removing masts, derricks, funnel, upper bridge, and other superstructure down to boat-deck level, a steel flight deck was fitted only 368 feet long and 60 feet wide, with simplified arrester gear and a small bridge and flying control box flush with the flight deck forward to starboard. Exhaust ducts were under the flight deck. There was no hangar and no catapult. Gun armament was four single 20-mm Oerlikons and four single 2-pounder pom-poms, with one 4-inch sited right aft under the round-down of the flight deck. Depth charges were also carried.

There were only two arrester wires aft instead of a fleet carrier's six, with a wire barrier forward. Just aft of this barrier was one additional arrester wire, which, unlike the other two, had no hydraulic retardation and thus a much shorter, sharper pullout. Contact with this wire

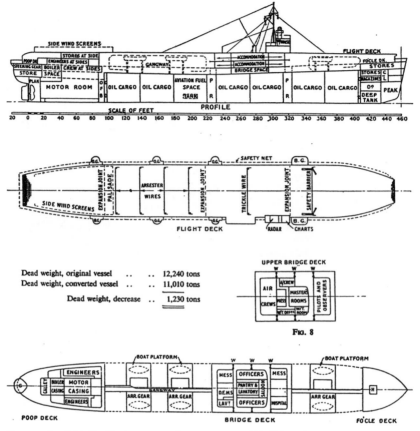

Dead weight, original vessel	.. ..	12,240 tons
Dead weight, converted vessel	.. ..	11,010 tons
Dead weight, decrease	..	1,230 tons

Fig. 8

Rapana class MACs. Outline general arrangement. (Shell U.K.)

by a pilot who had missed the first two would test the correct tightness of his harness and the strength of the plane's arrester hook.

Almost everything about the auxiliary carrier HMS *Audacity* was new, including the planes and pilots. The ship was to have had the hooked Sea Hurricane IBs, but these leftovers from the Battle of Britain had too many defects and were not ready.[4] The Admiralty, however, accustomed to coming in a bad second to the RAF in aircraft allocation, had been quick after the defeat of France to take over a batch of eighty-one American Grumman Wildcat F4F-3 single-seat fighters awaiting delivery to the French as G36As. Eight of these, renamed Martlet I's, were allocated to the *Audacity*'s Number 802 Squadron. Of their twelve pilots, six were temporary RNVR (Royal Navy Volunteer Reserve) officers, including a schoolboy, a teacher, a clerk, and a divinity student.

They found the Martlet reasonably easy to fly, though a fierce swing on takeoff could turn it, as its American pilots had found, into an "ass-buster." This was damped down by replacing the small, solid–rubber tired tail wheel with a much larger pneumatic type, which raised the tail wheel 9 inches and brought the rudder up into the slipstream in the three-point attitude. The Martlet I with its Wright Cyclone G-205A engine was not the fastest of contemporary fighters (top speed 304 MPH), but it had been built to withstand the special shocks and stresses of deck landing and catapult-boosted launchings. And so it proved when the squadron made its deck-landing trials. No one pranged. No one resorted to the hard-time "Jesus Christ" wire. Later the squadron received some Martlet IIs, with the Pratt and Whitney Twin Wasp engine and two more guns. Unlike the Mark I's, they had folding wings—unworkable at first, though in the *Audacity* this was largely irrelevant.

The new auxiliary aircraft carrier was commissioned on 17 June 1941, just beaten to the christening by her U.S. Navy counterpart, the USS *Long Island*. There were marked differences. The *Long Island* was twice the *Audacity's* tonnage, carried twenty-one aircraft, and had a hangar. The *Audacity* carried eight fighters in a permanent deck park. She was makeshift, but the need was urgent.

On 13 September 1941 the *Audacity* sailed from the Clyde to join the escort for OG 74 to Gibraltar, with six Martlets and eight pilots. Lack of a hangar complicated operations. For a patrol pair to take off, the remaining aircraft had to be parked right aft, leaving just 300 feet of deck. For the patrol's return, the parked planes had to be manhandled forward to the bows, probably in a high wind and salt spray. And each tired pilot had just two chances of snagging a wire before facing the Jesus Christ wire and after that the parked planes . . .

The air mechanics cursed, working out on the open flight deck in wind, rain, and cold, and the salt sea air that jammed throttles and guns; earthed firing circuits; and corroded gun wells, breechblocks and barrels, IFF switches, spark plugs, contact breakers, and all electrics. At dawn and dusk, hand torches masked by blue filters were the drill, screened by someone's hand or jacket.

At 1815 on 20 September, the dusk patrol sighted a U-boat. The Martlets dropped a marker, and the *Audacity's* RDF ranged on them at 12 miles. The convoy swerved aside and two sloops depth-charged, estimating damage. While the dawn patrol was rounding up strays, the Immediate Readiness section scrambled on reports of a Condor. Vectored by the carrier's well-run fighter-direction room, with particularly skillful use of RDF, they found the Fw at 600 feet. The fuselage of the new 200C-3 had been strengthened, but a 35-round full-deflection

The USS *Long Island*. (U.S. National Archives)

shot from Sub-Lt. Graham Fletcher's Brownings found a weak spot, and the whole tail unit broke off.

On the return voyage with HG 74, the ship met rough weather in the Bay of Biscay, with high winds and violent motion making takeoff dangerous. RAF Coastal Command crews had not been briefed on the new RN aircraft in their parish. One Martlet pilot was fired on by a suspected "friendly." Wounded in the mouth by windscreen splinters, he hit the emergency wire on landing and smashed his face against the gunsight, but HG 74 made the Clyde without loss on 17 October.

The *Audacity*'s activities had coincided with increasing success by Coastal Command. During October no ships were sunk within its operational range, about 400 miles. Twenty-six ships were lost in the gap beyond, only part of which was policed by the *Audacity*'s Martlets. They could fend off Focke-Wulfs from their convoy and they could spot U-boats for action by surface escorts, but they did not carry the means of sinking submarines. Slattery had suggested a switch to anti-submarine aircraft, if the Condor menace subsided.

That had not happened by the time the *Audacity* sailed with OG 76. In foul weather a section returning from a wild-goose chase found the deck pitching 65 feet and rolling 16 degrees. One Martlet slid into the sea but the flotation bags in its wings worked long enough for the pilot to be rescued. The Martlet commanding officer, Lt. Comdr. John Wintour, was killed attacking a Condor, which his wingman managed to finish off. Accidents, faults, and battle loss had reduced serviceable Martlets; young Eric "Winkle" Brown flew one with a bent airscrew, which put a strain on his engine. Brown and his wingman sighted two Condors and took one each. Brown destroyed his in a head-on attack.

The *Audacity* arrived at Gibraltar with one Martlet serviceable and was congratulated officially by the Admiralty for her big share in another passage without loss. There were in the vicinity of OG 76 six more Condors and the *Stoerbrecker* U-boat pack, trying to organize an attack on SL 91, bound for Britain from Sierra Leone. Had the two Fws shadowing OG 76 been allowed to continue unmolested, they might well have directed the wolf pack to that convoy. As it was, SL 91 also came in without loss.

By the end of November 1941, things were going better for the Allies in the Atlantic. Ship losses for that month were the lowest (thirteen ships, a total of 104,640 tons) since the spring of 1940 and almost the overall lowest in the war to date. There were then only fifteen U-boats operating in the Atlantic, eighteen others having slipped through into the Mediterranean to support the Afrika Korps. On 13 November one of these had torpedoed the *Ark Royal,* which had sunk the next day.

On 7 December the Japanese attacked Pearl Harbor, and four days later Germany declared war on the United States. American warships, which since early September had been escorting convoys as far as a midocean meeting point in the Atlantic, were now fully committed to the anti-U-boat war. The U.S. Navy would also be short of ships for some time, with commitments in two oceans.

The lower rate of sinkings by U-boats in November had been mainly due to better convoy defense. In Mid-December Capt. Johnnie Walker, RN, fought the first of his many successful battles with U-boats, in defense of HG 76 from Gibraltar to Britain. This convoy had the strongest escort it was possible to provide, with nineteen sloops and corvettes and HMS *Audacity* for thirty-two merchantmen. The Admiralty had wanted the carrier to add to her strength two or three Swordfish saved from the *Ark Royal,* but apparently they lacked complete crews. The *Audacity* made do with four patched-up Martlets.

One day out from Gibraltar, the Australian destroyer HMAS *Nestor* destroyed the *U-127.* Two days later a Martlet drove a U-boat down with its Brownings. Another submarine, the *U-131,* surfaced, and Walker sent Fletcher's Martlet to keep her busy while he raced to the spot. In attacking the U-boat with his machine guns, Fletcher was killed by a cannon shell. But four sloops arrived in time to destroy the submarine with shell fire, a victory they repeated the next day with the *U-434.* Walker's own *Stork* rammed and depth-charged the U-boat, which had sunk the sloop *Stanley.* Brown destroyed a Condor in a head-on attack; his wingman Lt. "Sheepy" Lamb damaged another. A net of U-boats, with special orders from Dönitz to make the carrier their prime target, was closing, however. At 2033 on 21 December a merchantman was torpedoed, and four minutes later a torpedo from the *U-751* hit the *Audacity,* followed by two more. A tremendous explosion blew off the carrier's bows, and ten minutes later she sank.

Dönitz was greatly relieved by this result. The new aircraft carrier had been the most dangerous addition to enemy escort forces. Her aircraft had repeatedly compelled his U-boats, when they had been trying to overhaul the convoy using their greater surface speed, either to submerge or to withdraw altogether. The Martlets had also prevented any protracted shadowing or homing procedures by German aircraft. Dönitz issued orders to all his submarine commanders to make any such vessel their main target in future convoy operations.

When the *Audacity* was sunk, the first of six new American conversions for Britain, HMS *Archer,* was on trials. The others were nearing completion.[5] They were larger than the *Audacity*—between 8,200 and 9,000 tons, 492.5 feet long, and 60 feet wide, with a 410-by-87-foot flight deck, a hangar, and a catapult. The *Archer* had a bridge box like the *Audacity's,* the others a small bridge island to starboard. Each was to carry fifteen aircraft. Diesel engines gave a maximum speed of some 17 knots. Gun armament comprised three single 4-inch antiaircraft guns and fifteen 20-mm antiaircraft guns (four twin and seven single).

With the entry of the United States into the war, much of the U-boat strength was switched to the thick traffic moving up and down the eastern coasts of the Americas, for which the U.S. Navy would be hard pressed to find escorts, at least for some time. Allied shipping losses reached 700,000 tons in June 1942. But with the completion of an American coastal convoy system, the U-boats' bonanza there was over. With his submarine production at its peak, Dönitz made a renewed onslaught on the transatlantic convoys, and the bloodiest period in the Battle of the Atlantic began.

The U-boats' targets were some fifteen inward-bound convoys a month. A normal convoy comprised about thirty ships, but gradually much larger groups, sometimes as many as sixty, would be assembled.

High-frequency direction-finding (HF/DF or Huff-Duff) sets were now in use in ships that could pick up the HF radio signals made by U-boats in the early stages of a pack attack. They could then fix a submarine's position by cross bearings.

The performance of asdic had been disappointing and had not proved to be the answer to the U-boat, mainly because of its short range. This was nominally 2,000 to 3,000 yards but was often reduced to less than 1,000 yards by high salinity conditions in the sea. Asdic could not register the exact depth of a target or scan the area immediately beneath it. Exploding depth charges set up turbulence that inhibited further sound waves until it had subsided. Asdic frequently led to the destruction of a U-boat once it had been located but was ineffective as an area sweep. For this reason it had proved better to use antisubmarine vessels to escort convoys than to hunt for U-boats independently. Nevertheless, asdic was responsible for 68 of the 104 U-boats destroyed in the first two years of the war, and now a special Q Attachment was invented to reach submarines diving below the normal beam.

Captain Walker invented the "creeping attack," which helped to counter the limitations of asdic. Once a U-boat had been located, the locating ship kept in touch with the target but did not attack it. Instead she used short-range radio to direct another escort, which crept up on the target with her asdic switched off. Walker also used a blanket attack, with three or more escorts saturating the area around the target with depth charges, thus providing a greatly increased chance of a kill.

Efforts to fit HF/DF in every escort were stepped up. In March 1942 the improved FH3 asdic, fitted with a second oscillator, went into action against submarines with the Lend-Lease destroyer HMS *Leamington,* escorting Convoy WS 17. Thereafter it proved to be an important antisubmarine device, and by the end of 1942 there were enough sets available for two or three escorts with every convoy to be fitted with it.

RAF Coastal Command patrols with ASV Mark II over the Bay of Biscay were increased, and Dönitz noticed that his submarines on transit there were being surprised more often. In May the powerful Leigh searchlight was fitted in Vickers Wellington bombers and used in conjunction with ASV to attack U-boats at night. The aircraft were brought close to the target by radar, whereupon the huge Leigh Light would be switched on.

Puzzled for a time by his suddenly increasing losses, Dönitz then diagnosed an increase and improvement in enemy radar. He ordered search receivers for fitment in his boats, then radar sets, and he initiated experiments to insulate submarines against radar. U-boats were ordered to transit the bay submerged by night, surfacing only when it was essential to charge batteries. U-boat losses there fell after fitment of the new Hagenuk FuMB radar search receiver. A U-boat could now tell when an aircraft with ASV approached, and it had time to dive. But in spite of improvements like these, U-boat losses overall rose. In the first six months of 1942, twenty-one U-boats were destroyed. In the second six months, sixty-four sunk in all waters, mostly in the North Atlantic—a near break-even figure. There was still a long way to go, however, before the Allies could in any way relax. In November 1942 losses were over 700,000 tons, caused by the drain of escorts to the North African landings.

The spread of airborne radar gave the Allies a boost, in particular the fitting of the excellent new 10-cm (3.9-inch) ASV Mark III in Coastal Command aircraft. This began in February 1943. The set was much better than the Mark II and could not be picked up by the U-boat FuMB search receiver, so the element of surprise was restored to Leigh Light aircraft. The Germans produced the Wanz receiver.

Bad weather in January 1943 helped to reduce Allied losses to 203,000 tons, but these rose in February to 359,328 tons. Twenty-seven new U-boats left the yards each month, a figure that exceeded losses.

March was crucial. Convoy SC 121 was detected by the German Radio Intercept Service, and thirteen boats of the *Neuland* group gathered south of Greenland's Cape Farewell. By the time of the U-boats' heaviest attack on the night of 9–10 March, the convoy had been scattered and battered by gales. Four of the eight escorts had RDF breakdowns, three lost their asdic domes, and others their Huff-Duff aerials. Twelve ships were sunk. Three more convoys followed at rapid intervals, routed 350 miles to the south of SC 121 but picked up by enemy radio intercept.

With HX 229 was the USS *Bogue,* the first of the U.S. Navy's escort carriers detailed to help the British in the Battle of the Atlantic. "Shall I run interference?" signaled Capt. Giles Short to the British senior officer of escorts, immediately on joining the convoy.[6] Unfamiliar with American football terminology and perhaps wary of a beginner's enthusiasm, the British officer declined the offer.[7]

In the fierce battle for the convoy, the *Bogue*'s new Grumman Avenger bombers were cheated out of beginner's luck by malfunctioning depth charges. The aggressive escort carrier then had to leave her second convoy early to find smooth water in which to refuel her escorts. Her aircraft had this time been deck-bound by the wild weather. Feeling their way in the techniques of U-boat hunting, the escort carriers had arrived.

Firepower, Arctic

The supply convoy PQ 17 sailed to Russia in June 1942. On a rumor that the *Tirpitz*, sister of the *Bismarck*, was out, the British First Sea Lord, in Whitehall, ordered the ships of the convoy to scatter. Thereupon, fourteen ships were sunk by air attack and another ten by U-boats.

When PQ 18 sailed in September, the long Arctic day had shrunk, providing a few hours of darkness to hide in. HMS *Avenger*, the second of the new escort carriers converted from American ships, with twelve Sea Hurricanes, joined the already extra-strong escort of sixteen fleet destroyers and the antiaircraft cruiser HMS *Scylla*.

The Hurricanes were at first misused, in attempts to shoot down shadowing Condors and Blohm und Voss BV 138s. The Germans simply brushed aside the fighters' small-caliber 0.303-inch bullets and eluded them in low cloud and mist, while fifty torpedo-bombers hit the ships. Flak destroyed five of these and a Hurricane one more, but eight ships were sunk.

At tea time nine He 115 torpedo-bombers attacked and the ships' antiaircraft-gun barrage spoiled their aim, with the Hurricanes once again chasing shadowers, and losing one of their section leaders. In the evening twelve Heinkels attacked. This time some of the Hurricanes assisted the barrage, and half the bombers were destroyed.

It was now clear that fighters armed with only 0.303-inch guns had little chance of destroying shadowers (especially the armored BV 138s) before they could report the convoy. When Heinkels and Ju 88s attacked the next day, they were met by nine Hurricanes. Twenty-five German aircraft were shot down by the defending fighters and the barrage—which also downed three Hurricanes. Next day, 12 Septem-

Sea Hurricanes in the hangar of an escort carrier. (Royal Navy)

ber, a large force of the enemy appeared but bombed through the cloud and did not appear again until the *Avenger, Scylla,* and the destroyers had left to join the homeward-bound convoy. At that stage fifteen Heinkels had only *Empire Morn's* CAM Hurricane to worry about. However, Flying Officer A. H. Burr not only destroyed one bomber and made several others miss, but he coolly navigated himself to a Russian airfield, tanks almost dry, rather than ditch and lose his aircraft.

PQ 18 arrived in Archangel with relatively fewer losses—ten ships by air attack and none by U-boats, lower than any other Russian convoy since PQ 12. Forty-one German aircraft had been destroyed for four Hurricanes and one pilot.

The excellent performance of the convoy antiaircraft-gun armament in PQ 18 illustrated the increasing firepower of Allied ships, the need for which had been realized early on in ship defense. Of the forty-one aircraft destroyed, the majority had fallen to the intense barrage thrown up by the powerful escort, especially the big fleet destroyers.

Merchant-ship armament was also increasing, from the odd elderly 3- or 4-inch to encompassing some of the more modern and sophisticated weaponry being fitted to escorts. Along with destroyers, many of the merchantmen were receiving the 4.5-inch high-angle gun that had been fitted in the *Ark Royal;* in the submarine depot ships *Forth* and *Maidstone;* in the older capital ships *Queen Elizabeth, Valiant,* and *Renown;* and in cruisers, including PQ 18's *Scylla* (called the Toothless Terror by its crew).

The most effective antiaircraft weapons were the quick-firing cannon pom-pom, Bofors, and Oerlikon. The 2-pounder pom-pom was to be found in all categories of Allied warships, and the size of a battery increased many times throughout the war—from four Mark VI mountings in the *Warspite* and *Ark Royal* early in the war to six in fleet carriers, and as many as eight in the *King George V*-class battleships by September 1945. These came in single (manual and power-trained), twin, quadruple, and even eightfold forms, though the latter were too

Bofors gun installation in an escort carrier. (D. J. Cole)

heavy for the smaller ships. The original manually operated HA Mark IIs, with elevation of plus 80 degrees to minus 5 degrees, were found in the older destroyers, in home-defense motor launches (HD MLs), and in other coastal craft.

Britain developed the Swedish Bofors 40-mm Mark I into a twin Mark II version, which, although effective, proved a difficult mounting to maintain under war conditions of service. The United States manufactured the Mark II version and developed a quadruple mounting. With their vast resources, the Americans built large numbers of both Marks, many being supplied under Lend-Lease to the British and other Allied navies. The appearance of the USN Bofors in RN ships usually indicated a North American refit.

Probably the most successful of all antiaircraft guns was the Swiss Oerlikon, a gun contrary to normal British practice in its working, and requiring cartridges lubricated with antifreeze grease. The breech was not locked at firing, the round being fired before it was fully home in the chamber, and the neck of the case swelling to form a gas seal. The explosion pressure blew the empty case back against the breech, forcing it to the rear against the barrel springs. Rate of fire was 465–80 rounds per minute, and the magazine held 60 rounds, driven along the internal track by a spring. Of the various Oerlikon Marks in Allied service, Mark I was the original Swiss-made gun; Mark II the British; IIUS and IVUS the American version. The differences between the Mark I and the others were mainly in the arrangements of the buffer springs and in the capability of the Mark I to fire single shots.

The American-converted escort carrier *Dasher,* which had reached Britain from the States, was to go with Convoy JW 53 to Russia in February 1943, though her squadron was not worked up. Off Iceland a gale sprang up. The *Dasher,* typically of the BAVGs (U.S.-converted auxiliary carriers allocated to the Royal Navy),[1] was rolling and pitching giddily and smashing through the heavy seas, when a seaman reported that he could see the escorts through the ship's side. Inspection revealed cracks in the plating around the leading ports, which had been hastily welded into position at the last minute in Hoboken. The violent motion was enlarging the cracks dangerously, and the *Dasher* was forced to turn back for repair.

On 27 March 1943, repairs completed, the ship was anchored in the Clyde River, Scotland. Her Sea Hurricane IICs were refueling in the hangar when a tremendous explosion blew a hole in the *Dasher's* bottom. Five minutes later she sank.

The board of inquiry attributed the explosion to the igniting of petrol vapor from a leaking valve in the petrol-control compartment, badly sited below a mess deck. A carelessly dropped cigarette butt had caused it, they concluded, blaming the American safety arrangements.

American experts blamed British inexperience with the fuel-safety arrangements, in which carbon dioxide was pumped through the system to purge it; they also criticized British slackness in safety drills.

The obvious presence of persistent and widespread petrol vapor and pools of petrol below decks was well known to the crews, who took it for granted that a torpedo hit would explode the petrol and blow the ship apart immediately. The volatile high octane was carried in compartments not designed for it. British safety arrangements were based on a drain-back principle, the operation of which still left petrol vapor in the system but no dangerous fuel deposits. As a result of the *Dasher*'s loss, RN engineers rigidly overhauled fuel-safety arrangements in all their auxiliary carriers.

After playing an important part in the North African landings in early November 1942, the *Avenger* was returning to Britain when the *U-155* torpedoed her just west of the Straits of Gibraltar. The tin fish struck amidships, crushing the thin merchant ship's plates like eggshell and igniting the aircraft fuel that was stored in crude, unprotected tanks in the bottom. There was a huge explosion, and the *Avenger* jackknifed amidships and sank quickly.

The engine troubles that afflicted the six BAVGs did not occur in the thirty-two other American escort carriers in service with the Royal Navy, nor in the ninety U.S. Navy CVEs. The majority of these had been new vessels built from scratch on merchant hulls only, whereas the AVGs had experienced hard sea time in merchant service. In addition to the carriers from the States, four were built in Britain on merchant hulls. These were HMS *Activity* and the *Nairana*-class *Campania, Nairana,* and *Vindex.*

They were solid in a traditional way; their hulls were riveted. The Admiralty considered this stronger than the all-welded construction of the American-built carriers (and, incidentally, of the *Ark Royal*), which, if sloppily carried out by wartime labor (witness the *Dasher*), could open up under the stresses of heavy seas or combat maneuvering.

The *Nairana*s were diesel propelled with twin screws, better for maneuvering than the single screws of the AVGs and providing backup if one shaft was damaged. Flight decks were steel plated in contrast to the Oregon–pine planked ships of the *Bogue* class. They had no catapults and only one elevator, which made readying aircraft difficult.

The *Vindex* gained a reputation as a mother of invention. Experiments with a Hurricane wing led to the fitting of two rocket rails beneath each wing of the ship's fighters, which still retained their four cannons. One machine had two of its cannons removed to make space for two marine markers to assist HF/DF tracking.

Improvements were also made in the ship's Swordfish. A crash into the wire barrier forward aboard the *Vindex* was not considered a great disaster. At the fore end of the hangar was rigged an assembly box with wings on either side, a complete tail plane assembly just above, an undercarriage below, and in front an engine unit with propeller requiring only four bolts to fix it to the front of a fuselage. The best turnaround was a thirteen-hour repair of an aircraft that had destroyed its starboard wing on a pom-pom and its port wing on the barrier, had buried its engine in the bridge island and damaged its after fuselage.

With no catapult, getting a Swordfish off the deck with a worthwhile war load was often a problem. The Robinson patent disengaging gear was sited on the curve of the round-down aft, with the aircraft attached to it by a single strop. The pilot opened up to full revs, the strop was released, and he went off with the equivalent of about an extra knot and a half of wind speed.

Then the *Vindex* received her new Swordfish Mark IIIs, with two innovations in equipment. These aircraft were all fitted with the new ASV Mark XI. This set had a rotating scanner housed in a big bulge under the nose. The observer now had a plan-position-indicator (PPI) screen in the cockpit, with a revolving scan in place of the old vertical scale. The positions of ships and landmasses all around the ship were

Sea Hurricane aboard HMS *Vindex* with four rocket rails installed aboard ship. (Royal Navy)

Fairey Swordfish Mark III with nose radar scanner. (Royal Navy)

revealed as the scanner beam passed over them. The telegraphist and air gunner had been eliminated.

The new machines were also equipped with rocket-assisted takeoff gear (RATOG). Rocket tubes were mounted in two clusters below the fuselage, one on each side. The principle was to fire the cordite charge toward the end of a takeoff run, thus reducing the amount of deck required and allowing a heavier war load. The pilot's front gun had been removed when rocket projectiles (RPs) had been fitted, and it was an obvious convenience to use the redundant control column gun button to operate RATOG, since the throttle was connected, through selectors, to the weapons.

Landing in the dark or in bad visibility was made easier when CPO Charles Waldram of the electrical staff put together a pair of illuminated "bats" for the deck landing-control officer to use in bringing down tired pilots. He took 12-volt bulbs and reflectors from the ship's toilet's lighting system. He and armorer Norman Pickup also fitted an illuminated target disk on the windscreen of each Swordfish to help the pilot aim the aircraft in the dark. Another valuable modification they made was the repositioning of the switches in the pilot's cockpit. All the switches had originally been fitted down the starboard side of the cockpit, making them awkward to operate, especially when wearing the usual thick gloves. One pilot thumbed a wrong switch and dropped a flare on one of the flight-deck crew. All the wiring was altered and the switch assemblies rebuilt.

But the *Vindex*'s pièce de résistance was the Morrison blind-approach system. Air radio officer Jock Morrison took a Mark XI ASV aircraft unit with its scanner uppermost and set it up outboard on the starboard side aft, connected to a modified aircraft PPI. After the air direction room had brought it to within some 3 miles of the ship, the approaching aircraft could be controlled via its radio altimeter to within 100 yards of the deck. The batsman, wearing headset and throat microphone, then took over with his Waldram illuminated bats.

Special measures were taken to remove the hovering menace of the *Tirpitz*. A midget submarine, or X-craft, had been developed early in the war for attacking big ships in anchorages protected from surface craft and conventional submarines. After experiments, the *X-3* and *X-4* were built between 1940 and 1943. They were 43–45 feet long and displaced 30 tons surfaced, 32.75 submerged, carrying two detachable amatol charges. These could be placed, from inside the boat, on the sea bottom beneath the target or on her keel. A diver from the X-craft attached magnetic clamps using a flooding chamber for exit and reentry. Six more X-craft were built, 52 feet in length, with a speed of 6–8 knots submerged. Range was 1,200 miles; depth limit 300 feet. Two detachable side charges weighed about 2 tons.

These six boats, towed by T-class submarines, left Scotland on 11 September 1943. Two were lost on tow; one malfunctioned. Lt. Henty Creer's *X-5*, Lt. Donald Cameron's *X-6*, and Lt. Godfrey Place's *X-7* continued to a point off Alten Fjord in Norway. Here their four-man attack crews cast off and navigated down Alten and into Kaa Fjord, where the *Tirpitz* and other major warships lay. The missing craft had been targeted on the *Scharnhorst* and the Panzerschiff *Lützow* (ex-*Deutschland*), the three survivors on the *Tirpitz*.

The *X-6* followed a harbor launch through the gate in the antitorpedo nets and located the *Tirpitz*. But the midget sub struck a rock and broke surface twice near the target, rising again under her port bow into heavy machine-gun and grenade fire. Cameron dived under the ship, placed his charges under her forward turrets, surfaced, scuttled the *X-6*, surrendered, and was taken aboard the *Tirpitz*. He said nothing under interrogation but the Germans guessed his mission. They were desperately trying to shift the *Tirpitz* when the *X-7* was sighted. Place dived under the ship and secured one charge under her forward turret, the other about amidships. Trying to escape, he tangled with the nets just as his and Cameron's charges, and probably Henty Creer's, went off. The *Tirpitz* rose bodily and crashed back into the water, listing heavily to port, a huge hole in her hull, her after gun turret torn from its mounting, the steering gear and engines seriously damaged, and lighting, radar, and damage-control systems wrecked. The *X-7* was badly damaged and sank just as her crew leapt onto a moored gunnery target. The *X-5* was never seen again and was probably sunk by a combination of damage from the *Tirpitz*'s guns, the destroyer *Z-29*, and patrol boats. The *Tirpitz* did not sink but took six months to repair. She was again disabled by carrier-borne aircraft and finally sunk by blockbuster bombs from RAF Lancasters.

The battlecruiser *Scharnhorst*, the last big surface threat to the Allied convoys, attempted to attack Convoy JW 55B on the dim Arctic day of 26 December 1943, in raging seas and freezing temperatures. A Royal Navy cruiser force turned darkness into day with its RDF, ranged on the German battlecruiser with its Type 284s, and destroyed the German's Seetakt. Finally the battleship *Duke of York*, with her big guns, cruisers, and destroyers with torpedoes, all radar-controlled, finished off the *Scharnhorst*.

Battle of the Boffins

In the first twenty days of bloody March 1943, the U-boats sank a staggering total of 627,377 tons—108 ships lost, two-thirds of them in convoy. In mid-month forty U-boats, acting on information from B-Dienst, attacked two convoys and in four days sank twenty-one ships for the loss of one U-boat.

The horror of March was in fact the dark night before the dawn for the Allies at sea. U-boat losses now equaled the number of new boats, and in April their kills were only half those of March.

On 21 May, a lovely late spring day, ceiling unlimited except for a few scattered clouds at 3,000 feet (useful for cover) and wind 15 knots from the east, the USS *Bogue* and her screen of five old four-stacker destroyers were 500 miles southeast of Cape Farewell, Greenland, escorting ON 184. At 2110 an Avenger TBF was cruising at 145 knots, on the second leg of the last patrol of the day, when a U-boat was sighted. The TBF dived and dropped four depth charges as the submarine crash-dived. A search by the escorts drew a blank.

The *Bogue's* westbound convoy and the eastbound HX 239, escorted by the hitherto unlucky HMS *Archer*, were now drawing close to one another, the latter to the south.

The *Bogue*, with her larger hangar, could carry up to twenty-eight aircraft and was sailing at present with twenty, comprising eight Avengers and twelve Wildcats. The *Archer*, with capacity for eighteen, was carrying twelve, a mix of nine Swordfish and three Martlets. The F4F-4 Wildcat (maximum speed 320 MPH at 18,000 feet; 242 at 15,000 feet) was a more advanced model than its Martlet II brother (304 MPH at 13,000 feet). There was a greater contrast between the Grumman Avenger TBF-1 and the Fairey Swordfish II. The stately

Swordfish biplane dated back to 1933 and had been rated obsolete in 1939. The Avenger, the most modern naval bomber in service, had a top speed of over 275 MPH; 132 in cruise. A Swordfish with no war load might just manage 125; 80 in cruise. Range of a Swordfish on internal tank at economical cruising speed was some 546 miles, and 770 with an extra 69-gallon tank. An Avenger could fly 1,105 miles on its basic tankage; 1,390 with two drop tanks. The pilot, radioman, and turret gunner of a TBF were accommodated in a comfortable "glasshouse," but a Mark II Swordfish pilot sat in a high, windy, open cockpit, with the observer (navigator) and telegraphist/air gunner in a bathtub-shaped open cockpit down behind him. The Avenger was all metal; the Stringbag was of wood and fabric.

Yet the TBF did not have all the advantages. The Swordfish, so much slower and thus more vulnerable in an approach to a well-defended target, had a better view from its open cockpits and could sight a U-boat sooner. It also had better ASV. The Avenger could lift four 500-pound bombs, the Swordfish one less, but some of the *Archer*'s Mark IIs had had their lower wings specially strengthened to operate the new rocket projectiles (RPs), with racks for eight fitted to each machine. In fact, the *Archer*'s Swordfish were the first naval aircraft to take RPs to sea. Swordfish had knocked out the Italian Fleet at Taranto, crippled the mighty *Bismarck*. Using cloud cover properly they could still be effective, though they could not use the American accelerator in the *Archer* to help them lift a bigger load.

Lt. (jg) Roger Kuhn's TBF stalked the *U-468* from a cloud on 22 May, dived, and let go three Mark 44 flat-nosed Torpex-filled depth bombs and one Mark 17 TNT (trinitrotoluene). The second fell almost directly under the U-boat's stern, while his bullets hit the submarine's 20-mm-gun crew. The U-boat began to trail a bluish oil streak, circled for a short time, then sank stern first.

Lt. Dick Rogers in his F4F was flying to assist when he sighted the wake of Kapitänleutnant Rudolph Bahr's *U-305*, which crash-dived. Bahr stayed down until Rogers had gone, then surfaced to resume his pursuit of ON 184 but was sighted from Ens. Stewart Doty's TBF. Doty hid in cloud, then dived and dropped his four depth bombs off the U-boat's port quarter. The boat jerked to port, lurched to starboard, and slowly sank, emitting a huge bluish oil bubble. The bow appeared briefly, then vanished. Another big blotch of oil arose. Doty claimed a kill. In fact the *U-305*'s pressure hull had been ruptured, and the submarine surfaced when he had gone only to face Lt. R. L. Stearns's TBF. He released his four depth bombs, and his turret gunner engaged the U-boat's 20-mms. Badly damaged, the *U-305* limped out of the fight.

The remainder of the Donau-Mosel wolf pack, which was scattered, made uncoordinated attempts to attack both convoys. Now it was the

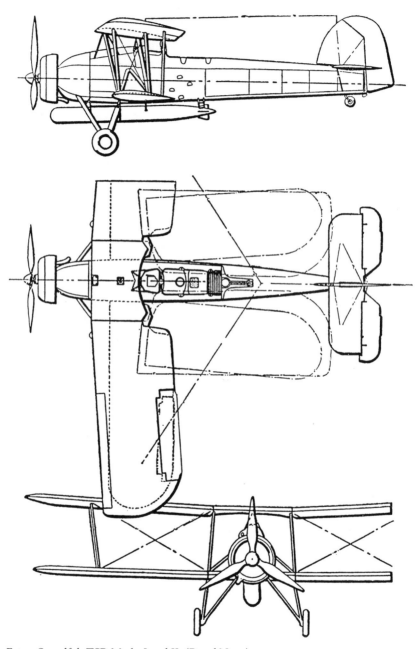

Fairey Swordfish TSR Marks I and II. (Royal Navy)

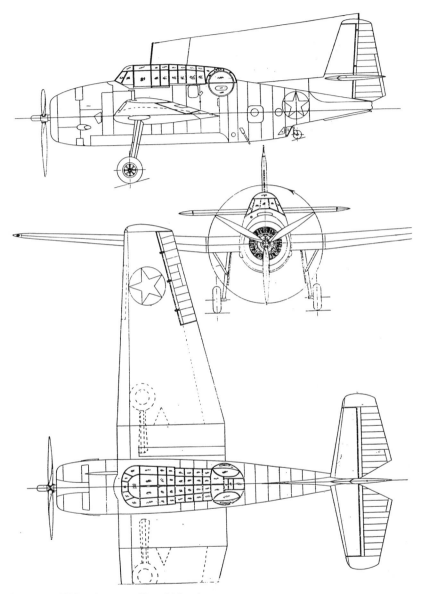

Grumman TBF-1 Avenger. (Royal Navy)

Archer's turn. In the early afternoon, Swordfish F sighted the *U-468*, Roger Kuhn's former antagonist, which was now looking for HX 239. Shadowing from cloud, the Stringbag, which in the light winds had lifted only two depth charges from the deck, waited for reinforcements. Then the U-boat dived and the TSR attacked with its two charges, but there was no sign of a hit.

At 1723 the *Bogue*'s new Huff-Duff picked up a U-boat transmission 23 miles off ON 184's port quarter. Lt. (jg) William F. Chamberlain's TBF was launched, headed down the bearing, and seven minutes later sighted the wake of *U-569*. The TBF circled in the broken cumulus to make an undetected approach from astern. Diving and increasing speed, it got down to 100 feet and let go four TNTs, scoring a perfect straddle. Chamberlain was back circling the *Bogue* when he heard Lt. Howard Roberts in a second TBF broadcast report the U-boat surfacing. Chamberlain flew back to the scene. Roberts attacked with his depth bombs as the *U-569* rose up, and men began leaping out of the conning-tower hatch and into the sea. Both TBF gunners opened up on them to drive them back to the U-boat and thus make them reluctant to let the sea-cocks be opened to flood the boat. A prime aim was to capture a U-boat intact for its valuable technology, signals, orders, and codebooks—especially its Enigma machine and sets of daily rotor settings.[1]

No more heads appeared out of the boat, and someone waved a white tablecloth. A destroyer steamed up and readied a boarding party but the U-boat's chief engineer had opened the flood valves, and the submarine disappeared. *U-569* was the first U-boat to be sunk by aircraft from an escort carrier. The American destroyer rescued twenty-four men.

Meanwhile the *U-218* had picked up HX 239, the *Archer*'s convoy, 700 miles north of Flores in the Azores, and informed Befehlshaber der U-boote at Lorient. Just before dawn, Karl Schroeter in the *U-752* sighted the convoy and signaled U-boat headquarters. The destroyer HMS *Keppel*'s Huff-Duff intercepted the signal, the escorts went hunting, and the *Archer* was asked to fly off searches. At 2055 Swordfish F sighted a periscope feather and dropped four depth charges around it. Swordfish G and Martlet B sighted a big milch cow supply U-boat and dropped some hopeful depth charges in its disappearing swirl.

At 2158 Lt. Harry Horrocks's Swordfish B, armed with eight of the new rocket projectiles, was launched, with orders to circle the port quarter of the convoy. Twenty minutes later a U-boat was sighted about 10 miles off. It was Schroeter's *U-752*, heading at 15 knots for the convoy.

Horrocks turned into cloud. Observer Lt. Noel Balkwill passed him a course of 195 degrees, which he calculated would take them into a good position for a surprise attack. They flew on blind for four and a half minutes. Balkwill calculated that the target should now be dead ahead, range just over a mile. He told Horrocks to dive out of the cloud.

The Stringbag nosed out of the cumulus at 1,500 feet. The U-boat was about a mile away, fine under their port bow. Horrocks dived,

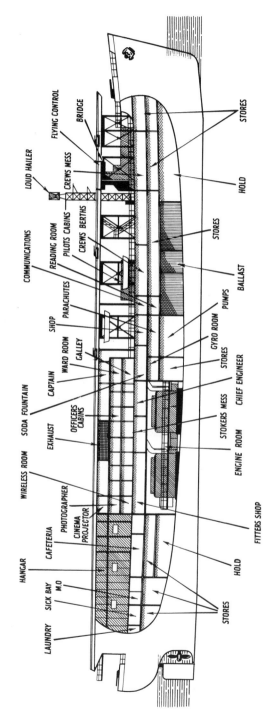

HMS *Archer*. (Royal Navy)

holding the submarine steady in the Swordfish's old ring-and-bead gunsight.

At 800 yards he fired a pair of rocket projectiles. The RPs lanced into the water about 150 yards short of the unsuspecting U-boat. Schroeter hastily triggered off the squawking siren and the submarine's bow tilted in a crash dive.

At 400 yards he fired a second salvo. The two small splashes went up 30 yards short of the conning tower. At 300 yards the third pair shot from their launching rails on trails of flame, plunging in just abaft the conning tower, 10 feet short.

The U-boat was tilting steeply, only the stern clear of the water, when the fourth and last pair of RPs hit. Two 25-pound solid heads, fired at 200 yards, smashed through the submarine's hull on the waterline about 20 feet ahead of the rising rudders.

The *U-752* continued downward at the same steep angle for a few minutes, then gradually rose to an even trim and surfaced. She began to circle to port, gushing oil. The conning-tower hatch opened and men leapt out, rushing to the 20-mm gun in the after conning tower. Horrocks opened the range and requested assistance from the *Archer*.

The pilot of Martlet B, on his way back to the ship from the scene of Swordfish G's attack, heard the call, turned back, and in a few minutes was over the damaged *U-752*. He fired his remaining 600 rounds of 50-caliber in one burst into the conning tower, killing Schroeter. The crew fired a few rounds, then scrambled down the hatch. Then the crew came up on deck and took to the water as the boat sank beneath them.

The *Archer's* U-boat was the first to be sunk by an escort carrier's aircraft using RPs, and Harry Horrocks had dealt the death blow to BdU's spring offensive. Total U-boat losses for May soared to forty-one—about one-third of all U-boats at sea. Twenty-four were lost on the North Atlantic convoy routes. Aggressive Coastal Command aircraft accounted for seven, in transit through the Bay of Biscay. The figure was more than new building could replace, not to mention the loss of over 2,000 highly trained men. The Allies lost forty-five ships, a total of 265,000 tons, about a third of the March total.

Dismayed by his May losses, Dönitz signaled to all his boats: "The situation in the North Atlantic now forces a temporary shift of operations to areas less endangered by aircraft."

Included in these areas was the central Atlantic, an American responsibility. Here in the next twelve months U.S. Navy CVEs savaged the U-boats, making full use of their surface-search and air-search radar, their sonar, HF/DF, and anti-U-boat missiles old and new. Most effective of the latter was the new homing torpedo known for security purposes as the Mark 24 mine. More familiarly, the British called it the B-bomb and the Americans Fido, or Wandering Annie. Using a hydrophone in its head, shielded so that it did not chase its own tail, Fido, its head filled with Torpex, a more powerful explosive than TNT, homed in on the noise made by a vessel's screws as they churned the water. With a range of 1,500 yards, Fido would continue to search for fifteen minutes beyond that distance, and many U-boats were fatally bitten by it.

Added to the great assistance that Huff-Duff and radar gave to the U-boat hunters was the decrypting service provided by Admiralty cipher specialists, especially the British government Code and Cipher School at Bletchley Park. Capture of the Enigma coding machine from Fritz Lemp's *U-110* and the ciphers from another vessel had helped Bletchley to break the German naval M-Home Waters Hydra code used for communications between U-boats and base. It was now possible to reroute convoys clear of U-boat packs.

In February 1942 the Germans had switched to the new Triton code, and in December Bletchley finally broke Triton. The Atlantic picture became clearer again. A delay in the British decrypting and an upsurge in the efforts of the German radio-intercept service in March 1943 partly accounted for the U-boat victories in that month, but the ultimate decoding machine, known at Bletchley as the Bomb, was back on song again.

Parallel but wider in scope was the U.S. Navy's Tenth Fleet, created by commander in chief Admiral King on 20 May 1943. It was a fleet without ships, sailing only some cramped offices in Washington. But it exercised unity of control over U.S. antisubmarine operations through Admiral King himself. Under its umbrella came all U.S. long range (LR) and very-long range (VLR) maritime aircraft as well as the CVE groups. It had its own Antisubmarine Measures Division for research, material development and training; units for statistical and analytical work; and its Operations Division for initiating action (accomplished by "recommending" what was in fact a mandatory course of action to Adm. Royal E. Ingersoll's U.S. Atlantic Fleet). Aid came from USN Combat Intelligence and the Royal Navy's Submarine Tracking Room and Intelligence Division, served by a network of Huff-Duff monitors stretching from Land's End to Newfoundland, Greenland, and the Arctic.

The Tenth Fleet contributed vitally to the *Bogue*'s pioneer U-boat sinking and to many more. German-speaking Commander Allbrecht of the U.S. Navy's Special (psychological) Warfare branch exploited the fact that Kapitänleutnant Bernhard Johannsen of the *U-569* had attempted to surrender his boat but could find nothing white to wave. In his role as Norden, Allbrecht broadcast the "correct" procedures for surrendering a U-boat, stressing the need to carry some white material, even a tablecloth. Dönitz ordered the jamming of these broadcasts. But it was too late to stop the commander of the *U-460*, who waved his white dress shirt, which he had smuggled aboard, at attacking bombers.

A wolf pack was not an independent force. Every move each U-boat made was controlled by radio signals from headquarters. The submarine was told her patrol position and estimated time of arrival, and it reported upon leaving the Bay of Biscay. Patrol lines were formed on the hour, positions in the line defined down to minutes by means of grid squares. Each boat transmitted situation reports on frequencies heard equally well on both sides of the Atlantic. If a U-boat did not report on time, she was called up. Losses were judged, by both sides, on this basis. No patrol could end without the signal permitting it, and each boat had to transmit her estimated time of arrival and request for radio beacons.

A U-boat's fuel state had to be included in every transmission. A refueling station at sea was always announced well ahead of time, together with the boats to be serviced and their fuel state. When she had completed a refueling session, the milch cow supply U-boat reported which boats she had replenished, quantities supplied, and her own fuel state. U-boat channels carried many technical details of modifications or repair and were choked with general orders, estimates, situation reports, crews' ailments, and even proxy marriages. All this information was entrusted to radio, and much of it was picked up and turned into Ultra intelligence by the Allies.

One of the early instances of the U.S. Navy's offensive use of Ultra was the *Bogue's* successful attack on the Trutz group's patrol line in June 1943.

On 16 May Dönitz had ordered the Trutz pack of seventeen boats to form a north-south barrier down the 43d line of longitude, with the northernmost boat patrolling on the latitude of New York and the Azores, the southernmost on that of Bermuda and Madeira.

This order was not locked in Enigma for long. Washington got it through Bletchley and the Admiralty, and the *Bogue* was ordered to leave Argentia, Newfoundland, and head south to provide offensive support for convoys GUS 7A, UGS 9, and Flight 10 against the Trutz line. The *Bogue* and her screen of five four-pipers steamed south to better flying weather than they had so far enjoyed.

The *Bogue* reached her first patrol station on 1 June, and from then on it was thirteen days of stubborn patrols and gritty battle typical of those fought in the central Atlantic. There, the energetic and aggressive American aircrews, under aviator captains such as Giles Short of the *Bogue* and Arnold "Buster" Isbell of the *Card*, addressed the U-boat assassins with a very special élan and tenacity.

Captain Short closed the southern sector of the Trutz line, into which westbound GUS 7A and then UGS 9 would be heading. His radar, sonar, and aircraft swept a 120-mile path through Trutz hunting grounds, and he sent a TBF to check on Flight 10.

On 4 June two TBFs were investigating a Huff-Duff lead when a U-boat was sighted. Both planes dropped depth charges and the boat sank stern first, leaving debris on the water. An hour later another Avenger sighted a surfaced boat 10 miles from Flight 10, 50 miles from the *Bogue,* and attacked. A brief gun duel was fought before the submarine dived. Meanwhile Lt. (jg) Bill Fowler's TBF was fighting it out with the *U-641* closer to the *Bogue.* He left the enemy down at the stern for squadron commander Bill Drane's Avenger to strafe in a hot fight from which he emerged with his IFF (identification, friend or foe) aerial shot away and his depth charges exploding under the U-boat's stern before it dived.

Next forenoon, Lt. Alex McAuslan's TBF and Lt. Dick Rogers's F4F sighted the surfaced *U-217* heading west at high speed. Rogers cleared her deck with his Brownings; McAuslan's charges straddled the boat, which sank, gushing oil.

Short joined UGS 9 on 8 June in clear weather. At 1700 three TBFs and two F4Fs slugged it out with Helmut Manseck's *U-758,* which remained surfaced and put up a hot barrage with at least two heavy-caliber cannons and three or four 50-caliber machine guns. The U-boat was straddled by depth charges but survived these and a destroyer hunt. Fowler returned to the *Bogue* with smoke in the cockpit, his engine leaking oil and running very rough.

Dusk was the time when U-boats surfaced to send Enigma, and a spate of signals suggested that a pack could be forming to mount an attack on the night of 9 or 10 June. As the dusk patrol returned, an army Liberator arrived from Morocco, and the *Bogue* left the convoy to turn west along the 30th parallel toward what Ultra thought was the center of the U-boat concentration. At dawn on the twelfth the hunt began again, when four Avengers, each paired with a fighter, took off to cover 70-mile sectors ahead and astern, with a patrol around UGS 9 at visual distance. They were relieved at noon, but one Avenger returned with engine trouble.

At 1345 Stearns in TBF12 sighted a surfaced U-boat lying stopped about a mile ahead. She was a milch cow, Czygan's big, 1,600-ton *U-118,* a combination minelayer and supply boat. Johnson's Wildcat strafed the boat from stem to stern; Stearns dropped his depth charges in a good straddle across the swirl of the crash-diving submarine. She came up again, trailing oil, then sank with her casing awash in a cloud of oil and air bubbles.

Bill Fowler's TBF and Lieutenant Tennant's F4F arrived, and Fowler made his third U-boat attack in a week. Three charges fell ahead, but the fourth hit the submarine's casing and exploded between bows and conning tower. Men came out of her conning-tower hatch, making for the four machine guns in the forward conning tower and a twin 20-mm cannon aft of them on a platform the Germans called the Winter-garten (bandstand). Tennant kept attacking to keep the men from their guns, and Fowler, then Johnson, joined in the grim game, chas-ing the Germans back and forth across the deck of the boat.

Lt. (jg) Harry Fryatt's TBF arrived just as they were running out of ammunition, dived, and got a close straddle with two depth charges a few feet aft of the conning tower. The U-boat listed to starboard and started sinking slowly by the stern. Fryatt tried to attack again but could not find a path through the seven aircraft now circling the sub-marine, which looked about finished.

New arrival Chamberlain persisted in the attack, his first stick of two depth charges exploding right underneath the stricken boat and lifting her out of the water. To his surprise, his second attack was met by some stubborn fire. Heim's F4F silenced the guns, and Chamberlain's second stick also burst under the U-boat's hull. One of them pene-trated a mine compartment where some six to a dozen mines were lying, and the boat blew up with a tremendous explosion, scattering big pieces of metal and debris high in the air. A huge gusher of arterial oil arose.

By August 1943 Dönitz had lost nine of his original twelve supply boats, the heavily armed submersible emporiums that carried, in addi-tion to fuel, shells, and torpedoes, such provisions as fresh strawber-ries, pears, asparagus, roast chickens, rabbits, and brandy.

The USS *Santee* was one of a quartet of tanker and escort carriers. Sixty-four feet longer than the *Bogue,* the *Santee* operated thirty-four aircraft to the *Bogue*'s twenty. She also carried large quantities of fuel to top up escorts.

At 0800 on 14 July the carrier was patrolling south of the Azores. An attack team of an Avenger (Ballantine) and a Wildcat (Lt. H. Brink Bass) was patrolling about 150 miles north of the ship when sharp eyes in the TBF sighted a U-boat 21 miles away. Closing on her, Bass strafed the boat, which began to dive, with Ballantine still 2 miles away. But the TBF had a Fido in the bomb bay. Lowering his wheels to lose airspeed for a torpedo drop, Ballantine came in from behind where the submarine had dived and let Fido loose at 250 feet, 200 yards ahead and about 100 feet to starboard of the swirl. He circled to port and saw an upheaval in the water. A moment later a 20-foot ring of foam arose, marking the end of the *U-160*.

Of the 489 U-boats sunk by the Allies between January 1943 and the end of the war, U.S. Navy forces sank 63 with direct use of Ultra information, some 30 more with its indirect aid. Details of many U-boat weapons, deception devices, and operating techniques were gained. Among these was the secret of Aphrodite, which consisted of a small hydrogen-filled balloon about 25 inches in diameter to which were attached silver wires tuned to radar frequencies. When a U-boat using radar receivers discovered that she was being hunted by radar, she could head into wind and release the balloon, which was carried to leeward, drawing her hunters away.

In June 1943 British intelligence realized that the Germans had cracked the British naval codes used to brief convoys on the location of U-boats. The codes were changed at once, and the new ones were never broken.

Much new antisubmarine hardware was introduced into the Atlantic battle. A modified type of standard depth charge was developed known as the Deep Depth Charge, which was 150 pounds heavier than the prewar 400-pound charge. It sank faster, and a "standard" and a "heavy" dropped together (but with different depth settings) would explode at two levels at the same time. The heavy's depth-setting calibration was altered to suit its range, and it could also be used if the submarine had gone very deep.

Twin rails and four throwers allowed the "ten-pattern" attack to be carried out. It was usual to load the port rails and forward throwers with heavies and the other group with standard charges, with the object of sandwiching the target between two layers of five explosions. Six-charge overstern depth-charge rails were superseded in escort frigates by eighteen-charge rails. Some ships had twin double-tiered rails holding a total of seventy-two depth charges, with four throwers on each side.

A new antisubmarine weapon, the Hedgehog, came into use in the spring of 1944. This was a 24-barrel mortar mounted on the forecastle; it threw a circular pattern of contact bombs ahead of the attacking ship. A later forward-throwing weapon was the Squid. More effective than the Hedgehog, it fired six fast-sinking depth bombs in a pattern that always exploded and could damage a U-boat even when not accurately placed. The Squid was used in conjunction with a new, small, Type 147 asdic set. This sent out a fan-shaped beam to find the depth of a U-boat and used its range recorder to operate the Squid, or sometimes a 3-barrel 12-inch mortar.

Sea trials of the Squid were held in the destroyer HMS *Ambuscade* in May 1943, and the first production unit was in the corvette HMS *Hadleigh Castle* in September 1943. The first frigate fitted was HMS

A Hedgehog mortar bomb pattern explodes ahead of the launching vessel. (Royal
Navy)

Loch Fada in April 1944. In general Squid was restricted to new construction, though one old escort destroyer, HMS *Escapade,* had two fitted in January 1945. By the end of the war, sixty to seventy ships had
been equipped with the weapon.

An ultimately successful version of the old "dunking" hydrophone,
with which the Americans had experimented in World War I, was the
electronic sonobuoy (called "sonobitch" in its more capricious
moments). Dropped in the sea from a hunting aircraft at an appropriate point, this device dangled a hydrophone at a preset depth and
broadcast a signal from any submarine within its range.

In September 1943 U-boats began using the Zaunkönig (gnat)
acoustic torpedo. At first they had some renewed success. Then the
Allies introduced the Foxer, a noisemaking device trailed in the wake
of a ship to explode the homer prematurely.

In October 1943 Terceira, in the Azores, was established by agreement with Portugal as a British air base. That month the U.S. carriers
Card, Core, and *Block Island* sank six U-boats with their aircraft. Other
aircraft sank ten more, and surface escorts a further ten.

During 1943 the Germans introduced two types of guided missile
for use by aircraft against ships. The first was the FX 1400, a heavy
free-falling bomb that could be guided visually by radio signals from a
parent plane and could pierce armor plate. In September 1943, when
the Italian fleet left Spezia to surrender, it was attacked by Dornier Do

217s using FX 1400. The battleships *Roma* and *Italia* were both hit, and the *Roma* blew up and sank.

When rough treatment by the *Audacity's* Martlets and by the guns of some well-fought merchantmen had exposed the shortcomings of even the better-armed and strengthened Fw 200C-3 and 4, the type was relegated mostly to the reconnaissance role. At 0750 on 27 August 1943, the sloop *Egret* and the frigates *Jed* and *Rother* of the First Escort Group were on antisubmarine patrol off Cape Villano on the Bay of Biscay, escorted by the destroyers *Athabascan* and *Grenville*. Two Condors appeared and circled above them at 8,000 feet, contrary to the Fws' normal practice of reconnoitering at low altitude.

The British force was prepared for the unusual. On board the *Egret* was a team of scientists with the mission of investigating the new radio-controlled rocket bomb that intelligence thought the Luftwaffe was ready to launch from aircraft flown from French coastal airfields.

At 1254 the ships' RDF picked up a big group of aircraft coming in fast from the northeast. Within minutes they were under attack by nineteen Dornier Do 290 bombers carrying the new missiles. The *Egret* was hit and blew up with heavy loss including the entire scientific team, and the *Athabascan* was damaged. Lt. Comdr. Roger Hill, captain of the *Grenville*, quickly assessed a weakness of the new weapon. Applying rudder, he drew a persistent bomb toward him and then suddenly went hard over the other way. The missile, or its operator, was not agile enough to follow, and stalled.

The Henschel Hs 293 "glider bomb" consisted of a small glider with a wingspan of 10 feet, carrying a 1,100-pound warhead and a rocket motor slung underneath. The 1,300-pound thrust of the rocket motor took the missile from a launch speed of 220 MPH to 370 MPH in twelve seconds. The navigator in the parent aircraft then guided the missile toward the target by radio signals.

After the promising attack on the *Egret* group, production of the Hs 293 was stepped up. The role of parent aircraft was entrusted to the Heinkel He 177 Griffon, though the rogue Wonder Bomber was still threatened by engine problems.

The Fw Condor had not been thought of originally as anything more than a stopgap measure, designed to carry on until the He 177 came into service. The latter was much faster, with a potentially far heavier bomb load and defensive armament than the Fw 200C-4. But more than a year had gone by, and the Greif (Griffon) bomber was still not in service.

By November 1943, all U-boats remaining in the North Atlantic were concentrated on the Azores-Finisterre patrol line. When a Condor reported the sixty-six ships of the combined MKS 30 and SL 139 from North Africa and Sierra Leone on 15 November, thirty-one boats were ordered to the attack. But radar transmissions gave them away. Strong air cover was flown from the Azores, Gibraltar, and Britain, and escorts multiplied. Between 18 and 21 November, the *U-211*, *U-536*, and *U-538* were destroyed. On the twenty-second, twenty He 177A-5s took off from Merignac in bad visibility with He 293 missiles to make up for the failure of the U-boats.

They reached the target, but a later debriefing estimated that only six-teen missiles were released. Most of these were aimed at a straggler 3.5 miles behind the convoy. The ship was finally hit and abandoned, but only one other merchantman was damaged. Three Griffons were destroyed. On 26 November fourteen missile-carrying He 177s from Bordeaux attacked an Allied convoy, but the group lost half its aircraft—four in action, three in crashes—as well as its Gruppenkommandant.

After this, the 177 unit had only seven dubiously serviceable aircraft left. On 28 December a patrolling RAF Sunderland attacked and forced down a Condor, one of four Fws on an antishipping hunt. The Condor was carrying two Hs 293A missiles, one under each outer engine nacelle. After the debacle of the first Greif sorties, eight Fw 200C-8s were specially built as Hs 293A carriers. These were com-pleted in January and February of 1944.

The remaining He 177s, fickle and vulnerable, were operated at night, preferably in bright moonlight, like giant werewolves. On dark

Heinkel He 177 Greif carrying a Henschel Hs 293 glider bomb. (Luftwaffe)

nights one Kette (three aircraft) would carry special 110-pound flares that it would drop on one side of a convoy. Another Kette attacked from the dark side, its target silhouetted against the light from the flares. The aircraft released their missiles at a range of 6 to 9 miles while flying directly toward the ships, thus simplifying the difficulties of aiming. The werewolves had little success, however, and in January 1944 they were transferred to Luftflotte 2 in the Mediterranean to help oppose the Allied landings at Anzio, Italy.

There the cruiser HMS *Spartan* and a tank-landing vessel (LST) were sunk by Hs 293 missiles. Reduced to six aircraft, the 177s were returned to Bordeaux, where they were reinforced in February by nine new Griffons, known as the tinfoil bombers to their Luftwaffe crews, and transferred to Trondheim-Vaernes in Norway to replace a Fw 200 squadron.

On 12 February the new American-built fighter escort carrier HMS *Pursuer* with two squadrons of Wildcats (the type having reverted to its American name) was accompanying OS 67 and KMS 41. As the last patrol of the day was being struck down, an Admiralty signal warned of impending air attack and the radar screens were registering three-plus bandits. Four Wildcats were scrambled, and at 1905 the *Pursuer* heard "Tally-ho!" simultaneously from two of the fighters as they attacked the German force of seven He 177s and Fws, which were carrying glider bombs. At 1910 one of them fell in flames, and the *Pursuer*'s guns opened up on the rest. Another bomber fell, and the enemy withdrew.

Four days later a Ju 290 launched a glider bomb at a ship in OS 68 and KMS 42, missed, and two New Zealand Wildcat pilots from HMS *Biter* shot it down. A few hours after this, another Ju 290 appeared. The *Biter*'s fighter direction room vectored an RAF Beaufighter on to it, and it was destroyed. This was the swan song of the glider bomb.

The successes of the U.S. Navy escort carriers continued through 1944, with five CVEs, operating at different times, accounting for seventeen U-boats. The USS *Guadalcanal* captured *U-505* and brought her in with a display of courage and seamanship.[2]

When trying to surface to recharge her batteries, the *U-505* used two types of radar detector receiver to give warning of approaching enemy aircraft. The inexperienced Oberleutnant Lange had insisted on retaining the Wanz receiver, which operated on the 120–180 band and was officially thought to give out too much detectable radiation. The newer Naxos receiver, designed to pick up transmissions on the 8–12 centimeter band and thought less likely a telltale, was delicate, unreliable, and erratic, and could not register a specific range. Furthermore, it had to be set up on deck on the surface, where it was highly prone to damage by salt spray. It was not pressure proof, and having given its

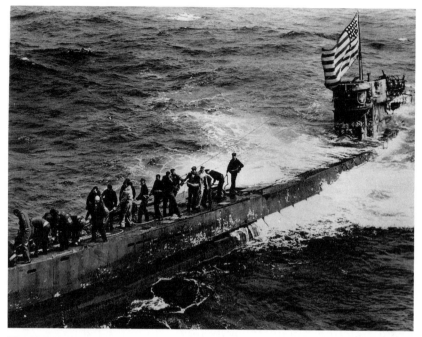

The *U-505* after capture by the USS *Guadalcanal*. (U.S. Navy)

distinctive nerve-shattering screech of warning through its connected bullhorn, it forced the submarine to wait vital seconds before crash-diving, while its handlers gathered up its aerial and trailing wire and bundled it below.

At the debriefing aboard the *Bogue* on 20 December 1943, after the TBFs of Lt. (jg) Harry Bradshaw and Lt. (jg) Wallace LaFleur had destroyed the *U-850* with Fido homing torpedoes, other aircrew who had been involved described a platform abaft the U-boat's conning tower thought to be a launch pad for a Flying Dutchman, a blend of kite and helicopter used for reconnaissance. This machine, featuring a three-bladed Hubschraube (lift propeller) overhead rotor, was attached to the submarine by 984 feet of wire. The boat went to full surface speed, the rotor windmilled and gave initial lift, and the pilot engaged a motor that operated the rotor, which gave full lift. If the boat was attacked while the Dutchman was flying, it was cast off.

Beginning in spring 1944, the Germans introduced some really impressive new technology, including the Schnorkel (snort), a breathing tube through which a submerged U-boat could draw air to run her diesel engines and recharge her batteries; a new Type XXI boat with an underwater speed of 17 knots; the Balkon hydrophone, which could detect an enemy at 50 miles; and the S-gear, a supersonic underwater detector that could do this even better. Experiments with the revolu-

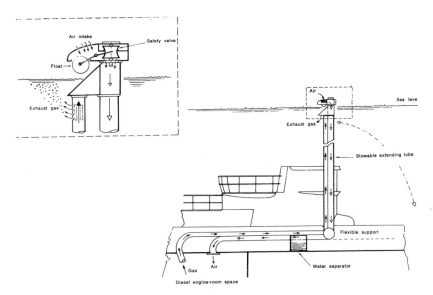

The Schnorkel. (Arms and Armour Press)

tionary Walter boats, which used hydrogen-peroxide fuel, had been successful. A hundred of these boats, which could maintain a speed of 25 knots underwater for 12 hours, were begun, but Allied bombing disrupted production. In April 1945 two of a new small U-boat Type XXIII, with an underwater speed of 13 knots, sailed on experimental cruises. The first and the last of the big Type XXXI, the *U-2511*, left Germany to make a surprise attack on Panama but was picked up by asdic. The boat spurted to 16 knots and got away, but on 4 March 1945 she heard Dönitz's order to cease operations.

The second great U-boat war was over. U-boats sank 2,603 Allied and neutral merchant ships, a total of just over 13,500,000 tons, and 175 warships. Of 1,152 U-boats built before or during the war, 781 were sunk by Allied action, 215 scuttled by the Kriegsmarine after the war, and 154 turned over to the Allies. Two boats, the *U-530* and *U-977*, escaped to Argentina.

Torpedoes at Taranto

"To gain and hold command of the Mediterranean in time of war is a high duty of the fleet," said Winston Churchill. "Once that is achieved, all European land forces on the shores of North Africa will be decisively affected."[1]

When Benito Mussolini declared war on the Allies in June 1940, he did so behind the shield of a navy of fast new or refurbished ships—six battleships, nineteen cruisers, and fifty-five destroyers. Massed on his airfields in Italy, Sardinia, Sicily, Pantellaria, North Africa, and the Dodecanese Islands was a large, equally modern air force.

His main opposition was the British Mediterranean fleet, comprising four old battleships, six cruisers, destroyers, the old carrier *Eagle*, and twelve aging submarines. When the proud Regia Aeronautica began bombing the Royal Navy's central Mediterranean base of Malta on 11 June 1940, the Italians were significantly shaken by a scratch air defense of three old Sea Gladiator biplane fighters. They were flown at different times by pilots drawn from the RAF air staff, from flying boats, or from antiaircraft cooperation units, who shot down several Savoia Marchetti SM79 bombers.[2] A training squadron of twelve Swordfish also flew to Malta. Without blind-flying panels, sensitive altimeters registering height over the sea in tens of feet, or long-range tanks, they bombed airfields and oil tanks in Sicily and in Tripoli harbor in Libya, and they went out at night over the sea on "rat hunts" for enemy shipping, often with student pilots at the controls.[3]

Admiral Sir Andrew Cunningham, commander in chief, Mediterranean, likewise established an early ascendancy in morale over the Italians. The modern Italian battleships and heavy cruisers were very fast and heavily armed but lightly armored, built to hit and run. At dawn on 11 June 1940, Cunningham put to sea from Alexandria with the fleet and swept the central Mediterranean as far as the heel of Italy. The old destroyer *Voyager* sank an Italian submarine off Crete, while two cruisers were detached to bombard Tobruk, the Italian port and base in Cyrenaica. The old submarine *Parthian* destroyed the Italian submarine *Diamante* off the harbor.

On 9 July the British fleet was on its way to cover some convoys from Malta to Alexandria. A submarine and a flying boat from Malta reported an Italian squadron of two modern *Cavour*-class battleships, with cruisers and destroyers at sea. Admiral Cunningham cut off the enemy force from its base at Taranto. The *Warspite* hit the *Cavour,* which fled wreathed in smoke for the Straits of Messina. The *Eagle's* few bombers failed to slow the battleship down, and she got away. The British fleet was then constantly attacked by high-level bombers, which scored one lucky hit—on the bridge of the cruiser *Gloucester.* The *Eagle,* like Malta, had improvised a fighter defense with four Sea Gladiators flown by Swordfish pilots, but the carrier had no radar and no means of directing the aircraft. Though bravely flown, they could achieve little. On 18 July the 6-inch cruiser HMAS *Sydney* sank an Italian cruiser and sent her consort running for home.

Winston Churchill, now British prime minister, wanted to send three armored regiments from Great Britain through the Mediterranean to Alexandria. His plan was to help counterbalance the huge numerical superiority of the Italian army in Libya over the British Eighth Army. Churchill wanted an escort of naval reinforcements, but the First Sea Lord feared the hazards of a passage past the airfields of Sardinia and Sicily and the Italian naval bases. So the tanks went via the Cape, while naval reinforcements ran the gauntlet between Sicily and Cape Bon in Tunisia, arriving unscathed in Alexandria.

With them was the new fleet carrier *Illustrious,* with Fulmar fighters and RDF to direct them. The antiaircraft cruisers *Calcutta* and *Coventry* also came out, with Type 279 RDF. Italian reconnaissance machines sighted the force, whose Fulmars shot down several of them. Upon first spotting the Fulmars, with the sleek shape of their cowled Merlins, the Italians cried, "Spittyfurers!" But the big two-seat fighters lacked the performance of Spitfires, and fighter direction was in its early stages. Voice communication was not good, and Type 279, with its early A-scope, manually trained aerials, and hand plotting, could not plot more than two or three aircraft at a time and could give little indication of height. Reflection off the sea also distorted the beam.

As the *Illustrious* passed through Maltese waters, her Swordfish, in between antisubmarine patrols ahead of the convoy, transported twenty-four sets of new blind-flying instrument panels and aerials and the same number of long-range fuel tanks, destined for Number 830

Squadron at Hal Far naval airfield on Malta. The small unit of ex–training aircraft flew fruitless warship hunts through September. After the last Augusta raid, attacks on Sicilian targets had been banned as provocative of retaliation that Malta was not equipped to resist.

On 14 September Malta's new RAF reconnaissance unit, Number 431 Flight, made its first sorties from Luqa airfield over Tripoli, Sicily, and Pantellaria Island with its three new American Martin Marylands, twin-engine planes with a range of 1,210 miles and a top speed of 278 MPH.

On the following day, instead of the usual Savoia Marchetti SM79s bombing from high level, a formation of aircraft not previously seen in the blue Malta skies appeared over the island—the ugly Ju 87s, the infamous Stukas, with their inverted gull wings. These particular machines were the Picciatelli (strikers) flown by Italian pilots and crews. Twenty of them, escorted by Fiat CR42 and Macchi 200 fighters, made their screaming dives on Hal Far, dropping a high proportion of delayed-action bombs.

Mass-bombing attacks from high level by the SM79s in July and August had proved unprofitable. Now the Italians had picked up the promising results of prewar torpedo-bomber trials with the SM79s, converting many of them to this form of attack and setting up a torpedo-bomber training school at Grasseto, on the Italian west coast. Fiat BR20 Bis bombers were also adapted as torpedo carriers. SM79s were converted to carry *motorbombas,* 880-pound "circling torpedoes" dropped by parachute and powered by gyroscopically controlled motors that were started at a depth of 9.84 feet by a siphon of mercury and drove the missile forward along a spinning path. Backed by a new launching sight, hung on a special rack offset from the plane's centerline, a 17.7-inch naval torpedo performed very well.

On the bright moonlit night of 17 September 1940, an Aerosilurante unit of torpedo-carrying SM79s attacked a British naval squadron returning from a bombardment of Bardia. They hit Admiral Cunningham's new addition, the heavy cruiser *Kent.* On 14 October a dusk attack on the British fleet returning to Alexandria resulted in a hit on the bows of the light cruiser *Liverpool.* The flash ignited a fuel tank, which ignited the forward magazine. The bow section hung by a few rivets. Towed by the cruiser *Orion* and destroyers, the *Liverpool* entered Alexandria harbor, where the bow section finally fell off.

Throughout October, Number 431 Flight was ordered out on regular reconnaissances of Taranto harbor, on the instep of Italy, the Supermarina's main base. On 2 November three battleships and eleven cruisers and destroyers were reported there. One Martin Maryland reconnaissance plane had a running fight with four Macchi 200s, managing to elude them in a cloud. On 10 November an aircraft encountered unusually thick flak and fighters but survived to report five battleships, fourteen cruisers, and twenty-seven destroyers in the harbor. The Italians had sensed something in the wind.

Occupying the *Illustrious*'s flag bridge was Rear Adm. St. G. Lumley Lyster, who, as captain of the *Glorious* in the late thirties, had trained his fliers for an attack on the Italian fleet in harbor. If the Supermarina was reluctant to fight, the *Illustrious* and the old *Eagle* together were to take the war to its fleet in Taranto harbor. For practice the new carrier's planes struck by moonlight at Italian ports on the Libyan coast, at airfields in the Dodecanese islands, and they laid mines in the harbors.

On 8 September Mr. Churchill had warned Cunningham of the importance of a strike against the Italian fleet in the fall, before the Germans could take over the faltering Italian war machine. On 30 September Admiral Cunningham covered a Malta-bound convoy with part of the British fleet, including two battleships. A force of five Italian battleships was reported near. Cunningham turned to intercept them, but once again they used their speed to escape.

It was time to act. The "fleet in being" must be struck at home.[4] Lumley Lyster was here with the nucleus of his torpedo droppers from the *Glorious*. The answer to a gun-shy enemy was the torpedo bomber. The decision was made: on Trafalgar Day, 21 October, the Swordfish would go to Taranto.

But then there was a hitch. As a long-range tank was being fitted into one of the *Illustrious*'s Swordfish, a battery short-circuited. A spark caught a fuel drip and set off a fire in the hangar that gutted two aircraft and damaged five others. Taranto was postponed for ten days. Meanwhile the commander in chief once more invited attack when he covered a convoy operation. The Fascist fleet avoided him, except for two destroyers that HMS *Ajax* caught by moonlight and sank, while the two carriers revisited the Dodecanese. This stirred up the Regia Aeronautica on Rhodes. The *Newcastle* was badly hit and was towed back to base. On 28 October Mussolini demanded the occupation of Crete. Greece refused and was at war with Italy. The attack on the Italian battle fleet in Taranto harbor was now more urgent than ever. It was finally planned for the night of 11 November, as Operation Judgement.

Two days before she was due to sail, the *Eagle*'s fuel system broke down, severely shaken by many near misses. The *Illustrious* borrowed five of her machines and aircrews to go it alone.

Photographs of the harbor taken on 10 November showed five battleships (two new *Littorios*, three of the recently reconstructed *Cavour* and *Duilio* classes) and three cruisers in the big outer harbor, with cruisers and destroyers in the smaller inner harbor. Antiaircraft guns lined the breakwaters. Balloons shielded one exposed flank of the battleships, nets the other. These inhibited torpedo attack, so half the attacking force would carry bombs, and some flares as well, for a part-diversionary attack on the cruisers and destroyers. The operation would be carried out in two separate waves.

On 6 November the Mediterranean Fleet, with the *Illustrious*, left Alexandria. On the eighth, seven SM79 bombers attacked. Fulmars shot down two of them, then a Cant 506B shadower. The Royal Air Force reported a sixth battleship in harbor. At 1800 on the eleventh, the *Illustrious* and the Third Cruiser Squadron were detached for Taranto.

At 2000 on an almost windless night, with cloud occulting the moon, 40 miles from Kabbo Point, Cephalonia, the first group of twelve machines took off to fly the 170 miles to Taranto. An hour later the second wave left the deck.

At 2245, after several false alarms, the Fortress, the Italian naval headquarters at Taranto, picked up the sound of the first wave of attackers. Very soon the flare droppers swept in, silhouetting the battleships for the torpedo droppers, which approached through the balloon barrage. The first dropped its tin fish from under 30 feet, aiming for a *Cavour*, then flak hit it and it fell into the harbor. The next three also aimed for a *Cavour*-class battleship, the fifth and sixth for a *Littorio*, a column of smoke from which shot up abaft the funnels. The rest of the strike pressed home their bombing attacks.

Swordfish TSR Mark I releasing a torpedo. (Royal Navy)

Less than an hour later, the second wave—eight aircraft with a straggler coming up in the rear—followed on, guided from 70 miles away by the fiery aftermath of the first attack in the sky.

To catch the defenses on the wrong foot, they attacked from the opposite direction to the first wave. This time both targets and attackers were illuminated by the moon. The Swordfish dived in line astern to 40 feet, flattened out, and attacked independently. When they had made their attacks, the straggler arrived and bombed a cruiser. As it left the target, the pilot saw two ships listing and down by the bows. Two days later RAF photographs showed the *Littorio* lying with a heavy list and her forecastle awash; one *Cavour* with her stern underwater as far as the after turret; and one *Duilio*, beached and abandoned. Two cruisers lay listed in a wide pool of oil, and two fleet auxiliaries lay with their sterns underwater. The seaplane base and the oil-storage depot had obviously been badly damaged.

Stuka Strada

The news of the Taranto triumph rang bells in naval circles throughout the world, not least in the mind of Adm. Isoroku Yamamoto, commander in chief, Japanese Combined Fleet. He sent officers to Italy to
study the attack from the Italian side, and from London in the diplo-
matic bag came a valuable expert assessment by assistant naval
attaché Comdr. Minoru Genda, naval aviator and tactician.

In Malta the news brought great relief and the shrinking of the
threat of invasion. Toward the end of November, RAF Wellington
medium bombers flew into Luqa airfield, and on 2 December ten of
them raided Naples and Messina. On the seventh, they hit Castel Benito airfield, near Tripoli. The Swordfish at Hal Far practiced dive-
bombing, and on the night of 10 December, eight aircraft dropped four
tons of bombs on Tripoli harbor, hitting three ships. On the fourteenth, nine Wellingtons attacked ships in Naples harbor, where the
Italian fleet had taken refuge.

Six submarines, HMS *Oswald, Osiris, Phoenix, Proteus, Rover*, and
Grampus, were sent initially to Malta, but they were all large oceangoing vessels of 1,750–2,060 tons submerged, very vulnerable in the
shallow waters of the Mediterranean. What were needed were some
of the S-class boats (715 tons surfaced, 990 submerged) designed for
coastal use, several of which had distinguished themselves in Norwegian waters.

Five boats were lost. The *Odin* was sunk by the destroyer *Strale* in
the Gulf of Taranto on 13 June, the *Grampus* by the torpedo boats *Circe*
and *Polluce* off Syracuse on the sixteenth, the *Orpheus* by the destroyer
Turbine off Tobruk. The *Oswald* and *Phoenix* were also lost.

More modern boats were sent out. In December, Lt. Comdr. Hugh Haggard in the *Truant* sank a 1,500-ton ship off Calabria and capped this with the 8,000-ton tanker *Bonzo*. Lt. Comdr. F. B. Currie's old *Regulus* and Lt. Comdr. G. S. Salt's new *Triad* were two boats destroyed by mines, which were a serious danger. When Italian records were made available after the war, Capt. George Phillips, formerly of the submarine *Ursula,* said, "Had we known of these minefields it's difficult to see how we could have operated submarines in the Mediterranean at all."[1] Nine boats were lost for a score of only six supply ships and one tanker, 29,000 tons' worth, plus the *Parthian*'s submarine and a destroyer sunk by the *Osiris.*

The losses were replaced by new U- and the larger T-class saddle-tank submarines. The small (540–730 ton) U class was the best type of boat for the shallow Mediterranean. The three original vessels of this class had been begun in mid-February 1937 as simple single-hulled "clockwork mice" utility boats for the training of surface warships in antisubmarine warfare. They performed so well that in the deteriorating international situation, it was decided to arm them for short-range offensive patrols. The bow was modified to allow for the fitting of six torpedo tubes: two on each side in the hull, and two—which could not be reloaded when submerged—in a bulge above the bow.

The "U-boats" were easy and cheap to build. All ballast and fuel tanks were inside the single hull. Surface propulsion was diesel-electric, with the engines connected directly to the generators, which provided the power for two electric motors connected to the propellers. This system greatly simplified the layout of the propulsion equipment and resulted in greater flexibility and ease of operation. For propulsion submerged, the electric motors were powered by two series of storage batteries, recharged in the normal way on the surface.

On trials these boats proved easy to handle and extremely agile, though they could only make 9 knots underwater and 12 on the surface. The only real snag was the telltale bow wave and the effect on stability caused by the bow bulge at periscope depth.

When twelve more U-class boats were ordered under the 1939 Supplementary Program, the bulge and the two exterior torpedo tubes were removed from the design in time to modify eight of the new boats. The penalty was the reduction in armament. The *Unique, Upholder, Upright,* and *Utmost* retained the fault together with their six-tube firepower. The newer boats were lengthened by some 6 feet astern to present a more streamlined shape aft and improve the flow of water over the propellers, which increased the displacement only minimally. The fuel capacity was increased by several tons, which lengthened the range considerably, though this was not a prime factor

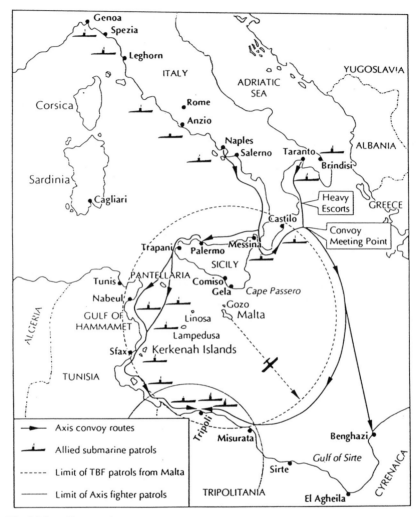

The Malta offensive. (K. Poolman)

in the Mediterranean. After the outbreak of war, a further forty-one of these boats were ordered.

Of the original three boats, the *Undine* had been sunk by antisubmarine craft, the *Unity* lost in an accident. Lt. Comdr. George Phillips's *Ursula* had proved the value of the design by getting among the sandbanks of the shallow Elbe estuary on 14 December 1939 and sinking the torpedo boat *F9* and a gunboat.

Not the least valuable addition to submarine technology was the "Ursula suit" invented by Phillips. George Phillips was disgusted with the protection against wind, cold, and spray offered his watch keepers

Utility submarine HMS *Undine*. (Maritime Photo Library)

on the surface by the normal foul-weather oilskins, southwester- and salt-soaked towels around their necks. After testing his navigator's Barbour motorcycle jacket satisfactorily with a fire hose, he persuaded the manufacturers to create a hooded jacket and separate trousers with elastic at the waist and ankles. Phillips paid for the prototypes himself. They were warm, comfortable, and waterproof, and Ursula suits became standard issue in the British submarine service.

Some of the new boats were earmarked for the Mediterranean, where they could be particularly effective in the shallows off Tripolitania and Tunisia in the paths of convoys coming from Italy. But when war began there, they were not ready for active service. The China boats had to soldier on.

The old guard of O-class, P-class, and R-class boats had sunk 44,544 tons of Axis shipping out of a total of 166,544 tons destroyed in all. The *Parthian* went to Malta with a cargo of essential supplies, and the old minelayers *Cachalot* and *Rorqual* were used almost exclusively for this work.

Patrols by the new boats were delayed for a time because of engine trouble and a shortage of torpedoes. Old destroyer torpedoes used were unreliable, and some new ones were brought in by submarine from Gibraltar.

The *Liverpool*'s replacement, the *Glasgow,* was anchored in Suda Bay, Crete, on 3 December 1940, when she was surprised by two torpedo SM79s of Carlo Buscaglia's 278 Squadriglia (squadron) from Rhodes, which scored solid hits from 3,000 yards. The *Glasgow,* following the

Kent and *Liverpool,* was only just able to reach an American repair yard.

Any damage done to Axis ships or stores on the quay was of extra importance now, as General Wavell's Eighth Army had counter-attacked from Egypt and was driving the Italians back along the Libyan coast. Mussolini had failed in North Africa as he had failed in his invasion of Greece in November, and there were signs that Hitler was moving to reinforce the Italians in Libya. Malta Marylands, patrolling Palermo, Catania, Gela, and Corviso on 5 January 1941, ran into snow showers, but more chilling was the sight on the airfields below of He 111s, Ju 87s and 88s, and Me 110 fighters. These were aircraft of General Geisler's Fliegerkorps X, containing some crack antishipping units.

The Ju 87 units were I Gruppe of Stukageschwader 1 (Hauptmann Paul-Werner Hozzel) and II Gruppe of Staffel G 2 (Major Walter Enneccerus), both from Fliegerkorps VII, which had been active in bombing English Channel ports and shipping, radar stations, and airfields. After dive-bombing attacks on Dover Harbor on 29 July 1940 by thirty-eight Stukas, destroyers were forbidden to sail in daylight. When the *Dainty* tried it, she was quickly sunk. On 12–13 August, Lympne and Detling airfields, near the English Channel coast, were blasted, and an overconfident squadron of Hurricanes was driven off by good defensive fire. This was an exception, however.

In an attack on a convoy in the Channel by eight Ju 87s, four were lost. Over Tangmere airfield, Kent, on 16 August, seven out of seventeen fell to a Hurricane and a Spitfire squadron. On 18 August the four Gruppen that attacked Gosport, Thorney Island and Ford airfields, and Polling radar station lost thirty planes, a whole Gruppe strength. This was the last time Stukas operated against targets in England, though they were very successful against British convoys in the Thames estuary in October and November and in night attacks on shipping in Dover and Margate harbors, guided by ships' wakes.

The experience of Hozzel's and Enneccerus's crews, then, had shown them that their machines were vulnerable to fighters. But there were few fighters on Malta—just a handful of overworked Hurricanes. And somewhere at sea in the offing was the *Illustrious,* with her small force of slow Fulmars.

Early on the morning of 9 January 1941, nine Stukas escorted by nine CR42s approached the island. Over Marsa Scirocco Bay, their BZA-1 computer dive sights took over and they plunged vertically, sirens screaming, toward the ships in the bay and the flying boats riding at their buoys off the Kalafrana seaplane station. The thrower arms under their engines jerked forward, pitching black 1,000- and 500-pound bombs. Geysers of spray rose from near misses, a jet of bright yellow flame and a column of smoke where a ship had been hit. Then the Stukas spread out over the island on their way back to Sicily, machine-gunning houses, farms, cars, people, and animals in the fields and on dusty goat tracks. They hit hangars and aircraft, putting three Wellingtons out of action at Luqa. Blitzkrieg had come to Malta—a first taste, with much more to follow in the months ahead.

There were no more attacks that day or the following morning, because the bombers were otherwise engaged. HMS *Illustrious* was with a Malta convoy in the Pantellaria Strait off Tunisia. Reconnaissance and antisubmarine patrols were up, a patrol of defending Fulmars overhead and a force of Swordfish away attacking an Italian convoy of three merchantmen, one destroyer, and an escort vessel. The three merchantmen, one a large liner, were sunk in minutes. The Swordfish were back on board at noon, when the ship's RDF reported several large groups of hostile aircraft closing rapidly.

First, two Italian torpedo bombers dropped their fish. Captain Denis Boyd skillfully avoided them all. The ship launched more Fulmars. They were climbing when a large force of Stukas peeled off overhead and screamed down from port and starboard bows and starboard quarter, diving in neat groups of three. They dovetailed together, cloverleaf fashion, down through the 4.5-inch barrage and into the pom-pom screen. When the spray from near misses subsided, the ship had lost her broadcasting system, radar, two pom-poms, and all eight after 4.5s. The after elevator was wrecked and a Fulmar on it destroyed. Aircraft in the hangar were on fire.

Men were fighting the fires when the second wave attacked, backed by high-level bombers. The ship began to flood forward, the forward elevator was punched out of shape, the wind blew through bomb holes and fanned the hangar blaze. Then a 1,000-pound bomb hit the flight deck on the center line, burst through the armor plate and the hangar deck beneath it, hit the after ammunition conveyer, and exploded, killing all the officers who were taking a hasty meal in the wardroom. Fire took hold everywhere, raging through torn and shattered compartments, fed by spilled aircraft fuel. The fire-control parties were getting to grips with the fires when a second 1,000-pounder plunged into the after elevator shaft, knocking out the steering gear below and sending the ship around in crazy circles.

Mercifully, this bomb signaled the end of the attack. Captain Boyd steered the ship on main engines for Malta. He wept when the maimed and badly burned were laid out on the decks—he could not tell one from the other. It was dark when the *Illustrious* made Grand Harbour and slowly came alongside the dockyard wall, listing to port and badly down by the stern.

It was, obviously, only a question of time before the Luftwaffe came to finish her off before turning to other targets on Malta: the airfields and submarine bases. But the days went by with only the occasional reconnaissance aircraft. Swordfish bombed shipping at Palermo, Wellingtons aircraft at Catania.

On 16 January a combined-services conference decided to put up a barrage over Grand Harbour through which the Stukas and 88s would pass at their peril. An hour after antiaircraft defenses had worked out the details, a force of these aircraft plunged down through the barrage, first the 88s, then the Stukas. Three ex-*Illustrious* Fulmars followed them down and destroyed a Stuka. The *Illustrious* and a cruiser were hit, an ammunition ship damaged. Hundreds of houses around the dockyard were destroyed.

On 18 January, eighty bombers hit Hal Far and Luqa, devastating both airfields and destroying planes, losing eleven aircraft themselves. Next day the main attack was on the *Illustrious* and Grand Harbour by some eighty aircraft. Nineteen were destroyed by the combined efforts of six Hurricanes, one Fulmar, the surviving Gloster Gladiator, and the ack-ack guns, but there were further hits on the *Illustrious*. The solitary Ju 88 that flew over Grand Harbour on 20 January must have decided that the destruction was sufficient unto the day, as the twenty-first and twenty-second went undisturbed.

The runways were patched up. Eight Wellingtons bombed oil tanks at Catania, home of the 88s. Temporary repairs on the *Illustrious* were completed, and on 23 January the carrier sailed under her own power for Alexandria, which she reached safely two days later, her berth booked in a United States repair yard. A proponent of air power but too weak alone, the *Illustrious* had been a victim of it. The ship had to wait until mid-March before the Suez Canal could be cleared of a new type of magnetic-acoustic mine sown in profusion by aircraft from Rhodes. Her sister the *Formidable* came out to replace her.

At the end of January the new T- and U-class boats began operating from Malta. On the night of the twenty-seventh, Lt. Comdr. David Wanklyn's *Upholder* on her first patrol torpedoed the 7,889-ton German motorship *Duisberg* off Kerkeneh Bank near the Tunisian coast, putting her in dock for four months. Three days later, the *Upholder* sank a 3,950-ton supply ship.

On 8 February the first convoy of troops and supplies for the new German Afrika Korps left Naples. Swordfish from Malta laid mines off Tripoli. On the twelfth, Lt. E. D. Norman's *Upright* hit an 8,000-ton supply ship with three torpedoes. Off Kerkeneh Bank on the twenty-second, Lt. Comdr. A. J. Mackenzie's *Ursula* hit the 5,788-ton *Sabbia* and the 2,365-ton *Silvia Tripcovitch*, which was finished off by the *Upright*. The valuable tanker disintegrated in a violent flash and sheet of flame.

With the Wellingtons at Luqa almost wiped out, only a depleted Swordfish unit and the handful of submarines were left in Malta to attack the Libyan convoys that were getting through regularly to Tripoli. The Malta Swordfish continued their rat hunts. Their torpedoes were now usually fitted with Duplex pistols, which were designed to be detonated by a ship's magnetism without the need for contact, but targets were not easy to locate.[2] Sometimes the Stringbags were alerted by recce report from a Maryland or a Sunderland, but these aircraft too were in short supply. Four roving Swordfish found and sank the 4,957-ton Italian motorship *Juventus* south of Kerkeneh Bank on the night of 15–16 February, but they had no ASV and missed the second Afrika Korps convoy from Naples.

Luqa was taking a pounding, but on 20 February seven Wimpeys bombed Catania and Comiso. The Malta submarines also maintained the offensive, though Manoel was also bombed. On 21 February, the *Regent* torpedoed a 5,609-ton German supply ship. Next day the *Ursula* attacked a convoy of two Italian steamers and a torpedo boat south of Kerkeneh, torpedoing one ship of 5,788 tons. The *Regent* later sunk the second freighter off Tripoli.

On 24 February nine Wellingtons bombed Tripoli. Next day a retaliatory raid on Luqa knocked it out for forty-eight hours, during which a troop convoy of four former liners sailed from Naples for Tripoli, covered by the light cruisers *Banda Nere* and *Armando Diaz*. The *Upright* sank the *Diaz* on 25 February, but the convoy got through. With only two Wellingtons left serviceable, the squadron was withdrawn from Malta. Then, on 5 March, sixty bombers hit Hal Far, leaving three Swordfish and a Gladiator burned out and all other aircraft unserviceable. The opportunity was taken to pass another convoy through to Tripoli and an empty one back.

A few Swordfish were patched up and flew rat hunts in bad weather to Kerkeneh or stood by armed for an enemy report. Between 8 and 12 March, two convoys reached Tripoli and another lost two ships to the *Utmost* and *Unique*. On 17 March all serviceable Swordfish—and some that were not—five with mines (known familiarly as cucumbers), four with bombs, took off for Tripoli. The first mine was dropped at 0140 in the face of heavy antiaircraft fire from ships and breakwaters, and in four minutes the "cucumber field" was sown. Stores on the quay and a pom-pom battery were hit by bombs.

To combat the German invasion of Greece, which was clearly imminent, in February 1941 over half of Gen. Archibald Wavell's army was transferred from Cyrenaica to Greece under the protection of the fleet. On 28 March off Cape Matapan the Supermarina tried to interfere, and Admiral Cunningham gave chase.

For a time it looked as if something like a fleet action in the classic style might be about to occur—the sort of heavy pounding, battle line to battle line between two columns of ironclads, that every flag officer who had matured in World War I secretly longed for. In that case the elderly battlewagons of the British Mediterranean Fleet, corroded by Jutland salt, would be more appropriate than the modern Italian battle fleet, which, fast and lightly armored, was built to hit and run from a sea of troubles. It was a fleet that, even more than the Kriegsmarine, "puts it not unto the touch/To win or lose it all."[3]

The main difference for Admiral Cunningham, pushing his scouting cruisers ahead in the time-honored manner, was that he had the *Formidable*'s squadrons to extend the hunt well beyond them, to cripple the gun-shy Italians for the battlewagons to finish off, perhaps even to sink the enemy themselves. At the Battle of Jutland in 1916, the British admiral John Jellicoe had ignored the static-stitched report from the pioneer seaplane carrier *Engadine*'s frail aircraft, but in 1941 Admiral Cunningham knew he had an edge with his Swordfish.

What actually happened was that aircraft from the *Formidable* reported an Italian cruiser force attempting to lure Cunningham toward the new battleship *Vittorio Veneto*, which opened fire on the British cruisers as they approached but turned for home on sighting aircraft from the *Formidable*. The battleship had no air shield and did not know Cunningham's strength.

Torpedo bombers from the carrier and from Crete, as well as RAF bombers from Greece, attacked the fleeing battleship. One torpedo hit and slowed her down temporarily, but another striking force hit the cruiser *Pola* by mistake. With no night-flying aircraft, Cunningham drove on through the darkness until the cruiser *Ajax*'s Type 297 RDF picked up a heavy ship lying stopped. This raised hopes, but it was only the *Pola*. She and two more 8-inch cruisers that appeared were sunk, and the *Valiant* put her 279 to good use for ranging. The *Formidable* was the only other ship in the fleet with radar (279), which she used to direct her aircraft.

The battle of Matapan destroyed any faith the Germans might have had in the Italian navy, and they realized that whatever they hoped to achieve in the Mediterranean could only be done through air power—an overwhelming fleet of dive-bombers. Since the latter were short-ranged, they would have to push their airfields ever forward to reduce the area in which the British fleet could operate, until the Luftwaffe commanded the whole Mediterranean.

They came near to this objective when the Allies were driven out of Greece into Crete, which was secured for the Axis by a big drop of paratroops. Its airfields rapidly filled with Stukas. When Gen. Erwin Rommel and his specially trained Afrika Korps drove Wavell's depleted army back to the Egyptian frontier, the Luftwaffe moved in behind him. The passage westward between Crete and Cyrenaica became dominated by German dive-bombers.

The picture for the Allies was not entirely dim, however. Malta, bombed incessantly, still held out, helped by some Hurricanes flown in from carriers. A flotilla of fleet destroyers working from Malta annihilated the five merchantmen and three destroyers of a Tripoli-bound convoy off Sfax. Tripoli itself was bombarded by the Mediterranean Fleet, installations were destroyed, and ships in the harbor were sunk. The Malta Swordfish, now equipped with ASV, used bomb, torpedo, and mine to cut off Rommel's supplies. RAF Wellingtons bombed Naples, and Blenheims and Beaufighters beat up shipping at sea. But keeping Malta supplied as a base from which to attack Rommel's supply convoys had to be done through Junkers Alley, and at times only submarines could make it. Besieged Tobruk was kept alive by coastal convoys of small craft.

The Malta-based submarines were sharp thorns in Rommel's side, particularly HMS *Upholder,* commanded by the black-bearded David Wanklyn. On 21 April he left Malta for his billet off Kerkeneh with orders to finish off a German troopship and a damaged Italian destroyer, the sole survivors of a convoy savaged by a Malta destroyer flotilla. On his way he sank the 5,482-ton *Antonietta Lauro.* On May Day he sighted a convoy of five transports and four destroyers. The *Upholder* strained forward at her best 9 knots, fired four tin fish, sank the 2,586-ton German *Arcturus,* crippled the 7,836-ton *Leverkusen,* went deep, then returned to finish her off. On 15 May the *Upholder* lost her asdic and hydrophones in a depth-charge attack in the Straits of Messina but survived to cripple the tanker *C. Damiani.* Ten days later the submarine sank the 17,897-ton former liner *Conte Rosso,* packed with troops for Rommel.

British submarines sank 89,797 tons out of the total of 209,714 tons of enemy shipping sunk in the Mediterranean between January and June 1941. The *Parthian* and other old ocean-going boats made what were called Magic Carpet runs from Alexandria to Malta with essential supplies and reinforcements. When the Allies evacuated Crete on 30 May, the old *Parthian* was reactivated and crippled the 5,000-ton *Strambo* in the Dardanelles on 3 June, but the loss of the *Usk* and *Undaunted* took the shine off the boats' achievements. "Shorty" Miers in the *Torbay* ran amok in the Aegean, sinking a tanker, a submarine, and caïques full of troops and stores.

On 17 September the *Upholder* had the center billet in a line of boats acting via Ultra to ambush three troopships heading for Tripoli. At 0300 the sub sighted the dark shapes of the enemy, and in four minutes her first tin fish left the 19,500-ton *Neptunia* sinking. The *Oceania,* holed aft and propellers smashed, settled stern first. On 8 November the *Upholder* sank an Italian submarine riding herd on a convoy that a cruiser-destroyer force from Malta later destroyed. The *Upholder* sank the destroyer *Libeccio* as she searched wreckage from the convoy. In all, during the last six months of 1941 the British Mediterranean submarines sank more than fifty Axis transports and four warships. The *Upholder* was sunk with all hands off Tripoli in April 1942.

In June 1941 Hitler attacked Russia, and the German dive-bombers in Sicily were switched briefly there. On 23 July seven SM79s torpedoed and disabled the cruiser *Manchester*. On 27 September twelve BR20 torpedo bombers damaged the battleship *Nelson* and sank a freighter. The Eighth Army was almost ready to attack Rommel, whose line of communications with Tripoli (his only large supply port) was attenuated. His lifeline to Italy was under constant attack from Malta, and pressure on it was stepped up when Force K of cruisers moved in. On 8 November they destroyed an Axis convoy.

Ten days later the Eighth Army began its offensive, and on 24 December it reoccupied Benghazi. With the Cyrenaican airfields lost to the Afrika Korps, it became easier to supply Malta. The fast supply ship *Breconshire* and its cruiser escort got through, undeterred by a timorous Italian battle squadron in the offing. On 13 December four Allied destroyers sank two Italian heavy cruisers.

But the Royal Navy was still losing ships. On 13 November the *Ark Royal* of Force H was torpedoed and later sank; on the twenty-fifth, the battleship *Barham* was lost. Two cruisers were destroyed by torpedo and mine.

On the night of 18–19 December, six of the Italian special assault unit known as the Sea Devils attacked the fleet in Alexandria harbor. They used three of the *siluro a lento corso,* or slow-running torpedoes (SLC), more familiarly known as *maiali* (pigs) to their crews ("human torpedoes" to the British). Developed before the war, each "torpedo" was 20 feet long with a detachable warhead. A two-man crew in frogman suits with breathing apparatuses sat astride the machine behind shields protecting them and the controls. They guided the weapon with their heads just above the water. They submerged close to the target and detached the warhead, clamping it magnetically to the victim's bottom, preferably to the keel. Then they set a time fuse and retired.

Outside the harbor on 18 December, the three *maiali* left their parent submarine. They waited until British destroyers passed through the net barrier, accompanied them in, and steered for their targets. One crew cut its way through antitorpedo nets around the battleship *Valiant,* became stuck in mud and cables, set the time fuse, and swam to a buoy. The two other crews attached charges to the battleship *Queen*

Elizabeth and the tanker *Sagona*. The six men waited, and at dawn three violent explosions signaled total success. They had done more damage to the British fleet than all the Supermarina's surface ships. The two battleships were out of service for several months. As a bonus, the destroyer *Jervis* was also damaged. Other SLCs, secretly housed in a tanker at Algeciras, did considerable damage to convoy vessels temporarily berthed in Gibraltar harbor. From a captured "pig" the British developed their own "chariots," using detachable warheads or limpet mines. Chariots from the submarines *Thunderbolt* and *Trooper* sank the new light cruiser *Ulpio Traiano* and badly damaged the troopship *Viminale* in Palermo harbor on 3 January 1943.

Early in January 1942 a small convoy got through to Malta, still free of Stukas, under cover of bad weather and low visibility. On the twenty-first, Rommel attacked in Africa and drove the Eighth Army back out of Cyrenaica. He complained about lack of supplies, and the Luftwaffe returned in force to Sicily to begin a maximum effort to neutralize Malta. Valetta and the dockyard were pulverized and much shipping sunk, but the island held out. In February a supply convoy from Alexandria was turned back by German bombers; another was bombed to destruction. Malta became untenable, and all naval forces there were withdrawn except for the dwindling squadron of fighting Stringbags and Albacores.[4]

In May a reinforcement of Spitfires, flown from HMS *Eagle* and the American carrier *Wasp*, inflicted severe casualties on the Luftwaffe, and in June a ten-ship convoy from Alexandria turned back under heavy air attack, losing one cruiser. Only two ships out of six in a western convoy that sailed on 11 June reached Malta, on 15 June, with the destroyer *Bedouin* sunk on the fifteenth and the *Liverpool* again crippled, both by SM79 torpedoes.

Rommel attacked again and this time captured the port of Tobruk, which then largely superseded Tripoli in his supply line. Hitler postponed a planned assault on Malta, which was simply kept quiet with air raids. The Eighth Army was to be built up to attack Rommel once again.

With the latter at El Alamein, near the Egyptian border, this could not be done from the east. Early in August, in Operation Pedestal, a convoy of fourteen fast merchantmen left Gibraltar escorted by four cruisers and eleven destroyers. Two battleships; the carriers *Indomitable, Victorious,* and *Eagle* (recently fitted at last with RDF Type 291); three cruisers; and fourteen destroyers took them as far as the Sardinian channel. With them also was the old carrier *Furious,* with more Spitfire reinforcements for Malta.

The first casualty was the *Eagle*, torpedoed and sunk on 11 August by a U-boat. Ten SM79s loosened the convoy's formation with *motor-*

bombas, and after that there was a continuous air and underwater battle. The cruiser *Cairo* was sunk by aircraft; submarines sank the cruiser
Kenya and badly damaged the *Nigeria.* E-boats sank the cruiser *Manchester* and damaged three merchantmen. These were finished off by
SM79 torpedoes, which also sank the destroyer *Foresight.* The
Indomitable was seriously hit. Five merchant ships reached Malta, four
of them damaged. This was counted a success.

Allied long-range bombers attacked Axis staging ports, and from
July to September 1942, British submarines sank 80,000 tons of Rommel's supplies. By 4 November, defeated at El Alamein, he was in
retreat from the Eighth Army, galvanized by Gen. Bernard Mont-
gomery and heavily reinforced and resupplied. On 20 November
Cyrenaica was again in British hands, and Rommel was driven back
headlong on Tunisia.

Here the Eighth could join hands with the First Army, which on 8
November landed at Oran and Algiers in Operation Torch, simultaneously with an American landing near Casablanca on the Atlantic
coast. The two British landings had been covered by Fleet Air Arm aircraft from fleet carriers and three of the new escort carriers on loan
from the United States—HMS *Avenger, Biter,* and *Dasher*—whose planes
bombed airfields and fought off Vichy French fighters.

The same formula was adopted in the American assault, with the
fleet carrier USS *Ranger* and the brand-new large escort carriers *Sangamon, Santee, Suwannee,* and *Chenango.* The operation proved that escort
carriers could be used to great effect in other roles, as the Pacific war
would bear out, not only in amphibious operations but in replenishing
other warships and transporting aircraft. (HMS *Archer* and USS *Chenango* ferried fighters to Casablanca.)

The next step on the road to Rome was the invasion of Sicily, Operation Husky. This was the first big test for Allied amphibious forces. To
achieve this major landing on a hostile shore, special craft were
needed to put ashore tanks, guns, and infantry. In the North African
landings, the landing craft were mostly small types easily carried in
British infantry-landing ships (LSI) and American attack transports
(APA). Bigger craft were now available, notably the tank-landing craft
(LCT) and infantry-landing craft (LCI) for short sea crossings, and the
bigger tank-landing ships (LST) for long passages. Many of the LSTs
later crossed the Atlantic.

The tasks of the Allied navies were to organize the passage and landing of the American force on the south coast and the British on the
east, and to support the landings with guns and planes. With Allied
warship strength, including forty-seven submarines and the aircraft of
HMS *Formidable* and *Indomitable,* interference from Axis warships was
not feared; land-based fighters would prevent heavy air attacks.

A dress rehearsal was afforded when the island of Pantellaria was eliminated by bombing and surface bombardment, to prevent interference by its aircraft and motor torpedo boats. The main assault was made on 10 July. After a counterattack on the Americans by German armor at Gela, and some stubborn resistance to the British in the plain of Catania, the campaign was swiftly concluded. The *Indomitable* mistook a lone Ju 88 for a returning Albacore on 16 July, was torpedoed, and limped back to Malta. On 3 September the Eighth Army crossed to the Italian mainland in landing craft under cover of army artillery and naval guns. The advance through Calabria was slow, and in Operation Avalanche a landing was made on 9 September 1943 by the American Fifth Army on the east shore of the Gulf of Salerno.

This was only 30 miles from Naples but 150 miles in advance of the nearest Allied fighters in Sicily. These operated on a fixed program that allowed Spitfires and Mustang A-36As twenty minutes over the beachhead, P-38 Lightnings forty. An inshore Force V of four American-built escort carriers, HMS *Attacker, Battler, Hunter,* and *Stalker,* plus the training carrier *Unicorn,* were stationed 20 to 30 miles offshore. Thus their Seafires, 106 in all, could spend more than an hour airborne and quickly reinforce standing patrols. Force H, with the fleet carriers *Formidable* and *Illustrious,* provided deep cover for all the inshore forces.

The successful landing of seven RAF Hurricanes without arrester hooks aboard the doomed *Glorious* at the end of the Norwegian campaign significantly weakened the case against modern fighters for the Fleet Air Arm. The Air Ministry was persuaded to hand over a number of Hurricanes, although many of them were unserviceable veterans, for conversion. Sea Hurricane IAs would have catapult spools for operation from fighter-catapult ships and CAM ships; IBs would be equipped with arrester hooks for carrier work.

The rugged Hurricane, with its wide-tracked undercarriage folding inward out of the wings, was quite easily adaptable to the rigors of carrier operation. The faster Spitfire, however, with its spindly fuselage-mounted underpinnings, was not ideal. Even so, rear admiral, aircraft carriers, Lumley Lyster reiterated his forceful demand for 200 Spitfires, and in early summer 1941 the Air Ministry was requested to transfer 400 of the latest VC mark. They squeezed out 250, 48 of them VBs. A Mark VB had been fitted with an arrester hook and slinging points and successfully tested aboard HMS *Illustrious* at Christmas 1941.

To overcome the poor view forward over the long nose, a continuous curved final approach was recommended, sighting the bridge island over the port-side wing root as a reference point. Two types of Sea Spitfire were then adopted: the IB, an interim type converted from existing Spitfire VBs; and the IIC, a machine adapted on the production line or built entirely from scratch and based for the first production model on the sturdier VC, with its heavier armament capability. Strength was added—to the middle fuselage to counter the onward thrust of an arrested landing, to the wing to allow for the lifting of heavier weapons, and to the main undercarriage. Heavier armor was fitted. The penalty of reduced performance was accepted, the IIC being some 15 MHP slower than the IB, which therefore just led the IIC as the fastest naval fighter in service. The increase in weight was too great to allow a hoped-for extra pair of cannons. But the strengthened undercarriage permitted the IIC to carry a larger external jettisonable "slipper" fuel tank than that of the IB, with a corresponding increase in range and endurance.

The IIC, with the Rolls-Royce Merlin 46 engine, was designed, like its Spitfire progenitor, to achieve its maximum speed at 20,000 feet, but most naval fighter interceptions had occurred below 10,000 feet. At low level the IIC's performance was inadequate, and the Merlin 46 was replaced by the 32. Advantage was taken of the marked increase in power resulting from a modified supercharger: the three-blade propeller was replaced with a four-blade Rotol type.

"The Seafire LIIC immediately displayed an outstanding low-level performance. Rate of climb and initial acceleration were far in excess of any other naval fighter produced during the war,"[5] asserts David Brown in his fine study of the aircraft. The increase in power also shortened the takeoff run remarkably, to less than 100 yards into a 30-knot wind, with a 500-pound bomb. The only feature desirable in a carrier fighter that was lacking in the Seafire LIIC was folding wings, which were introduced in the next Mark, the FIII.

The American-built escort carriers of Force V had large-enough elevators to handle the LIICs with which they had all been equipped just in time for Avalanche. On 8 September, while the Allied Avalanche invasion fleet was on passage, the Italian government surrendered. The Germans, however, did not, and the Allied landings went ahead as planned.

The first Seafires that circled Capri on D-Day, 9 September 1943, were vectored toward a flight of six Ju 88 "Jabo" fighter-bombers by the fighter direction ship HMS *Palomares*. The Jabos shed their bombs and fled, as did a score more just after noon, but echoes off high ground behind the beachhead swamped the *Palomares*'s radar screens, and pilots had trouble seeing through the prevailing thick haze. Nevertheless they continued to repel raids by faster Focke-Wulf Fw 190s and Me Bf 109s. Some attacks were made by Dornier Do 217s of Kampfgeschwader 100, carrying the new Henschel Hs 293A glider bombs. One of these aircraft sank the Italian battleship *Roma* as she headed for Malta to surrender.

Seafire LIICs aboard an escort carrier. (Royal Navy)

For the Seafire pilots, operating from the small carriers in the prevailing conditions was difficult and dangerous. Inexperience starting
from the top was a deadly factor. Many pilots had had insufficient
training. Adm. Phillip Vian, commanding Force V, was not an aviator
and had no experience handling carriers. The five flattops were given
far too little sea room, working with their circuits almost overlapping
in a box far too close inshore, all too conducive to bad landings, especially when there was no wind to land into and the deck was blurred
by glitter off the glassy sea. Aircraft pitched too fast into a wire and
pecked the deck, scattering splinters of Oregon pine, or landed heavily,
splaying the Seafires' over-delicate landing gear, shattering airscrew,
airscoop, ailerons, and tail wheel, often slamming into the bridge
island or skidding overboard. Pilots were killed, badly hurt, or burned,
and there was a lesser crop of wrinkled fuselages, impacted engines,
and tail hooks ripped off. The sortie rate was high, the schedule tight.
"Patrol maintained all day—landing on and flying aircraft every hour,"
the *Stalker*'s log recorded for D-day, 9 September.

On D-Day Plus One the pattern was the same, but in the evening,
twelve BF 109s decided that Lieutenant Commander Simpson's patrol
of the *Unicorn*'s 897 Squadron gave good odds, and they stayed to
fight. The agile LIICs outturned and outdived them. Simpson shot
down two 109s, and his wingman damaged two more. That day the
Seafires of Force V aborted forty enemy sorties, with their own avail-
ability down by 40 percent.

On the third day only thirty-nine Seafires were serviceable, but they
achieved thirty more sorties than scheduled. Glider bombs hit inshore

gunfire support ships. The all–New Zealand 834 Flight in the *Hunter* kept all their six aircraft serviceable, their only accidents four deck pecks. Pecking was reduced overall in the *Hunter* by Captain McWilliam, who ordered 2 inches trimmed off the 10-foot-diameter airscrews, with no drop in performance, and the modification became standard.

On the fourth day a landing strip at Paestum became available, and the twenty-six serviceable Seafires operated ashore for two days, battling dust (with no dust filters), the pilots maintaining and refueling their own aircraft. They used 5-gallon drums, twenty-three for each machine. Then U.S. Air Force fighters moved in, Montecorvino airfield was captured, and their work was done.

For the landings in the south of France in August 1944, a combined force of Royal Navy and U.S. Navy escort carriers supplied lavish fighter and bomber support over the beachhead and the Riviera hinterland as the troops struck inland. They spotted for the big guns of the Allied bombarding fleet and flew long intruder sorties with fast and rugged RN and USN Hellcat fighter-bombers. A month later a British escort carrier squadron's six ships neutralized Axis air power in the Greek islands and destroyed communications on the mainland. Their aim was to prevent evacuating German troops from going west to join their retreating comrades in France.

Although submarines and surface ships had made invaluable contributions to the Mediterranean war, the long, drawn-out struggle had ultimately been won by air power—and had almost been lost for the lack of it. Had Britain rearmed fully in the late thirties, the air strength needed might perhaps have been provided by aircraft carriers. This the Americans were to do in the Pacific.

More practical and economical for the comparatively restricted theaters of the European war might have been strong, peripatetic units of shore-based aircraft trained to make and defend their own airfields where needed. But, as in the Norwegian campaign, there had been no such foresight. Engrossed with the burdens of defending Britain and preparing for the destruction of German industry, the Royal Air Force had done very little to provide cover for warships within range of enemy airfields. It must have been clear that in a war with Italy, Malta might well become cut off and would certainly be heavily attacked from the air. Nevertheless, no precautions had been taken to accumulate supplies on the island, to provide proper air defense, or to excavate pens in the soft rock for submarines and minesweepers. The citizens and defenders of Malta paid a heavy price for this neglect.

The New Dreadnoughts

Immediately after World War I, for which the dreadnought race between Britain and Germany had been partly responsible, a de facto contest began between the United States and Japan in the development of the new capital ship—the aircraft carrier. This ship was to increase the range at which naval battles were fought, from a mere score to hundreds of miles, with the ships themselves never sighting each other.

Both parties were inspired by Britain's first custom-built carrier, HMS *Hermes*, 10,950 tons, laid down in 1919. Japan's *Hosho*, begun a year later, was a smaller ship but already embodied Japanese naval architects' skill in combining low displacement with high aircraft capacity. Over 3,000 tons lighter, the *Hosho* carried six more aircraft. Whereas the *Hermes* pioneered the bridge and funnel island structure, the *Hosho* favored HMS *Argus*'s system, vomiting smoke through three hinged exhaust pipes on the starboard side that were lowered to the horizontal for flying operations, as were the masts. Both ships had a top speed of 25 knots. The *Hosho* followed the *Hermes* in carrying a light cruiser–type gun armament, the latter with six low-angle 5.5-inch guns, the former with four of the same. These were to fight off conventional warships, a fallacy that was to persist for over a decade.

In 1917 the U.S. naval staff had been shown the plans of the *Hermes* and had absorbed the British dictum that a main armament of 6-inch guns should be carried, "together with one or two antiaircraft guns."[1] They intended to incorporate these features in a 24,000-ton, 35-knot ship, but a frugal Congress refused funds, allowing as a substitute the conversion of the 5,500-ton fleet collier *Jupiter*. In the new form of the USS *Langley*, she proved to be astonishingly good value. It was cheaper

119

to modify the coal holds than to fit the ship with a hangar deck, but these changes gave the *Langley* a quantum lead on the *Hosho*, with capacity for fifty-five aircraft. The much lower speed of only 15 knots became an asset, in that it necessitated the perfecting of the type of arrester system that became standard. The British fore-and-aft wires were abandoned in favor of Eugene Ely's old transverse principle combined with a crash barrier as a last ditch for landing aircraft and protection for planes that had just landed.

Another important spin-off, and a major innovation, was the fitting of two catapults for launching aircraft in low-wind conditions. The *Langley* also pioneered tying-down points on the flight deck to replace the protective palisades of contemporary British carriers. The masts were unobtrusively telescoped for flying operations; the single, later doubled, hinged port-side smoke vent was reminiscent of the *Hosho*'s. Both carriers were pioneers in the development of naval fighters, bombers, and torpedo planes, and in their combination as a unified fighting force.

Much practice enabled the *Langley*'s aircraft in 1928 to carry out an impressive raid, embarrassing to entrenched battleship diehards, on the U.S. Pacific Fleet's major base at Pearl Harbor on the Hawaiian island of Oahu. Her planes took the defenses completely by surprise, leaving the moored battlewagons no chance to sortie, and shore-based aircraft no time to intercept.

Meanwhile, both Japan and the States had taken up the option allowed in the Washington Treaty of converting redundant capital ships on the stocks into carriers. Japan converted the battlecruiser *Akagi* and the battleship *Kaga*. The *Akagi* had a top speed of just over 31 knots; the *Kaga* of some 3 knots less. Both carried to excess the idea of a flying-off deck below the main flight deck featured in HMS *Furious*. In the *Akagi* and *Kaga*, two flying-off decks were stepped down from a flight deck that extended to only two-thirds of the ship. The idea was to allow an absolute maximum number of sorties. But operations proved dangerous and in rough weather impossible, while also restricting aircraft capacity to seventy-two, still an impressive total. In 1935 the flying-off decks were scrapped and the flight deck extended to the bows.

The American giants *Lexington* and *Saratoga* did not take such byways in design. Like the Japanese pair, they were nominally of the 33,000 tons permitted by treaty, but advantage was taken by both nations of a clause that allowed existing capital ships an extra 3,000 tons for the new requirement of antiaircraft defense. All four carriers sailed through this loophole, with the American duo coming out at 36,000 tons, the *Akagi* at 36,500, and the *Kaga* at 38,000.

The *Akagi*. (Maritime Photo Library)

The American ships' huge hangars had capacity for ninety aircraft. A hearty 180,000 horsepower drove four shafts through turboelectric engines to produce a top speed of 34 knots, making the twins the fastest warships of their size in the world. Whereas the *Akagi* and *Kaga* featured horizontal exhaust vents, in the *Lexington* and *Saratoga* a huge distinctive flat-sided 76-foot funnel contained the uptakes from sixteen boilers.

Advanced as they were in carrier evolution, the four vessels suffered from the prevailing cruiser-carrier concept. To protect them in surface actions, the *Akagi* was fitted with six 8-inch guns and the *Kaga* with ten, and 10- and 11-inch armor, respectively. With the short range and restricted striking power of existing naval aircraft, it was not foreseen that, far from being mere ancillaries to main-fleet big-gun actions, carriers would be the principal agents in naval battles conducted without the ships ever sighting each other. A carrier's main protection then would be her own planes and light, quick-firing anti-aircraft guns.

With the same blindness, the *Saratoga* and *Lexington* were fitted with eight 8-inch low-level guns in superimposed turrets forward of the bridge island and aft of the funnel. Not only did their shell hoists and magazines take up space better occupied by aircraft, but their improbable use in action would likely be restricted to the starboard side. Firing to port was impossible when aircraft were operating, and blast from gunfire made crew stations untenable when they were not.

The lust for conquest felt by the Bushido junkers who dominated Japan was clearly confirmed when they invaded Manchuria in 1931, violating the Nine Power Treaty that bound signatories to "respect the sovereignty, independence and territorial integrity of China."[2] On 2 April of that same year, Japan launched the custom-built small carrier *Ryujo*. To keep within the tonnage left available by treaty, an attempt was made to hold the size under 10,000 tons—with capacity for fifty planes. This was achieved by building in two hangar decks, producing a top-heavy vessel 600 tons above target. The *Ryujo* was the first Japanese carrier to abandon the low-level gun, though her armament of eight 5-inch antiaircraft guns was less advanced than the main armament of sixteen high-angle 4.7-inch antiaircraft guns fitted in the *Glorious* in 1930.

In 1932 Adm. H. E. Yarnell, one of the first naval aviators to reach flag rank, conducted another, even more decisive, mock attack on Pearl Harbor, using planes from the *Lexington* and *Saratoga*. The "defenses" included an American battle fleet and submarine flotilla at sea, a division of troops and heavy mobile artillery and antiaircraft batteries ashore, and 100 defending fighters. Yarnell used the vast spaces of the ocean, rain squalls, and low cloud to attack when least expected—on a Sunday forenoon, with personnel relaxed in harbor routine and contemplating church parades. Fighters and bombers took off from a position 60 miles off Oahu. The fighters strafed the straight lines of parked defense aircraft; bombers targeted ships, barracks, and oil-storage tanks. In view of later events, it is probable that Japanese agents in Honolulu reported this successful evolution to Tokyo.

In 1933 the new Roosevelt administration authorized an increase in naval construction, and on 25 February the U.S. Navy launched its answer to the *Ryujo* with the USS *Ranger*. The 14,500-ton *Ranger* attempted to solve the problem of combining comparatively small size with a proportionately large air group when she pioneered the principle, later standard in the U.S. Navy, of hangars wider than and separate from the hull. She was 4 feet wider than the *Lexington* and *Saratoga* and could carry almost as many (86) planes. Unfortunately this also made the small carrier dangerously top heavy. Reduction of the bridge structure and the raising of the forecastle in 1935 did not eradicate the fault. Another disadvantage resulting from trying to cram too many planes in too small a ship was that machinery space suffered. Two-shaft turbines produced 53,000 horsepower, 13,129 less than the *Ryujo*'s, achieving the same modest 29.5 knots.

In 1934 U.S. naval building was stepped up again by the Vinson-Trammell Act to achieve parity with the rapidly expanding Japanese navy, already right up to treaty strength and bursting at the seams. Japan suggested the abolition of capital ships altogether, a less-generous offer than it appeared, as Japan itself was moving toward adopting the carrier as its major naval weapon.

Part of the Vinson program was the laying down of two new large carriers, the *Yorktown* and *Enterprise*. Learning from the underpowered *Ranger*, designers increased displacement to 20,000 tons to accommodate more powerful engines that delivered 20,000 horsepower on four shafts, producing 34 knots. An increase of 40 feet in length and just over 3 in beam allowed larger double hangars with a capacity for 100 aircraft, using three elevators. An additional forward set of arrester wires and an athwartship hangar-deck catapult proved to be impractical. The two forward-firing flight-deck catapults were unnecessary for World War II American aircraft, aided by the ships' high speed into wind.

These otherwise excellent ships were flawed, however, in perpetuating the American unarmored, wood-planked flight deck, reflecting a rather naive belief in the protective powers of a carrier's own aircraft against enemy bombers. More shrewdly, their British contemporary *Ark Royal* embodied the principle of the "armored box" hangar, which was made an even stronger feature of her successors of the *Illustrious* class. Even the deck armor of the latter did not stop Stuka bombs in the Mediterranean, and the Americans would later pay dearly for their unrealistic approach.

In November 1934 Japan laid down the new *Soryu*, which was followed by her improved big sister *Hiryu*. At a modest 15,900 tons, the *Soryu* still put Japan well over its treaty allowance of 81,000 tons, and a month later Japan formally disowned both the Washington and the London naval treaties.[3] This was three months before Hitler publicly rejected the restrictions imposed by the Versailles Treaty, and after a new agreement with Britain had sponsored new naval construction including the carrier *Graf Zeppelin* of 23,200 tons and designed speed of 33.5 knots.

Generally speaking, the States honored treaty terms, which, after the *Yorktown* and *Enterprise*, allowed it just enough tonnage for another smaller carrier. The 14,700-ton *Wasp*, ordered in 1935, was shorter and slightly broader than the *Ranger* and had a similar aircraft capacity of eighty-four. Almost identical machinery produced the same speed. One important innovation was the addition to the normal two centerline elevators of an outboard elevator, which aided distribution of aircraft on the flight deck.

In 1937 Japan cooked up an expansionist war with China. In December the small U.S. Navy gunboat *Panay* shepherded three Standard Oil tankers 28 miles up the Yangtse to avoid the fighting at Nanking. On 12 December the *Panay* was strafed and bombed by Japanese aircraft, and the gunboat sank with the loss of two killed and fourteen wounded. Japan's instant apology and offer of reparations were accepted but not the explanation of mistaken nationality.

Japan acted promptly to counter the American Vinson-Trammell program of naval expansion. In 1937 it adopted the Marusan Program, the third wave of naval construction undertaken since the Washington Treaty. This program focused on special, high-quality vessels designed to offset the numerical superiority that the industrial might of the United States could produce. The battleship lobby was satisfied by plans for the *Yamato* and *Musashi*, at 40,000–45,000 tons and with nine 18-inch guns the most powerful battleships in the world.

In 1936 the Washington Treaty limitations formally expired, though realistically they were already dead. In May 1938 the Naval Expansion Act raised the American limits on construction by 20 percent, including an additional 40,000 tons of new carrier building. In September 1939 the third *Yorktown*-class carrier, the USS *Hornet,* was laid down.

On 1 June Japan had launched the new *Shokaku,* a fast (34-knot) carrier of 25,675 tons with capacity for eighty-four aircraft. The carrier *Zuikaku* followed in November.

The States decided to build the new *Essex* class of large carriers, displacing 27,100 tons, with greater fuel storage capacity and cruising economy to measure the vast spaces of the Pacific. In June 1940 an extension to the Naval Expansion Act increased new naval construction plans by a further 11 percent, which included three of the new *Essex* class.

In July, after the fall of France and the rapid German acquisition of the European coastline from North Cape to the Spanish border, President Roosevelt signed the Two-Ocean Navy Bill, which authorized a huge 70 percent increase in warship construction, including eight more *Essex* carriers. Restrictions were imposed on gasoline exports, and six months' notice was given of the American intention to break the Japanese-American commercial treaty.

In September the destroyers-for-bases agreement was signed with Britain. Fifty old but refitted, fully equipped and stored U.S. Navy destroyers were to be exchanged for leases for naval and air bases in Newfoundland and the West Indies.[4]

In the same month Japan signed the Tripartite Pact with Germany and Italy. In October the United States also placed restrictions on the export of scrap iron and steel, much of which had been going to Japan for warship and other weapon construction.

In March 1941, the Lend-Lease Act made the States, in President Roosevelt's words, the "arsenal of democracy" and permitted the repair of Allied warships in the States.

The new battleships USS *Washington* and *North Carolina* were commissioned in the spring of 1941. The latter was a 35,000-ton ship, with nine 16-inch guns in triple turrets and a speed of just over 27 knots. Four of her sisters were under construction. Keels were laid for four 45,000-ton giants of the *Iowa* class, and seven even bigger *Montanas* were projected (over 60,000 tons), with cruisers of 6,000–10,000 tons and six super-cruisers of over 20,000 tons.

In June all German and Italian consulates in the United States were shut down, all assets frozen, and more than eighty ships taken over. Further, to replace shipping losses, the U.S. Maritime Board had already begun a big program of new merchant-ship construction, which added a million tons of new vessels in 1941. Fifteen hundred utility Liberty Ships were planned; it was discovered that with prefabrication one of these could be built in eight days.

In April 1941, by arrangement with the Danish minister in Washington, the United States took over the protection of Greenland and in July sent forces to Iceland. That same month, Japanese troops moved into southern Indochina. Britain and the Netherlands imposed a concerted oil embargo on Japan. For Japan this was really the point of no return in the prospect, now generally accepted as a foregone conclusion by the military, of war with the United States. The Imperial Navy was seriously embarrassed by the loss of oil imports. Its seemingly large reserve of 6,450,000 tons could not be stretched to much more than three years' supply.

In September 1941, U.S. Navy ships were empowered to fire on German submarines flouting international law, after a U-boat had attacked the U.S. destroyer *Greer* on 4 September. In October a German torpedo hit the destroyer USS *Kearney,* killing 11 men. Two weeks later a U-boat sank the destroyer *Reuben James,* with the loss of 100 American sailors.

If Japan's vital oil supplies could not be produced at home or by trade, the high command decided to capture the major petroleum-producing centers in southeast Asia. This would automatically initiate war, and must, the Imperial Naval General Staff decreed, be carried out before the U.S. Pacific Fleet, based at Pearl Harbor, could intervene. Adm. Isoroku Yamamoto, commander in chief Combined Fleet and Japan's naval supremo, thought it essential to prevent this possibility by using the heavy carriers to knock out the U.S. fleet at Pearl simultaneously with the launching of the attack on the East Indies.[5]

The general staff protested that all fleet strength would be needed in the southern campaign, air protection for which could not be covered by shore-based aircraft. Further, a successful Pearl Harbor strike depended entirely upon surprise. If that was lost the gamble would fail, and the carriers would be vulnerable to retaliation.

These views were shared by Vice Adm. Chichi Nagumo, who, though not an aviator, commanded the First Air Fleet, which would carry out the operation. Yamamoto threatened to resign and vowed to command the strike personally if Nagumo was halfhearted.[6] The staff gave way, and 8 December on the Japanese calendar was fixed for the attack.

"Hit 'Em When You Can"

The latest signals from agents in Oahu had identified eight battleships and the four carriers *Yorktown, Hornet, Lexington,* and *Enterprise* in harbor at Pearl. At 0500 on 7 December, with only a few hours to go before the first strike was due to take off, an intelligence message reported no carriers in harbor, though the eight battleships were still there.

Nagumo in the *Akagi,* leading the *Kaga, Soryu, Hiryu, Shokaku,* and *Zuikaku,* rejected cancellation. By the time his planes hit Pearl the U.S. carriers might have returned, and the battleships were in any case an important target. Just before dawn the force reached a point 200 miles north of Pearl Harbor, and at 0600 the first wave of the 353-plane attack force, led by Comdr. Mitsuo Fuchida, took off.[1]

Fuchida flew in the lead, followed closely by forty-nine other Nakajima B5N2 level bombers (later called Kates by the U.S. Navy). Each carried one 1,760-pound armor-piercing bomb. To starboard and close below flew Lt. Comdr. Shigeharu Murata from the *Akagi,* with forty torpedo planes drawn from all the carriers. Above and to port were fifty-one Aichi D3A-1 (Val) dive-bombers led by Lt. Comdr. Kakuichi Takahashi from the *Shokaku.* These machines' 14-cylinder air-cooled radial engines gave them a modest cruising speed of 200 MPH at 10,000 feet, with a cruising range of 450 miles. With their fixed, faired undercarriages, they resembled the German Stukas and were equally effective in spite of their old-fashioned appearance.

Forty-three escorting Zero fighters kept guard overhead, led by Lieutenant Commander Shigeru Itaya from the *Akagi.* The weather was cloudy down to 1,640 yards off the water, but as they flew, the sun rose. An hour and forty minutes after leaving the carriers, Fuchida

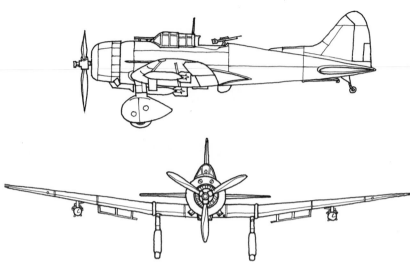

Aichi D3A-1 Val. (J. Poolman)

saw a line of surf breaking on the north shore of Oahu. He led the formation off to the west. Over Pearl Harbor the sky was clear. He raised
his binoculars. Still no carriers, but eight battleships slumbered at their
moorings. At 0749 he ordered his wireless operator to send the message "Attack!"

No warning had been received by the defenses. Soon after 0700, a
noncommissioned officer instructing a private first class in the use of
the army's new radar set detected a large number of aircraft 130 miles
to the northward. He reported it to his commanding officer, who
assumed the formation was a number of Flying Fortresses due from
the mainland. The air group from the *Enterprise,* returning from a
delivery of Wildcats to Wake Island, was also due. The *Lexington* was
still at Midway, on a similar mission. Ens. Manoel Gonzalez's plane, on
a reconnaissance mission from the *Enterprise,* was over Oahu when
Fuchida swept in. The *Enterprise* heard him shout, "Don't shoot! I'm
American!"[2]

While Takahashi's Vals climbed for height, Murata's torpedo bombers dived for the crowded Battleship Row. Smoke rose from nearby
Hickam Field as Vals dive-bombed and Zeros strafed the neatly parked
planes. Worried that the smoke might obscure his targets, Murata cut
short his group's approach and released his torpedoes. Inland, Wheeler
Field was bombed and strafed, and a section of Vals appeared over the
harbor, followed by high-level bombers.

The battleships *California, Oklahoma, West Virginia,* and *Nevada* were
hit by Murata's tin fish, the *West Virginia* at least six times. The *Mary-*

land and *Tennessee* were protected by the *Oklahoma* and *West Virginia* but were hit by bombs from high-level Kates. The *California* and *West Virginia* sank at their moorings; the *Oklahoma* capsized. A 1,600-pound bomb went down the *Arizona*'s funnel and detonated the forward magazine. She blew up, with great loss of life. Two cruisers were hit by torpedoes and a third by a bomb. The destroyers *Cassin* and *Downes* were sunk, though their main machinery was salvaged. The destroyer *Shaw,* in drydock, received several bomb hits but was at sea again in July 1942 with a new bow.

At 0854 Fuchida heard Lt. Comdr. Shigekazu Shimazaki from the *Zuikaku,* commander of the second wave, order his 170 planes to the attack. They had taken off at 0715, one hour and fifteen minutes after the first wave, and were now over the target. Fifty-four Kates armed with two 550-pound bombs or one 550- and six 132-pound bombs targeted the air bases.

The original targets for the dive-bomber group, led by Lt. Comdr. Takashige Egusa, the *Soryu*'s flight commander, in his distinctive red-tailed Val, had been the enemy carriers. Egusa could not be certain, peering down through the lingering smoke and the heavy antiaircraft barrage that rocked his plane, but Fuchida's binoculars told him that Nagumo's forlorn hope of catching any of the absent American carriers returning to Pearl was doomed. Egusa directed his eighty Vals with their 550-pound bombs to ships that appeared to be still undamaged or only slightly damaged by the first wave. The *Nevada,* holed in the port bow by a torpedo, was struggling to make the open sea. Six bombs hit her, and she was beached to avoid sinking in the fairway. The *Pennsylvania,* in drydock, was hit by one bomb.

Fuchida returned to the *Akagi* chagrined that the American carriers, their prime targets, had eluded them. Convinced that the latter were exercising to the south of Oahu, he begged Nagumo not to withdraw but to sweep in that quarter to locate them, and, failing that, to mount a third strike on Pearl Harbor.

But Nagumo, lacking the information on the enemy that more intense air reconnaissance could have provided, did not want to risk an encounter with four American carriers, by now doubtlessly informed of his presence. To spend time attacking Pearl again—even worse, to take his tired force southward into harm's way—was to invite disaster. He rejected both ideas and turned north to rendezvous with his tankers for the homeward run.

There were, of course, no U.S. carriers in the offing. The *Enterprise,* alerted by poor Gonzalez and warned to stay clear by another of her planes, was steering east out of trouble. With no air group, she had no choice. The *Lexington* was still in the Midway area, the *Saratoga* was refitting in San Diego, and the *Hornet* was in the Atlantic. The two U.S.

carriers present in the Pacific were not strong enough to oppose Nagumo directly, but as a fleet, or part of a fleet in being (with their air groups the most potent part), they had forced him to hold back and had thus achieved a strategic victory.

As a result, Nagumo left his job at Pearl unfinished. Not only were its docking and repair facilities still unscathed, except for minor damage to one drydock, but the big oil-storage depot, with 4.5 million barrels of fuel oil in its tanks, was completely unharmed. With this destroyed, the U.S. Navy would almost certainly have abandoned Pearl Harbor and withdrawn to California. Also intact were five submarines under overhaul. The *Narwhal* and *Tautog* had actually each shot down a torpedo plane.

The most significant result of the "day of infamy"[3] was its effect on the American people. An avenging fury now fueled a dynamic drive not only to salvage and repair the *Colorado, Maryland, Nevada,* even the *West Virginia,* and to replace a thousandfold the 208 aircraft destroyed at Pearl, but to build with the awesome potentiality of American industry a fleet the like of which the world had never seen, and which Japan had no hope of matching.

Until then, however, the United States had to rely on its small force of carriers and cruisers, plus its remaining three old battleships and two new 16-inch ships hurriedly completing their shakedown cruise off the West Coast, and, not least, its submarines, to protect the country against any follow-up of the Pearl attack. The U.S. Navy had shrunk to a task force, which would have to be used wisely until the seventeen *Essex*-class fleet carriers already being built, the nine light fleet carriers, and the fleet of escort carriers planned could be put into action.

When the news of the Pearl disaster reached Norfolk Navy Yard, Virginia, the *Yorktown's* chief engineer Lt. Comdr. Jack Delaney "thought it was another of those Orson Welles things," but soon discovered that "it was Orson Yamamoto."[4] His first concern was to speed up the rebricking of six of the carrier's boilers, without which flank speed would be impossible. Soon the *Yorktown* planes were taxiing down the streets of the naval base from East Field air station to the ship at Pier 7. Gunnery officer Ernie Davis was about to replace the ship's .50-caliber machine guns with twenty 20-mm cannon, as ordered, but Davis liked his fifties and decided to keep them as well. The *Yorktown* also had eight dual-purpose 5-inch guns, mounted in pairs just below the flight deck at the four corners. The 20-mm guns were manned by Marines, who used 5-inch shell bursts as practice targets. The ship's four sets of quadruple "Chicago Piano" 1.1-inch machine guns usually jammed after two or three seconds' fire, requiring the permanent presence of a gunner's mate with wrench and hammer under the mounting.

The *Yorktown* cleared Panama and steamed up the Mexican coast. She had been the first carrier to be fitted with radar, a CXAM set developed from the U.S. Naval Research Laboratory's proven XAF set, working on a frequency of 1.5 meters. The CXAM, with its 17-foot-square rotating "mattress" antenna, was successful in detecting aircraft and ships. But it was the first operational type of American radar in service, and the *Yorktown*'s was temperamental. All the other U.S. carriers had been fitted with the improved CXAM-1. Now, however, the old CXAM, in the hands of radioman Alvis "Speedy" Attaway, enabled the ship to make 27 knots at night, by ranging on the coastline. This was the ship's best speed until the boilers were finally repaired.

At San Diego 42 more aircraft were taken aboard, and fuselages were lashed up on the deckhead in the hangar, with wings and spares stacked along the bulkheads. The additions gave the *Yorktown* a record 129 planes. On New Year's Eve Rear Adm. Frank Jack Fletcher came aboard as commander of the new Task Force 17.

Meanwhile the Japanese were overrunning Malaya. To attack an enemy landing on the east coast, Adm. Tom Phillips took the new battleship *Prince of Wales* and the battlecruiser *Repulse* up from Singapore. He was supposed to have a carrier with him, but HMS *Indomitable,* the ship intended, had been damaged. The *Ark Royal* had just been sunk, the *Illustrious* and *Formidable* were still under repair in the States, the *Victorious* was with the Home Fleet, the *Furious* too old and worn, the *Eagle* and *Hermes* too slow and with too few aircraft.

Phillips pressed on without air cover, knowing that the nearest Japanese-held airfields were ex-Vichy strips over 400 miles away and believing that no torpedo bomber could boast that range. He had been promised the support of some inferior RAF U.S.-loaned Brewster Buffalo fighters for part of the way.[5]

A Japanese submarine sighted the British force at about 1600 on 9 December and reported it to Saigon, where Air Flotilla 22 of Eleventh Air Fleet of the Japanese navy was now based. The Genzan Squadron under Captain Sonokawa was equipped with the Betty, the big twin-engine Mitsubishi G4M2 navy Type 1 land attack aircraft. Fitted out for bombs, it was also the first aircraft to carry a torpedo internally. With a crew of seven and a top speed of 272 MPH at 15,000 feet, its best feature was a range of 3,765 miles, its worst a strong tendency to catch fire at the sight of tracer, later earning it the nickname Flying Lighter. When the sighting report of the British capital ships came in, Genzan was bombing up for a raid on Singapore but was hurriedly rearmed with torpedoes. Taking off at 1800, they made a wide box search but returned at midnight unsuccessful.

At 0700 next morning the 22d's main strike force of twenty-seven high-level bombers and sixty-one torpedo bombers comprising Bettys and the older Mitsubishi G3M2 took off. This machine, the brainchild of Admiral Yamamoto when he had been head of the technical division of the Naval Bureau of Aeronautics, had been a great advance in torpedo-bomber design in 1934 and was still very effective. It had a speed of 258 MPH carrying a 1,764-pound torpedo, and a range of 3,871 miles.

The three squadrons, Genzan, Mikoro and Kanaya, took off at 1100 on 10 December, and at 1130 they found the British ships. At 1115 high-level bombers hit the *Repulse,* and the torpedo bombers attacked. Genzan aimed seven torpedoes at the *Repulse* and claimed four hits. Kanaya launched twenty, with ten apparent hits, and Mikoro struck the old battlecruiser with four of its seven tin fish. Genzan claimed four hits on the new *Prince of Wales* out of nine torpedoes dropped, Kanaya four out of six. Even allowing for exaggeration, the two ships were overwhelmed. The *Repulse* sank at 1233 and the *Prince of Wales* at 1320, taking Phillips with it.

Though on a smaller scale, this action was a better demonstration even than Pearl Harbor of the vulnerability of conventional warships without strong fighter protection against air attack. The capital ships had been steaming fast at action stations, while the battlewagons at Pearl Harbor had been tethered goats. The lessons of the Mediterranean had not been learned.

Simultaneously with the attacks on Pearl Harbor and Malaya, the Japanese struck at and captured Wake Island, Guam, Hong Kong, and the Philippines, using greatly superior air strength in well-planned amphibious operations. Burma soon fell, and by the end of February 1942 the Japanese had occupied the whole East Indies with the exception of New Guinea. The old *Langley* was sunk attempting to ferry P-40 fighters to Java. A scratch Allied naval force was annihilated in the Java Sea.

U.S. submarines were among the first units to fight back against the Japanese, beginning with the *Narwhal's* and *Tautog's* Kates. Lt. Cdr. Willis A. Lent's *Triton,* patrolling south of Wake Island, was surfaced for a battery charge on the night of 10 February 1942 when a Japanese destroyer sighted her and subjected her to three hours of depth charging. Exasperated, Lent came up and emptied his four after tubes at his attacker. In this first U.S. submarine attack of the war, one torpedo hit and sank the Japanese.

It was the Irish-American John Holland who in 1897 invented the first modern submarine, powered by a gasoline engine on the surface and a battery-fed electric motor submerged, with a single bow torpedo tube and two fixed guns aimed by aligning the whole boat. For several years after World War I the U.S. Navy, reflecting its country's isolationist stance, concentrated on boats for coastal defense, producing the excellent, long-lived S class ("Sugar boats") in 1918–21. A range of 5,000–8,000 miles at 10 knots surfaced and a top surface speed of 14–15 knots were good for their time, though a crash dive took all of a minute.

In the later twenties the style was changed to larger, faster, wider-ranging boats, initially intended for fleet work, to sink enemy capital ships and cruisers. The first of these, developed from the Sugar boats, were the three 2,000-ton surfaced, 2,620-ton submerged, B class *Barracuda, Bass,* and *Bonita.* They had a good range of 12,000 miles at 11 knots surfaced and a speed of 18 knots, produced by the first U.S. Navy use of combined diesel and electric drive on the surface. They got to 8 knots submerged, but otherwise their performance was disappointing. From these was developed the big (2,710- and 4,164-ton) *Argonaut,* the only specialized mine-laying boat ever built for the U.S. Navy, with the heavy gun armament of two 6-inch guns in addition to four torpedo tubes. The *Argonaut* had a long range (18,000 miles) but was slow and unwieldy. Of a similar size, built with Japan now in view as a possible enemy, were the *Narwhal* and *Nautilus* of 1927–30.

The next class, the P boats (*Porpoise, Pike, Shark, Tarpon, Perch, Pickerel, Permit, Plunger, Pollock,* and *Pompano*), built in 1933–36, were the first really modern fleet boats in the U.S. Navy, with the first totally diesel-electric propulsion. At 1,310 and 2,005 tons, the Ps were large enough to be roomy for long patrols and had good sea-keeping qualities. They were also strong and well armed, as were their fifteen derivatives of the *Salmon/Sargo* class and twelve boats of the T class.

It was with the next class, however, the *Gatos,* that the U.S. Navy found its perfect formula for the fleet boat. This double-hulled type became the standard form of American World War II submarine, introduced in the 1940 program. A first batch of six was followed by an order for sixty-seven more. These boats had an all-welded hull, a more sophisticated and powerful all-diesel-electric drive, higher speed (20–25 knots surfaced), and a long range of 11,800 miles. A new series, the *Balao* type, was added in the 1942 war program.

On 7 December 1941 the U.S. Navy had 111 boats in commission, 38 being the old S boats, but the majority modern *Gatos.* There were 60 boats in the Atlantic and 51 in the Pacific, together with 50 British and Dutch boats. The Japanese had 63 oceangoing submarines and were building "baby" submersibles for coastal defense and short-range operations.

The saving grace for the United States on 7 December was that all the carriers and seventeen of the twenty-two submarines based at Pearl were absent at sea. Based at Cavite Navy Yard in Manila were the twenty-nine boats attached to the Asiatic Fleet. On 8 December

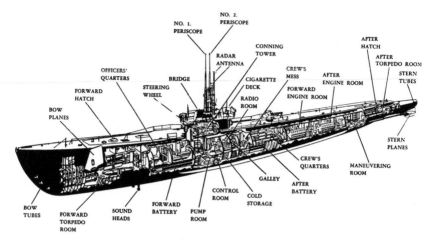

U.S. Navy fleet submarine *Gato* class. (U.S. Navy)

the *Seawolf* and *Sculpin* were escorting the doomed *Langley* and her ferrying convoy, and other boats formed an inner scouting ring around the Philippines, an outer ring stretching east around the Palaus, northwest to the Gulf of Hainan.

On the tenth, Japanese aircraft bombed and destroyed Cavite. The *Sealion* was sunk and the *Seadragon* damaged, but the submarine rescue ship *Pigeon* patched her pressure hull, stopped leaks, and the *Seadragon* limped out to sea. The other submarines in the harbor were unharmed. Silently they put to sea, to look for the enemy.

On 15 December Lt. Comdr. Freddie Warder took the *Seawolf* into the bay of Aparri on the northeast coast of Luzon, the scene of one Japanese landing, and fired four torpedoes at the big, 12,000-ton seaplane tender *Sanyo Maru*. There was a dull thud in the hydrophones as one tin fish hit but did not explode. U.S. boats used both the old Mark 10 contact torpedo and the new Mark 14, designed to detonate either on contact with a ship's hull or by the influence of the vessel's magnetic field on a magnetic actuating pistol, or exploder, in the warhead.

The torpedoes fired at the *Sanyo Maru* were Mark 14s, forerunners of all the 14s doomed to explode prematurely, pass under the target, or simply thump it without detonating. Both marks had suspect depth-keeping mechanisms, but the older "kippers" were far more reliable.

U-boats had had trouble with their torpedoes in the battle for Norway, but not as serious as the problems that plagued U.S. submarine skippers for nearly two years before a special troubleshooting program put things right. The Japanese suffered no such troubles in the use of their large, 24-inch, long-range, oxygen-aspirated torpedo of great reliability and explosive effect, far superior to the American tin fish.

Nevertheless, Chester Smith's *Swordfish* sank two Japanese marus (Japanese merchant ships) up in the South China Sea and on 16 December destroyed the 8,663-ton *Atsutusan Maru* with three torpedoes. The *Sargo*, however, fired thirteen torpedoes in eight attacks with no success; the *S38's* tin fish prematured when dead on target; the *S39's* torpedo hit a maru with a dull and impotent thud; and the *Pickerel* fired five tin fish at a patrol boat, scoring zero. And so it was with eight other boats.

But of the four boats that went into the shallow Lingayen Gulf during the Japanese landing there, the *Seal* sank the small freighter *Hayataka Maru*, and, after missing with four old Mark 10s preset for the wrong depth, the *S38* had better luck when a reset tin fish sank the 5,445-ton *Hayo Maru*. In the depth-charge hunt that followed, the *S38* damaged a propeller on a reef and ignited accumulated gas in the battery compartment, while noise from the damaged propeller set off another hunt. The sub then crash-dived into a mud bank and sank to 350 feet, 150 feet below her designed maximum depth, buckling the ballast tanks. But she struggled to the surface and limped away to Pearl.

On 25 January 1942, Lt. Comdr. "Jumping Joe" Grenfell's *Gudgeon* was trudging the 3,400 miles back to Pearl from the Sea of Japan with a zero score when she sighted and sank a big (1,173- and 1,785 tons) Japanese I-class submarine with two detonations out of three. Between 24 January and 19 February the *Swordfish* braved unknown currents off the Celibes to sink two freighters and a tanker, but on 2 February the *Shark* was lost in the Makassar Strait between Borneo and the Celebes. On the twenty-fifth, the *Perch* became involved in the Java Sea battle and was scuttled.

"Fearless Freddie" Warder took the *Seawolf* to Christmas Island west of Java in the Indian Ocean to see if the Japanese had made a move on the valuable phosphate mines. He arrived in the forenoon of 31 March. There was no sign of life, but on April Fool's Day he sighted four enemy cruisers in column heading his way. Offshore he fired four torpedoes and saw a column of spray, steam, and flame rise from one cruiser's side before he went deep. At first light next morning he sighted another cruiser steaming offshore, fired three more tin fish from his dwindling stock, and his hydrophone man reported breaking-up noises. A destroyer steamed out; another cruiser launched her seaplane. With her last two "torpeckers" the *Seawolf* bagged this one too, then survived a destroyer hunt to escape to Fremantle in southeast Australia, where a new base had been set up.

In April 1942 Admiral Nagumo took five carriers, his veteran Pearl Harbor carriers less the *Kaga* (which was under repair), and four battleships with cruisers and destroyers into the Indian Ocean. The Allies feared the capture of Ceylon, to sever British communications with India and menace even the vital traffic up the east coast of Africa. But the Japanese, knowing that American strength in the Pacific was growing rapidly, intended only a raid in force. They wanted to break up communications in the Bay of Bengal, draw opposing troops and aircraft as far as possible to the southward and away from Burma, and generally damage British prestige in India.

A British Eastern Fleet of three old battleships, a few cruisers and destroyers and the old carrier *Hermes,* based for safety at Addu Atoll in the Maldive Islands, missed contact with Nagumo. Just before dawn on 5 April, fifty-four dive-bombers and ninety level bombers took off from his five carriers 200 miles south of Ceylon. As they closed the coast they sighted twelve unescorted Swordfish below them. Itaya's fighters shot them all down. The dive-bombers sank an armed merchant cruiser and an old destroyer and damaged installations in the harbor; the level bombers destroyed twenty-five planes on the airfield. A floatplane reported two enemy heavy cruisers in the vicinity, and Mitsuo Fuchida was reassembling his planes for a quick dash to protect his carriers when some twenty Hurricanes appeared. The Zeros were left to deal with them and lost a number of planes. A second-wave dive-bomber group of eighty planes found the cruisers *Dorsetshire* and *Cornwall* and in twenty minutes sent them to the bottom.

On 9 April the same force attacked Trincomalee on the east coast of the island. Hurricanes again came out to intercept, but this time they were dealt with decisively by the Zeros, allowing the bombers to destroy carrier-type aircraft on the airfield and damage installations there and in the naval base with 1,760-pound bombs. A munitions dump went up like a firework display.

As the first wave returned to their carriers and as the second wave prepared to take off for Trincomalee, a search plane reported an enemy carrier with a destroyer. Egusa's dive-bombers of the second wave were switched to the new targets. While Fuchida's level bombers were being rearmed with torpedoes to back up Egusa, six columns of white water rose off the *Akagi's* bows as bombs from nine British Bristol Blenheim light bombers fell. Caught off guard, the Zeros of the combat air patrol protecting the carriers shot down five of the attackers. Then Egusa's dive-bombers found HMS *Hermes* and her escort. The carrier was heard calling for her aircraft, but they were now burned-out wrecks on Trincomalee airfield. The Vals sank both ships in fifteen minutes.

To oppose Japanese attacks on the east African trade route and prevent the Vichy French from handing over Madagascar, the Allies occupied the island. It took them four months to do this, while Japanese submarines and armed merchant cruisers sank over forty Allied merchant ships in the area. A midget submarine damaged the battleship *Ramillies*.

Admiral King, commander in chief of the U.S. fleet and chief of naval operations, knew that a showdown with the Japanese fleet was inevitable but avoided such a challenge until his new ships could be commissioned and his Pearl Harbor wrecks repaired. He told Adm. Chester Nimitz, new commander in chief, Pacific, "Hold what you've got and hit 'em when you can."[6] On 11 January 1942 the *Saratoga* was badly damaged and sent off stateside for repairs and the replacing of her redundant 8-inch guns with 5-inch dual-purpose guns. The *Saratoga* was greatly missed, but at the end of January task forces under Admiral Halsey (in the *Enterprise,* with three cruisers and six destroyers) and Adm. Frank Jack Fletcher (in the *Yorktown,* with two cruisers and four destroyers) started a series of raids on Japanese airfields and anchorages in the Gilbert and Marshall Islands. The *Yorktown's* generally unreliable radar made itself useful picking up Japanese search planes. More than fifty .30-caliber machine guns, mounted on cut-down deck-scrubbing broom handles to fit into lifeline posts, were added to the *Yorktown's* already formidable antiaircraft defenses.

The *Hornet* arrived hotfoot from the Atlantic. She was held back to test the feasibility of launching a B-25 medium bomber, so much larger than normal carrier planes, from the limited space of a carrier's flight deck. Two machines took off successfully on 2 February, and selected pilots were given a month's intensive practice in short takeoffs and with bombed-up planes.

The eyes of the Japanese naval staff were on Australia, a potential springboard for future offensives in the southwest Pacific. On 19 February 1942 they showed their hand with a strike on Darwin by 135 land-based and carrier-borne bombers, which sank three ships and damaged three more, as well as hitting port installations.

On 20 February the *Lexington* attempted a raid on the big base at Rabaul in New Britain, was spotted and attacked by shore-based aircraft, but won the ensuing air battle. Lt. Butch O'Hare destroyed five Kates in one dogfight. Halsey shelled and bombed Wake and Marcus Islands, 800 miles farther west and only 1,000 miles from Japan.

The *Hornet* sailed on 2 April 1942, sixteen B-25s on the flight deck, with her own aircraft confined below. The *Enterprise* accompanied her with air cover. The target was Tokyo. There was no way in which the B-25s could land again on the carrier, which in any case was too precious to wait for their return. With the raid accomplished, the bombers were to fly on to friendly Chinese bases.

On 7 April the U.S. Navy Combat Intelligence Unit at Pearl deciphered a signal detailing a plan to seize Port Moresby in New Guinea in early May. With the possession of New Guinea, the Solomon

Islands, and the Bismarck Archipelago, and later New Caledonia, Fiji, and Samoa, even New Zealand, the Japanese could dominate the Coral Sea, Australia, and the South Pacific, cutting off Australia from the United States. An amphibious force was assembled at Rabaul.

The aggressive U.S. Navy submarines were carrying the war right to Japan's doorstep. On 16 April the *Thresher,* having just sunk a merchantman south of Tokyo Bay, helped a very special carrier force to do the same. Pulling out of range of Japanese direction finding, the submarine sent Admiral Halsey the weather report that gave him the all-clear to attack Tokyo.

It had been planned to launch the *Hornet'*s B-25 strike against the Japanese capital in darkness, 500 miles from the Japanese mainland. But early on 18 April 1942, in broad daylight, the task force ran across the Number 23 *Nitto Maru,* a former fishing boat, at her station in a picket patrol line some 720 miles east of Tokyo. At 0630 the Japanese ship radioed Combined Fleet headquarters reporting three carriers, and Halsey knew he had been spotted.

The Japanese would now be expecting a normal carrier raid, which could not have reached the target intended. The B-25s were ready to go, and with much of the element of surprise gone, the strike was launched. The force was at this point fighting a 40-knot gale that sent spray over the *Hornet'*s pitching, rolling flight deck. At 0725 Lt. Col. Jimmy Doolittle, the former air record breaker, with only 467 feet in which to get airborne, led the strike off the deck. The pilots aimed to open the throttle at the start of an upward pitch of the flight deck. Only one plane threatened to stall, but made it safely. The whole take-off operation took exactly one hour and one minute, then the bombers set course for Tokyo, and the task force withdrew eastward at 25 knots.

The B-25s had been unable to lift a load heavy enough to do serious damage, but when they arrived over their targets, Tokyo residents assumed they were part of a Japanese air-raid practice that was just finishing. Thus the American planes had an uninterrupted run in. Little concrete damage was done, though the city's biggest hospital was unfortunately burned down. Strict orders to avoid the emperor's palace, damage to which would have been counterproductive, were observed. Three bombers scattered incendiaries over Kobe, Nagoya, and Osaka. The raid was an enormous propaganda victory for the Allies and a boost to American morale.

In the course of exhausting operations, American aircraft had developed faults. *Yorktown* Dauntless dive-bomber pilots complained that their new telescopic bombsights fogged up with condensation in dives from high altitudes, and on reaching release point, electrical bomb releases failed. This forced pilots to open the canopy, line up the target visually, and use the old manual bomb-release handle. When the *Lexington* left for the States to have her redundant 8-inch guns replaced by light antiaircraft guns, she gave the *Yorktown* five Wildcats to replace some of her worn-out machines. Six aircrafts had crashed, the sixth on takeoff, with a case of engine failure that plagued the F4Fs for some time. The fault was eventually traced to an inferior fuel that wore away the rubber liners of the self-sealing tanks, sending crumbs of rubber into carburetors, choking the engines.

On the night of 6 May 1942, Lt. Comdr. J. W. "Red" Coe in the submarine *Skipjack* invented an important new tactic. Overtaking a Japanese freighter from astern in the moonlight, he speeded up to get ahead of his quarry to avoid being silhouetted. He succeeded too well, finding himself right in the path of the maru, about 300 yards away. Normal reaction was an instant crash-dive, but on the spur of the moment Coe fired three torpedoes on the instinct that if the enemy sighted their tracks he would swing away and present his whole flank to the tin fish. If not, one of them might well hit her bows-on. This was precisely what happened to the *Kanau Maru*, which swallowed the torpedo and sank by the head. The maneuver became known as Down the Throat and was often used.

Admiral Yamamoto and his staff of Combined Fleet favored an offensive to the east to occupy the western Aleutians in the north Pacific and the American base of Midway Island in the central Pacific. Yamamoto thought that this would draw out the remnants of the U.S. fleet, including the carriers he had missed at Pearl Harbor. Heavily outnumbered, the Americans would be crushed once and for all.

The Doolittle raid on Tokyo gave MI, the Midway plan, final credibility, and on 5 May it was decided to activate it as well as the Moresby venture. Organization of the Midway attack was begun. But the cryptographers of U.S. Combat Intelligence, known as Hypo, broke the Japanese codes and identified the Moresby operation. They caught the wind of a plan for a central Pacific move, but as yet they could not nail it down.

On 1 May the *Yorktown* joined the *Lexington* at Point Buttercup, south of the Solomons, to cover, under the command of Rear Admiral Fletcher, the anticipated Japanese drive on Port Moresby and the Solomons. They had 141 aircraft between them and were accompanied by a joint U.S.-Australian force of cruisers and destroyers under Rear Adm. J. G. Crace. The *Yorktown* refueled from the tanker *Neosho* and the *Lexington* from the *Tippecanoe*, which also put right the *Yorktown*'s shortage of toilet paper, a serious matter on the eve of battle. The carriers were still refueling when the *Yorktown*'s torpedo bombers sighted a Japanese submarine and depth-bombed her. Fletcher, thinking erroneously that he had been discovered by the Japanese command, left the *Lexington* refueling and headed northwest around the tip of New Guinea, hoping to find the Japanese transports before he was attacked. He ordered the *Lexington* and the Crace force to catch up with him, while doubling the radar watch in the *Yorktown.*

On 3 May a small Japanese force seized Tulagi in the Solomons as an advanced seaplane reconnaissance base. Fletcher took the *Yorktown* alone, and the next day his planes attacked ships off Tulagi. All their torpedoes missed, many of them set too deep. Fogged bombsights and windshields plagued the dive-bombers. In three strikes, only two seaplanes and four landing barges were definitely destroyed, and a destroyer damaged. The Americans believed they had sunk two destroyers, a freighter, and four gunboats, with another destroyer and a seaplane carrier damaged.

On 6 May the Japanese Port Moresby expedition sailed, escorted by the light carrier *Shoho.* Completed in 1939 as a submarine depot ship, she had been designed to be converted if necessary into a carrier, which was affected in 1941–42 with the fitting of steam turbines giving a top speed of 28 knots. Fletcher's planes searched for the MO (Moresby) force in vain. U.S. Army Air Corps B-17 bombers based in Australia did sight it but failed to score.

At 0730 a Japanese search plane reported an American carrier and cruiser southwest of Guadalcanal in the Solomons. Fifty-one bombers from the *Shokaku* and *Zuikaku,* the nucleus of a general covering force heading west from the Solomons, found the *Neosho* and the destroyer *Sims* waiting for their carriers at a refueling rendezvous. The *Sims* was sunk at once, the *Neosho* scuttled later. Meanwhile the *Shokaku* and *Zuikaku* had received a report of Fletcher's force farther to the northwest, and they felt vulnerable without their aircraft.

But Fletcher had in turn been distracted by an incorrect scout-plane report of two Japanese carriers and four heavy cruisers 130 miles east of New Guinea, and he had launched ninety-three planes from the *Yorktown* and *Lexington.* The target actually comprised two cruisers and two destroyers, but the commander of the *Lexington's* dive-bombers, which were off course, happened to sight the *Shoho* and her covering force of cruisers and destroyers. The carrier dodged and weaved, but American torpedoes for once behaved themselves. Dive-bomber pilots used their manual releases, and, in the patch of temporarily clear sky, bombsights did not fog up.

The *Lexington's,* then the *Yorktown's* aircraft gave the enemy no mercy. The eighteen escorting Wildcats shot down eight of the Zeros that managed to get airborne. The *Shoho* took thirteen bomb and seven torpedo hits in twenty minutes, and, as she was making 20 knots, simply slid right under. One American bomber was shot down.

At 1747 the *Yorktown's* radar picked up a formation of aircraft 18 miles to the west. This was a group of twelve dive-bombers and fifteen torpedo-bombers from the *Shokaku* and *Zuikaku* under Lieutenant Commander Takahashi, who had led the first wave of Vals at Pearl Harbor. It was his idea to attack at sunset to present the American antiaircraft gunners with poor targets, but the weather worsened. He had just decided to turn back when he was attacked by fighters from the *Lexington*, soon joined by seven Wildcats from the *Yorktown*, and lost eight planes. When at about 1855 the *Yorktown* began recovering her fighters, it was soon spotted that there were aliens in the circuit. Some of the Japanese pilots had either become so disorientated in the misty melee that they had mistaken the *Yorktown* for one of their own carriers, or, more likely, as they knew the latter were some 100 miles away, had followed the Wildcats to do some damage. Whatever the reason, nine of them were splashed near the American carriers, and eleven more ditched on the homeward run when they ran out of gas. Only seven of the original twenty-seven returned to their carriers, and Adm. Takeo Takagi had lost a sixth of his air strength even before the anticipated battle of the carriers had begun.

This came next forenoon. Search planes from both sides were up with the dawn. Fletcher learned Takagi's precise losses of the previous day from an intercepted signal, but the weather had now changed sides. The foul front that had given him cover was now moving northeast, over the Japanese carriers.

At 0600 Takagi launched a search group, which fanned out to the south and west. At 0630 the *Lexington* launched eighteen search planes to make a wide circle round Task Force 17. The *Yorktown* launched a CAP of F4Fs, followed by eight Dauntlesses with depth charges for submarine attack, that could be jettisoned to engage oncoming bombers. Fletcher zigzagged along a southeasterly course, waiting. At 0820 a *Lexington* scout sighted the Japanese and reported two carriers, four cruisers, and many destroyers about 175 miles northeast of Task Force 17. About twenty minutes later the latter picked up a Japanese search plane's accurate report of their position and constitution.

At 0848 Fletcher ordered his strike of nine Devastators, twenty-four Dauntlesses, and six Wildcats from the *Yorktown*; and twelve Devastators, twenty-two Dauntlesses, and nine Wildcats from the *Lexington*.

At 0900 Takagi launched eighteen Kate torpedo bombers, thirty-three Val dive-bombers, and eighteen Zeros. His force was weakened by the losses of the previous evening but was protected by more fighters than the American strike force. It was also more accurately directed and formed one integrated whole, unlike the Americans, whose two air groups operated as separate units. The first pure carrier battle was about to be joined. The fate of Australia hung on the outcome.

As the American strike headed northeast and the Japanese along the reciprocal, southwest, bizarrely the two forces passed each other some way off, the Japanese to starboard of the Americans. Neither had enough fuel to investigate the other. It was no occasion for 1914–18 gallantry. Some U.S. pilots waved cynically at their opponents.

The enemy position given to the American strike proved to be innaccurate by 45 miles, which caused an initial delay while Fletcher's Dauntlesses, which had outdistanced the slower Devastators, located the Japanese force. Then they had to wait twenty-three minutes for the Devastators to catch up. While they waited, the *Zuikaku* slid out of sight under a rainsquall, and more Zeros scrambled from the *Shokaku* to engage the enemy.

Lt. Comdr. William Burch of Scouting 5 thought he had better catch the one visible Japanese carrier while he could, and he led his seven Dauntlesses down from 17,000 feet. As he nosed over, the Zeros attacked. Five SBDs were hit in their fuel tanks, but the rubber liners saved them. All seven were riddled with 7.7-mm and 20-mm holes, but the rear gunners shot down four Zeros. Then their windshields and telescopic gunsights began to fog up in the foul weather, and no hits were scored.

While they were fending off the Zeros, Lt. Comdr. Wallace Short's Bombing 5, too low to start with, had time to go around again. Lt. "Jo-Jo" Powers, badly wounded, his machine in flames, held on and dropped his 1,000-pounder from 200 feet above the *Shikoku*'s flight deck, then plunged to his death, taking radioman Everett Hill with him. This hit started fires and so mutilated the forward end of the Japanese carrier's flight deck that she was unable to operate aircraft. Nine Zeros had been shot down, for the loss of two Dauntlesses.

Then Lt. Comdr. Joe Taylor attacked with his Devastators. Having hugged the ocean so that the Zeros could not attack their vulnerable bellies, they had passed clear under the Japanese strike force. When they approached their target, the *Shokaku*'s CAP fighters were so busy with the Dauntlesses that only two attacked and were shot down by the rear gunners. But all Taylor's torpedoes ran so slowly that the carrier easily combed most of their tracks, and the remainder either ran wild or merely thumped the carrier's flank harmlessly.

Of the *Lexington*'s air group, one TBD turned back with engine trouble shortly after takeoff; three Wildcats lost their way and had to return before they ran out of gas; and, in worsening weather, all twenty-two dive-bombers got off course and were also forced to return. The eleven Devastators, in company with nine Wildcats and four reconnaissance Dauntlesses carrying only light bombs, pressed on to attack through the overcast at 1107. The F4Fs were outnumbered by Zeros and could not be of much help to the crawling Devastators, five of which were shot down with no hits scored. Two of the SBDs were shot down, but a Dauntless bomb added to the *Shokaku's* damage. The *Lexington's* returning survivors reported the Japanese carrier sinking, but in fact she managed to get her fires under control, though she still could not receive her aircraft. Some of these landed aboard the *Zuikaku*.

Meanwhile, at 1000 aboard the *Yorktown*, Bob Milholin, a storekeeper converted to radar watchkeeper, identified at a range of 68 miles a big formation of planes, phenomenal for the carrier's temperamental scope. "It was one heck of a pip," recalled radar man Vane Bennett.[7] A big formation of planes, covering a whole inch of the 5-inch screen, was heading for them as they steamed under sunny skies—clear, solid targets. Neither Japanese ships nor planes had radar, but leading the strike force in was the search plane of WO Kenzo Kanno, who had first reported the U.S. force that morning. Well past his point of no return, he had sacrificed himself and his crew to lead his own force to the enemy.

The *Lexington's* fighter-direction officer, coordinating the combined CAP, ordered more F4Fs aloft. Nine took off to join the eight already airborne and flew out to a radius of 20 miles at 6,000 feet, thereby missing the Japanese attackers, who were coming in at over twice their height. Aerial defense of Task Force 17 devolved upon the eight Dauntlesses, thus doubling as antisubmarine/torpedo plane and fighter protection.

The *Yorktown's* Capt. Elliott Buckmaster anticipated the Japanese attack would hit them at about 1100, and at 1106, *Yorktown* radar reported the enemy 20 miles away. Five minutes later they were 5 miles closer, visible with binoculars.

The torpedo planes approached in a huge arc, then divided into two sections, one for each target. Through a too widely dispersed barrage from a surrounding ring of cruisers and an outer circle of destroyers, eighteen Kates made for the *Yorktown* at 5,000 feet, making 180 knots, almost twice the attacking speed of a Devastator. They brushed aside the fighter Dauntlesses to drop their lethal torpedoes. Fortunately they all attacked from the port side, making it easier for Captain Buckmaster to evade the torpeckers. He combed all eight, and the *Yorktown's* bristling gun batteries shot down all but one of the Kates. The group that attacked the *Lexington*, however, came in from both flanks in an "anvil" attack. The older ship, slower to answer her helm, and with a wider turning circle, made Capt. Frederick Sherman's work hard for him, and at 1120 the ship was hit by two torpedoes on the port side.

The fighter Dauntlesses fought a stalemate with the Zeros, four aircraft being destroyed on each side. At 1124 the Japanese dive-bombers began their attack on the carriers, unopposed by the handful of Wildcats. These were now fully occupied with the superior number of Zeros, several of which they shot down. The *Yorktown* dodged ten bombs and shot down four Vals. An 800-pound bomb plunged down through four decks and caused much damage and many casualties, but the engines were left intact and the flight deck still operational. Concussion damaged the boiler intakes but damage control made emergency repairs, and the ship was still capable of 24 knots.

More serious was the damage caused by two near misses. The *Yorktown's* 4-inch side armor plate had been designed to withstand 6-inch shells and 400-pound torpedoes, but bomb fragments blew open seams in the carrier's port-side fuel tanks beneath the armor plate, and vital oil gushed out. With the *Neosho* sunk, the *Yorktown's* life blood was ebbing away. But she continued to maintain speed, and at 1231 she began recovering her returning air group, twenty-two of them with damage and wounded crewmen. Permanently missing were seven dive-bombers and one fighter, and their crews.

The *Lexington* appeared to be holding her own. The 7-degree list caused by the two torpedo hits was removed by switching oil across from starboard tanks, and flight-deck operations were resumed. Then, at 1247, the whole ship was shaken by a great internal explosion, blowing her amidships elevator high in the air and starting fires. A spark from a generator had ignited fuel from ruptured tanks and gasoline vapor that had gathered between decks, a hazard that was to threaten American-built carriers for some time.

These fires were put out. But then, at 0245 in the graveyard watch, there was a second huge explosion. Fire burst out again, this time unquenchable. By 0430 the *Lexington* was dead in the water. At 0510 her crew began to abandon ship and were taken off by destroyers, leaving the ship a flaming beacon in the night that was of necessity put out by torpedoes from the destroyer *Phelps*. She finally sank at 0800.

The first great carrier-versus-carrier battle was over. Many mistakes had been made by both sides, many lessons stood to be learned. In terms of ships sunk, the Japanese were ahead. The loss of the *Lexington*, which the Americans could not afford, did not balance the scales against that of the lightweight *Shoho*. The Japanese were far numerically superior in carrier strength, though the *Shokaku* would be out of action for some months. The air groups of the *Shokaku* and *Zuikaku* could muster between them only 9 effective Val dive-bombers and 6 Kate torpedo planes. In all, from various actions, more than 100 Japanese aircraft, including search planes and those lost with *Shoho*, had been destroyed. More seriously, many experienced air crewmen had been lost, including Lt. Comdr. Kakuichi Takahashi, Pearl veteran. The resulting abandonment of MO (the Port Moresby operation), however, constituted a resounding strategic victory for the Allies. The battle itself, though the first of its kind, was no classic, but largely an improvisation by air power. With the U.S. Pacific Fleet apparently dealt another severe blow, Imperial Japanese headquarters now gave Yamamoto's MI (the Midway operation) operation full backing, in order to finish the job. Nimitz sent Halsey's *Enterprise* and *Hornet,* the only remaining U.S. carrier force available to him, to hover off the northern Solomons in case MO was reactivated, but it soon became obvious that a bigger move was in preparation.

The Carrier Weapon: Midway

In their astonishing, swift leap from a feudal society into the twentieth century, the Japanese had in some important ways short-circuited organic history. For all their brilliant, though patchy achievements in technology (such as superb torpedoes, but no radar), their warriors flew into battle with one hand on the throttle, the other figuratively on the hilt of a samurai sword.[1] In the cockpit, on the compass platform, they listened still for the Divine Wind.[2] There was an obsession with attack, paying scant regard to the need for the painstaking buildup by intelligence, reconnaissance, and communications that precedes a successful campaign. Their leaders too often suffered from the paralyzing hand of Bushido and a hierarchical system that promoted by seniority rather than brilliance, the exception proving the rule. All these handicaps afflicted them in the vital encounter that now began.

The U.S. Combat Intelligence Unit Hypo had warned early in 1942 of an impending Japanese strike somewhere in the Hawaiian Islands. On 12 May, four days after the end of the Coral Sea battle, the unit came up with "AF" as the Japanese code symbol for the new target. Hypo thought this meant Midway Island. To make certain, the U.S. air base on Midway was ordered to make a signal in plain language that the island was suffering from a water shortage due to a failure of its distillation plant. Sure enough, a Japanese signal was picked up and deciphered by the cryptanalysts; it reported that AF was short of water.

The MI/AF plan depended on Operation AL, an attack to capture the westernmost Aleutian Islands in the north Pacific, partly as a distraction for the depleted U.S. fleet while the main Japanese force captured Midway. The Americans would then attempt to retake Midway, and the Combined Fleet would be waiting for them, to finish unfinished business.

Numbers would tell. The Japanese had intended to sail their six fleet carriers *Akagi, Kaga, Hiryu, Soryu, Zuikaku,* and *Shokaku,* but the latter was under repair after Coral Sea, and the *Zuikaku,* though herself undamaged in that encounter, had suffered heavy losses in aircrews. There was no time to train replacement crews at sea. However, Nagumo's carrier force, with four carriers, would still outnumber that available to Nimitz. With the *Saratoga* under repair after her ambush by submarine, the *Ranger* and *Wasp* in the Atlantic, and the *Lexington* gone, the *Enterprise, Hornet,* and *Yorktown* would bear the brunt. They would bring 233 aircraft to the fight (plus 115 on Midway) against some 400. The 225 fighters and bombers of Nagumo's force would soften up the Midway defenses for a 5,000-strong invasion force buttressed by two support groups. They would also locate and destroy the American carriers. Behind Nagumo, Yamamoto in the giant *Yamato* would lead the main force of seven battleships, cruisers, destroyers, and the carrier *Hosho.*

By this time aviators on both sides had had several chances to evaluate the opposition. In torpedo bombers, the American Douglas TBD-1 Devastator had been, when it had been produced after competition in 1935, a paragon for its time. The first U.S. Navy carrier-borne monoplane, it featured novelties like power-operated upper folding wings and a semi-retractable undercarriage. It had a pedigree stretching back through the 124-MPH, 422-mile-range Douglas T20-1, which had first flown from *Langley* in 1927; the DT-J of 1921, Douglas's first military aircraft; and the 100-MPH, 565-mile modified Curtiss R-6L of 1920. By 1941, however, when it was still in common service, the Devastator had passed its replacement date. It was slow, its 900-horsepower Pratt and Whitney giving it a top speed of 206 MPH at 8,000 feet and an attacking speed with torpedo of 100 MPH. Aircrews were waiting eagerly for the new Grumman TBD-1 with internal torpedo stowage, which had begun to reach some units. Failing these, they would have settled for a Kate.

The Nakajima B5N-2 Type 97 attack plane was a newer design, first produced in 1937, with an improved version reaching carrier squadrons in 1939. The Kate had a family tree that included the 205 Mitsubishi-sponsored, British Blackburn-designed Ka-3 Type 89 B2Ms, serving aboard the *Akagi, Kaga,* and *Ryujo* from 1933 to 1937; the Mitsubishi B1M1 Type 13 attack bombers; and the 123-MPH, 300-mile Blackburn Mark 2 Swift, which the Royal Navy's Lieutenant Commander Brackley had used to train Japanese pilots in torpedo-dropping from their pioneer carrier *Hosho* in 1922. The Kate had a top speed of 235 MPH at 11,800 feet and a maximum range of 1,237 miles, carrying a standard torpedo. It was a veteran of attacks against targets on the Chinese mainland, launched from the *Kaga, Ryujo* and *Hosho,* and was also a good level bomber. It was the first Japanese aircraft to go into the attack at Pearl Harbor. The superiority of the aircraft over the Devastator was never more obvious than in the attack on the *Yorktown* in the Coral Sea by eighteen Type 97s. Racing toward the carrier at 180 knots, twice the speed the TBD-1 could manage with a torpedo, they leveled off to release their torpedoes from between 100 and 500 feet. With American torpedoes, the dropper had to get down as low as 30 to 40 feet for the missile to survive. Japanese torpeckers also traveled faster, allowing far less time for a moving target to comb their tracks.

In dive-bombers the odds were about even. The Douglas SBD Dauntless had a range of 773 miles to the fixed-undercart Aichi D3A-1's 915, but a higher top speed of 255 MPH to the Val's 240. Both types were strong and sturdy machines.

In fighters, combat between the American Wildcat and the Japanese Zero, both first-rate machines, was an encounter of opposites. The Grumman F4F was stronger and tougher than the Mitsubishi A6M2 Reisen (Zero), its Pratt 6 Whitney Twin Wasp more powerful than the Nakajima NK1C Sakae 12, but the Zero could reach 331 MPH to the Wildcat's 318, could climb at 3,000 feet a minute, and could range at least 500 miles from base. At 6,025 pounds' operational weight to the F4F-4's 7,956, it was also much more agile. Its twin 7.7-mm machine guns and two 20-mm cannon could outrange the 4's six .50-inch machine guns. But to achieve these high parameters, protection had been sacrificed. A Zero pilot had no armor plate, and with no self-sealing tanks a Zero would too often explode in flames when hit. American naval pilots would in fact often aim for the tanks, located near the wing roots, for a total kill. A good Wildcat pilot could nail a less-experienced Zero pilot, but at the time of the Pearl attack many Japanese pilots were also China veterans.

On 20 May Hypo deciphered a signal from Yamamoto to Combined Fleet confirming the impending attack on Midway, even obligingly specifying 4 June as D-Day, twenty-four hours after the start of the Aleutians attack.

On 28 May Task Force 16, with the *Enterprise* and *Hornet;* and Task Force 17, with the *Yorktown,* sailed from Pearl. The *Yorktown* had been readied for sea by telescoping weeks of repairs into just forty-eight hours. Halsey, who was to have taken operational command of the fleet, was in the hospital with a skin disease. Nimitz had appointed Rear Adm. Raymond C. Spruance, a non-aviator but a cool, clever tactician who appreciated the value of the carrier and was less prone to impulsive acts than "Bull" Halsey. Thus he was better suited to carry out the commander in chief, Pacific's, warning not to engage the enemy without good prospect of success, though not to shrink from taking a calculated risk.

Well briefed by intelligence, Spruance had left the stable and was in position with his three carriers poised northwest of Midway long before the fifteen Japanese submarines ordered to watch for him had shut the door, two days behind schedule, west of Pearl Harbor.

The commander in chief, Pacific's, own submarines were well established in their patrol areas. Of the twenty-nine boats based at Pearl, the *Thresher* and *Argonaut* were in dock for overhaul; the *Triton*, which had made a fruitless pursuit of the damaged *Shokaku* after Coral Sea, was returning from the South China Sea too low on fuel and torpedoes to divert to a battle; and the new *Silversides* was on patrol off Japan, under orders to remain there. Eight others were fresh in from patrol and in need of repair, while six more were far off and unlikely participants. Six of those available had not yet made a war patrol, but twenty-four boats were designated Task Force 7 and divided into three task groups, one to fan out around Midway to the west to screen it from the approaching armada; three boats to patrol an area east-northeast of the island; four boats to maintain a position about 300 miles north of Pearl Harbor.

By the forenoon of 3 June, all these boats were on station. In the evening, they received a signal that the enemy had attacked Dutch Harbor in the Aleutians. At 0700 the *Cuttlefish* reported an enemy tanker 600 miles west of Midway, then more ships appeared and drove the boat deep. A Japanese plane attacked the *Grouper* and she crash-dived.

At 0900 a Midway-based Catalina flying boat, not equipped with radar, sighted the Japanese invasion force 470 miles west of Midway. There were no carriers with this group, and Admiral Fletcher, in tactical command of the U.S. force, withheld his planes. Catalinas and army Flying Fortresses from Midway attacked the transports, leaving only the *Akebono Maru* slightly damaged.

At 0300 on 4 June the planes of the Midway attack force began to warm up on the flight decks of Nagumo's four carriers, which were grouped in the center of a compact ring. They were steering a south-easterly course in the general direction of Midway, the two medium carriers *Hiryu* and *Soryu* leading, followed by the *Akagi* and *Kaga*. The perimeter was formed by the battleships *Haruna* and *Kirishima*, the heavy cruisers *Tone* and *Chikuma*, the light cruiser *Nagara*, and twelve destroyers.

"The enemy," the aging admiral informed his officers, "is not yet aware of our plans." He thus began the day of battle in basic ignorance. "He has not yet detected our task force," he went on, which was true. "There is no evidence of an enemy task force in our vicinity."[3] Complacently, he did not intend to send out search planes until the strike force itself set out, just before sunrise, which would be about 0500. Even then, it would be only a single-phase search, with one plane each from the *Akagi* and *Kaga*, two seaplanes each from the *Tone* and *Chikuma*, and one from the *Haruna*. It was to be a seven-pronged search, radius 300 miles except for the *Haruna*'s floatplane, which was limited to 150 miles. With no radar in the aircraft, they would begin the effective stretch of their search only at sunrise, leaving a stretch of darkened sea unsearched behind them. This was to be covered by a second search wave. It was an example of the Japanese habit of devoting all effort to the business of attack.

At 0430 the first of the 108 planes took off. Thirty-six dive-bombers, 36 level bombers, and 36 fighters were led by Lt. Joichi Tomonaga. The scout planes went off at the same time. One of the *Chikuma*'s floatplanes developed engine trouble and was launched late, then turned back when it hit foul weather and its engine began to act up again. Another aircraft, from the *Tone*, was delayed half an hour by a jammed catapult.

In fifteen minutes Tomonaga's planes were all in formation, and at 0445 they climbed to 13,200 feet and headed southeast for Midway. At 0500, with the sun coming up, the carriers' bullhorn blared out, "Prepare second attack wave!"[4] The planes were ranged, thirty-six dive-bombers (eighteen each from the *Hiryu* and *Soryu*), thirty-six torpedo planes (eighteen each from the *Akagi* and *Kaga*), and thirty-six Zeros. This force was held ready to attack any enemy carrier force reported. Eighteen fighters were left for CAP.

When the Midway force was about 150 miles from the target, it was sighted by a Catalina, which alerted the island's defenses, and the formation was then picked up by Midway radar. At 0600 all aircraft on the island were scrambled, either to intercept the enemy or to escape the bombs. The Catalina shadowed the Japanese force undetected until about 20 miles from the island, when it climbed above the formation and released a parachute flare. Midway fighters 5,000 feet above the enemy attacked, but Lt. Masaharu Suganami's Zeros held them off the bombers, destroying all but two of the twenty-six. The bombers pounded installations, airstrips, and empty hangars, the Vals with 550-pound bombs, the level bombers with 1,760-pound bombs from a height of 11,550 feet. The Japanese lost three level bombers and one dive-bomber to flak, and two fighters in a dogfight. Midway fighters had suffered badly, but Tomonaga considered the primary aim of his mission, the destruction of enemy air resistance, unfulfilled. He radioed, "There is need for a second attack."[5]

Meanwhile, at 0525, the PBY that had first seen Tomonaga's planes sighted the Naguma force. Japanese CAP climbed to attack it but it disappeared into cloud. Nagumo's radio monitors reported it transmitting its sighting report.

On receiving the signal, Fletcher immediately sent Spruance with the *Enterprise* and *Hornet* ahead to attack Nagumo, while his own *Yorktown* held back to take aboard her ten search planes. From then on the two American carrier task forces acted separately.

Spruance sent his planes off just after 0700 to catch the enemy carriers. At that time, Capt. Miles Browning of his staff thought, the Japanese would be busy retrieving the Midway strike. In the general melee of aircraft, the *Enterprise*'s Fighting 6, ordered to remain at high altitude to protect both *Enterprise* and *Hornet* dive-bombers, somehow got attached to the *Hornet*'s Torpedo 8.

At 0700 Tomonaga's message recommending a second strike on Midway had reached Nagumo. It was almost immediately given weight by the appearance of four of the new Grumman Avenger torpedo bombers from the island. CAP shot down three well clear of the ships and was pursuing the survivor when a column of B-26 Marauder medium bombers made an attack with torpedoes, scoring no hits and losing two aircraft.

With no knowledge of any enemy battle force within range, Nagumo decided to follow Tomonaga's advice and mount a second strike on Midway. This necessitated dearming the torpedo-bombing element of the waiting strike force in the *Akagi* and *Kaga* and rearming them with bombs. Their elevators began working flat-out to shift the planes ranged on the flight decks below.

At 0728, however, the search plane from the *Tone* that had been launched half an hour late reported "Ten ships, apparently enemy, sighted. Bearing 010 degrees distant 240 miles from Midway. Course 150 degrees. Speed more than 20 knots."[6]

Nagumo's staff intelligence officer rushed to plot the data. What was the constitution of this enemy force only 200 miles away? Above all, were there carriers present? The *Akagi* radioed urgently, "Ascertain ship types and maintain contact." At 0745, while he anxiously awaited a reply, Nagumo, with half the *Akagi*'s and *Kaga*'s torpedo planes rearmed with bombs, reversed the order—"Prepare for a possible attack on the enemy force."

About this time, fourteen U.S. Army B-17s from Midway dropped a total of fifty tons of bombs in the sea around the Japanese force and turned back, feeling safe in their concentrated firepower from the 20-mm guns of the Zeros. As all the latter scrambled, sixteen Dauntless SBDs were seen heading for the ships. They were flown by green Marine Corps pilots, unpracticed in dive-bombing, who approached in shallow dives and attempted to glide-bomb the *Hiryu*. She disappeared in clouds of spray but emerged unscathed, with eight of her attackers downed and six more limping home damaged beyond repair.

At 0758 the *Tone* plane reported an enemy change of course, with no mention of ship types. At 0809 came "Enemy ships are five cruisers and five destroyers." Ten minutes later, the amended report: "Enemy force accompanied by what appears to be aircraft carrier bringing up the rear."[7] The latter was the *Yorktown,* steaming apart from Spruance and the other two American carriers. The *Tone* search plane stuck stubbornly to the *Yorktown,* with clever use of cloud cover, and the carrier became a marked ship. Nagumo felt justified in his order to restore torpedoes to the *Akagi* and *Kaga* bombers. But speed was vital, and this process was only half completed. Moreover, all Zeros had been scrambled to tackle the Midway B-17s and Dauntlesses; they were airborne and short of fuel. The only planes fully prepared for an attack on the enemy ships were the thirty-six dive-bombers aboard the *Soryu* and *Hiryu*. But these or any bombers launched now to attack the enemy, including whatever *Akagi* or *Kaga* torpedo planes might be ready, would be without fighter protection. They would be decimated.

Then, as Nagumo was pondering the problem, about 0830, an outlying destroyer signaled the approach of some 100 more planes. They were the Tomonaga planes returning from Midway. Some of them were damaged; others, particularly the fighters, were running very low on fuel, and their recovery was urgent. The decks must be cleared— either by launching the bombers to attack the enemy without fighter cover, or by striking them down into the hangar to recover the Midway planes, thus dangerously delaying a strike against the enemy. At this point Rear-Adm. Tamon Yamaguchi in the *Hiryu* rubbed salt into the sore by signaling, "Consider it advisable to launch attack force immediately."[8]

Unmoved by this gung-ho advice from the aggressive Yamaguchi, Nagumo thought of the massacre of the unescorted American bombers from Midway by his fighters and antiaircraft guns. He saw his own planes flying into the jaws of death without profit. Feeling ultimately secure about the Combined Fleet's immense superiority in numbers over the American rump fleet, he ordered all bombers struck below, clearing decks to receive the Midway strike. Any bombs still on the Kates' racks were to be removed and torpedoes substituted; all planes were to be readied swiftly for a maximum strike against the enemy fleet.

By 0918 the recovery of the Midway attack force and the second strike-force fighters diverted to CAP had been completed. In the *Akagi* and *Kaga,* complex movements went forward. Bombers below were rearmed with torpedoes, and those already so armed were respotted on the flight decks. There was general refueling. The whole force made a radical alteration of course to the northeast. The flight decks of the *Kaga* and *Akagi* were filled with bombed-up, gassed-up, torpedo-heavy planes; the hangars, slippery with leaked liquid gas and vapor, with discarded 551- and 1,764-pound bombs in rows and loose piles.

With the two carriers in this sensitive and volatile state, at about 0920 enemy carrier-type planes were reported approaching. As their numbers visibly increased, it seemed likely that they came from more than the one carrier reported by the *Tone's* tardy plane. Nagumo had not been well served by his reconnaissance force, and here he was with carriers lying like four huge fireworks awaiting the match.

The torpedo squadrons from the *Enterprise* and *Hornet* located the position the enemy would have reached had he maintained the course he was steering when the Catalina had first spotted him. They found an empty ocean. Since that original sighting Nagumo had made his northeasterly change of course, and the American planes had no radar.

Lt. Comdr. John C. Waldron, skipper of the *Hornet's* Torpedo 8, turned north, following a hunch that he would find the Japanese in that quarter. He was fully aware that his fuel state was uncomfortably near the point of no return, but he was conscious too of the enormous odds at stake. His intuition paid off and revealed Nagumo's ships. Calmly he radioed the all-important sighting report, then led his fifteen Devastators into the attack, calling urgently for fighter support. The rest of the *Hornet's* air strike, however, Dauntlesses and Wildcats, had altered course to the southeast to look for the Japanese. Running low on fuel, they were forced to divert to Midway to top up, and they missed this stage of the battle altogether. The *Enterprise's* Fighting 6 was overhead, but having mistakenly followed Waldron from takeoff, they were now running too low on gas to intervene. Their commanding officer finally radioed Lt. Comdr. Clarence McClusky, leading the *Enterprise's* dive-bombers, that he was forced to return to the ship. Fighting 6 had originally been briefed to protect the dive-bombers.

In training in the States, Waldron had emphasized to his green young pilots the need to bore in as close as possible before dropping torpedoes. As the Zeros shot down the lumbering bombers piecemeal, the rest tried desperately to follow his instructions—until they were all lost, without scoring one hit. Just one man, pilot George Gay, was left alive, floating in the water wounded and sick.

The fourteen Devastators from the *Enterprise* followed them at 0951, unprotected by their fighters, which waited in vain for the squadron's operations officer to call them in. But he had been shot down. Ten Devastators were shot down, and again no hits were scored.

The *Yorktown's* air group followed a course worked out for them by their air-group commander, Comdr. Oscar Pederson, with Lt. Comdr.

Lance Massie of Torpedo 3 flying low, watching the wind streaks on the water and correcting for drift accordingly. The dive-bombers and fighters followed him from high above. They were all airborne by 0906 and had sighted the enemy by 1000. As they approached, Lt. Comdr. Max Leslie, skipper of Bombing 3, pressed the button of his new bomb-arming system. The fitter had crossed the wires and the system malfunctioned, releasing the bomb as well. He quickly warned the squadron to use their old manual releases, but in three other cases he was too late.

Torpedo 3 first sighted the smoke laid down by Japanese destroyers shooting at Torpedo 8 and Torpedo 6. Massie changed the squadron's course 30 degrees to starboard to make his attack from the north bows-on to the enemy. Above him hung Lt. Comdr. John S. Thach's six Wildcats.

An antiaircraft burst from a cruiser pinpointed the Wildcats, and some fifteen Zeros, now finished with the torpedo bombers, jumped them, shooting down one Wildcat in the ensuing wild dogfight. Other Zeros fastened on Torpedo 3 as it made its run in.

The four Japanese carriers were preserving their loose box formation, heading north. The two medium carriers were ahead, the *Hiryu* to starboard of the *Soryu*, the two heavy carriers behind them, and the *Kaga* to starboard. The *Hiryu* had drawn ahead of the others and was hidden from the high-flying dive-bombers by cloud, but she was the first to draw Massie's attention as he came in from the north. He delivered his attack on her, forming Torpedo 3 into two divisions of six planes each to catch the carrier in a crossfire.

Some twenty-four Zeros jumped them about 14 miles northeast of the main enemy fleet, before they reached the destroyer barrage. With the outnumbered Thach still dogfighting up in the blue, the Devastators were as helpless as their predecessors. Massie's plane burst into flames and went in, and only two others escaped the slaughter, riddled with shrapnel. CPO William Esders blessed his armor, run up at the last minute from boiler plate in the machine shop at Kaneohe, Oahu. Harry Corl's elevator controls were so badly damaged that he could not hold the nose down. He jettisoned his torpedo and broke away. Esders dropped his torpedo 500 yards from the *Hiryu* and saw the carrier comb its tracks. He and Corl then ran north, their wounded rear gunners firing at pursuing Zeros. When Corl's gunner Lloyd Childers ran out of ammunition, he took on the Mitsubishis with a .45-caliber pistol.

It was now just after 1020. After attack by Avengers, Marauders, Fortresses, and Dauntlesses, fifty-two planes in all, and forty-one from the U.S. carriers, Nagumo's force was still unharmed. Through lack of coordination and the employment of the inadequate Devastator, thirty-five American aircraft and all but one of their men had been lost from the carrier force.

Like Waldron, Lieutenant Commander McClusky, leading thirty-three Dauntlesses from the *Enterprise*, had watched his fuel clock closely but decided to press on just a little longer in search of the Japanese force. At 0925 he spotted the wake of an enemy destroyer steaming at high speed. McClusky guessed rightly that the *Arashi*, which had been diverted by a submarine contact, probably the *Nautilus*, was speeding northeast to join the Japanese force. He followed her.[9] Sure enough, she led him to the Japanese carriers. He divided his group into two, directing one division to the *Akagi* and the other to the *Soryu*.

The preparations for a strike against the American carriers by the Nagumo air groups had gone forward throughout the American torpedo attacks. Greatly heartened, as was the whole Japanese force, by their decisive repulse, at 1020 Nagumo gave the order to launch aircraft. The *Akagi* began turning into wind. Visibility was good, though clouds at 3,000 feet gave good cover for attacking planes. At 1024 the order to start launching came from the bridge. The air officer dropped his white flag, and a Zero roared forward and left the deck. As it did so a lookout screamed, "Helldivers!" Up above three Dauntlesses, unimpeded by CAP (which was at sea level pursuing American torpedo-plane survivors), winged over.[10]

The huge explosion, blinding flash, and wave of hot air of a direct hit on the flight deck was followed by a second, then the lesser shock of a near miss, close aboard. A great jagged hole had been torn in the wooden deck aft of the amidships elevator, which sagged down into the upper hangar, soon ablaze. The second bomb had torn another hole aft. Bombs piled in the burning hangar began to cook off, fire spread among the planes packing the flight deck, and their torpedoes exploded. Flames spread to the lower hangar deck, and soon the whole ship above the engine room was in the grip of fire. Reluctantly, Nagumo shifted his flag to the cruiser *Nagara*.

Away to the starboard the *Kaga* could be seen also buried in smoke and flame. The *Akagi* was still heading into wind, which was fanning the flames. Capt. Taijiro Aoki rang down to stop. The order was obeyed, and then all communication with the engine room broke down. The dynamos went out, cutting power to the water pumps, and all the ship's spaces went dark. As the fires spread and increased in fury, hot air flowed down through the intakes, and the engine-room crew began to faint from suffocation. Chief engineer Comdr. K. Tampo struggled up through the inferno to the bridge. Aoki ordered abandonment of the engine room, but the messenger sent never returned. No one survived from below. At 1800 Captain Aoki gave the order to abandon ship, and the survivors were taken aboard destroyers. At 1920 he signaled Yamamoto, asking permission to sink his disabled ship. The admiral was reluctant, but finally, at 0350 the next morning, he gave the order to scuttle. Four destroyers also fired some of the powerful new Type 93 torpedoes into the wreck. Twenty-seven minutes later the *Akagi* sank, a huge underwater explosion signaling her final disintegration.

Meanwhile, the *Kaga* had suffered her own ordeal by bomb and fire. At the head of the *Yorktown*'s Bombing 3, Max Leslie, looking for the enemy, radioed Massie for information on their whereabouts. But there was silence from Torpedo 3. Then his gunner sighted ships and smoke dead ahead, 30 miles away. He descended to 14,500 feet. At 1023 he was over the easternmost section of the Japanese force, untroubled by Zeros, which were all away chasing Esders and Corl or dogfighting with Thach. Below him was the *Kaga*, with the *Akagi* and *Soryu* well away to the west and the *Hiryu* still obscured by cloud to the north.

Patting his helmet in the familiar signal, he nosed over for the attack, leading his seventeen bombers down even though he had no bomb now. Behind him his wingman Swede Holmberg released his 1,000-pounder. The *Kaga*'s flight deck burst open, and her hangar and its armed and gassed-up planes began to burn. Three more direct hits set the whole ship on fire. Damage-control parties fought the flames, but at 1840 the *Kaga* sank, after a final huge explosion.[11]

In the *Soryu* they were first made aware of the American dive-bomber onslaught by the sight of flames and smoke rising from the *Kaga*. Then thirteen Dauntlesses singled out the *Soryu*, and three hits wrecked the flight deck and started fires below. The ship stopped, with the engines disabled and the steering system and fire mains out of action. Within twenty minutes Capt. Ryusaku Yanagimoto had ordered the ship abandoned. She finally sank at 1913.

When the American dive-bombers departed, the *Hiryu* was the only Japanese carrier left undamaged, and Rear Admiral Yamaguchi assumed command of air operations. When the American force had been discovered, the *Soryu* had launched one of her new Type 2 Judy search plane and dive-bombers. Nothing had been heard from the plane, but on seeing his carrier disabled the pilot diverted to the *Hiryu* and announced that "The enemy force contains three carriers—the *Enterprise, Hornet,* and *Yorktown.*"[12] Yamaguchi now knew where he stood.

At 1040 a force of eighteen Val dive-bombers and six Zeros took off, as they thought, for the *Enterprise* and *Hornet.* But a plotting error had been made and they found the *Yorktown.* On their way they encountered some returning American planes and lost ten Vals.

Eight got through to the *Yorktown*. Learning from the Coral Sea experience, the carrier was at a high degree of readiness, gasoline lines drained of high octane and refilled with inert carbon dioxide. The first bomb burst on the flight deck and set fire to aircraft in the hangar. Another bomb plunged deep and disabled the engines, leaving the ship dead in the water. Fletcher transferred his flag to the cruiser *Astoria*.

At 1245 Yamaguchi launched all of the *Hiryu*'s surviving aircraft: ten torpedo-carrying Kates (including one from the *Kaga*) and six Zeros (with two *Kaga* refugees). They were led by Tomonaga, Midway's attacker, in a plane whose damaged tanks meant a certain one-way ticket for him. At 1246 he sighted the *Yorktown*, now able to manage 18 knots, thanks to fine damage control. She seemed so fighting fit that Tomonaga took her for one of the other carriers. His Zeros kept the *Yorktown*'s Wildcats busy while the Kates closed on the carrier. At 1432 he ordered the torpedo planes to split up and attack from all quarters. Four Kates bored in from the port side, and the crippled carrier had insufficient speed to avoid all their torpedoes. Two hit the ship, undid all the good damage-control work, and knocked out her power supply, which had been keeping the pumps going. At 1445, abandon ship was ordered.

Four surviving Kates and three Zeros flew back to the *Hiryu*, which was now reduced to six fighters, five dive-bombers, and four torpedo bombers. Yamaguchi's men were hungry and exhausted, and he decided to make another attack under the cover of twilight. Meanwhile everyone except the pilots of the Zero CAP enjoyed a meal of sweet rice balls.

Spruance in his turn was gathering together in the *Enterprise* the nucleus of a last strike to complete the day's saga of destruction— eleven *Enterprise* Dauntlesses and fourteen refugee dive-bombers from the *Yorktown*. The bombers would go to the *Hiryu* unescorted by fighters, which had to be held back to repel any further Japanese attacks. At 1530 this tired remnant took off. One turned back with engine trouble, but the remainder were unexpectedly backed up by eleven *Hornet* Dauntlesses that had landed at Midway earlier in the battle to refuel after failing to find Nagumo. Topping up tanks and ammunition boxes aboard the *Hornet*, they joined the last remaining five dive-bombers aboard her to form a second wave for the attack on the *Hiryu*. The latter had no radar and was thus unable to pick up the American scratch force coming in from the southwest, so that the sun was behind them.

At 1703 a fast search plane forerunner of the *Hiryu*'s intended strike was about to take off when the Americans appeared overhead. As the ship's antiaircraft opened up, thirteen Dauntlesses winged over. With a deft touch of rudder, Capt. Tomeo Kaku avoided the first three bombs, but four direct hits began a by-now all-too-familiar story. The forward elevator was wrecked, and fires cut off all escape from the engine room. At 2123 the *Hiryu* stopped and began to list. At 0230, after desperate attempts at damage control, all those who were able to abandoned ship. At 0510, with Admiral Yamaguchi lashed by his own order to the bridge, torpedoes from the destroyers *Kazagumo* and *Yugumo* struck the carrier and she began to sink.

At 0255 on 5 June Admiral Yamamoto sent out a general signal to all MI task forces informing them, "The Midway operation is canceled."[13]

The Japanese had lost the Battle of Midway long before Nagumo's first plane had been launched. After the Pearl Harbor attack, child of Yamamoto's far-sighted strategical thinking, it was as if the Japanese naval staff had exhausted themselves in the effort to keep up with him. If his line of thought had been followed, MI, the Midway operation, would, employing the maximum possible strength, have preceded MO, the move on Australia. In the event, MI was fatally weakened by the absence of the resources committed to the more conservative, cautious drive on Moresby. With the *Shokaku* and *Zuikaku*, even the *Shoho*, added to the Midway carrier force, two carrier task forces could have sailed. Thus Nagumo would not have been saddled with the mutually incompatible jobs of supporting the invasion force and dealing with the American carriers.[14] When the worst happened and he was asked to do both at the same time, he was ground between a rock and a hard place. The disorganized, in one department ill-equipped, American attack achieved, technically, more than it deserved.

Microwaves and Long Lances: Guadalcanal

Progress in the fitting of radar to U.S. warships had been made since September 1939, when there had been just two U.S. Navy ships equipped and six sets on order. The CXAM sets ordered in October 1939 were fitted in May 1940 in the battleship *California*, the carrier *Yorktown*, and the cruisers *Chicago*, *Pensacola*, and *Northampton*. During 1940 fourteen more improved CXAM-1 sets were ordered and fitted in the other seven carriers, five battleships, and the cruiser *Augusta*. Work also started on new projects. Western Electric was given a contract to develop a 60-cm surface fire-control radar (Type FA); the Naval Research Laboratory was contracted to develop a surface search set.

By the end of 1940 the FA was accepted for service, and ten were ordered to fit in the heavy cruiser *Wichita* and nine light cruisers. A shortwave set was desirable for surface search, but at the time the greatest transmitting power available was from the Klystron valve, which produced only 10 watts. The SC radar was therefore designed, with a wavelength of 50 centimeters. It was compact enough to fit in small ships and proved rather better for air than for surface warning. Finally, an omnidirectional telescopic air-warning radar on a metric wavelength, Type SD, was developed for submarines.

In the autumn of 1940 a British mission visited the United States for an exchange of information. They brought with them a magnetron, which made powerful microwave radar possible, and details of the British 175-cm airborne search radar ASV Mark II. The U.S. Navy at once went to work to design microwave sets for fire-control and warning radar. They also designed their own airborne ASV set, which was ready for production by the end of 1941. The fire-control set in the *Wichita*, though designed mainly as a range finder, was found to be very useful for giving warnings of the approach of surface vessels. But it was not accurate enough for blind fire. The design of two new microwave sets, Types FC and FD, was begun for surface and anti-aircraft fire control respectively.

FC fitted in the USS *Philadelphia* in October 1941 improved on the FA and made blind firing possible. FD with the new Mark 37 fire-control system for 5-inch guns was fitted in the USS *Roe* just before Pearl Harbor, following which SC or the improved SG were fitted extensively. At the end of 1941 the plan position indicator (PPI) was developed after the British example.

Frustrated in the central Pacific after the battle of Midway, the Japanese moved to advance the occupation of the Solomons in the southeast. With a toehold in Tulagi Harbor on Florida Island in the southern Solomons, in May 1942 they had moved into neighboring Guadalcanal, which looked out across the Coral Sea to Australia. There they began laying out an airfield 650 miles from the U.S. Navy advance base on Espiritu Santo Island to the southeast.

Reversing the Japanese drive on the central Pacific, an idea was taking shape of advancing on Japan by an island-hopping thrust through the islands above the equator. Meanwhile, it was important materially and psychologically that the Japanese be driven back in the south along the way they had come.

After Midway, and with still-limited resources committed to the impending landing in North Africa, the United States had just sufficient strength for a comparatively modest attempt to drive the Japanese out of Guadalcanal. To attack before the Guadalcanal airfield was completed, a landing was planned for August. After a chaotic rehearsal on Fiji beaches, an invasion force of 19,000 U.S. Marines in twenty-three transports protected by eight U.S. and Australian cruisers and fifteen destroyers sailed from New Zealand. South of Fiji they joined Admiral Fletcher's covering force comprising the *Enterprise, Saratoga,* and *Wasp;* the new 16-inch battleship *North Carolina;* six heavy cruisers; and some destroyers. At dawn on 7 August 1942, the force entered Savo Sound from the west. The marines landed near the embryo airfield while another force took Tulagi, covered by warship bombardment and carrier attacks. By the afternoon of the eighth, the airfield had been captured and the marines seemed established, if hampered by disorganized supply.

The Japanese reacted strongly, attacking from the air shortly after the landing, destroying plane for plane and damaging some ships. Five heavy cruisers, two light cruisers, and a destroyer left Rabaul in New Britain, 700 miles to the northwest. They were sighted in the central Solomons but Fletcher's covering force had withdrawn, short of fuel, and poor Army Air Corps sighting reports suggested that they were a reinforcement for the seaplane base on Santa Isobel Island 120 miles northwest of Guadalcanal. For the protection of the invasion force on the night of 8–9 August, the heavy cruisers *Australia, Canberra,* and *Chicago* patrolled east-west between Guadalcanal and Savo Island, with the heavy cruisers *Vincennes, Astoria,* and *Quincy* between Savo and Florida Islands just to the north, patrolling around a square. Light cruisers *San Juan* and *Hobart* and two destroyers watched the eastern entrance to Savo Sound.

The Allied crews were tired after thirty-six hours at action stations in the tropical climate, and not at peak efficiency. Warning of the approaching enemy might have been expected from the cruisers' radar sets, though they were comparatively primitive and unreliable, with inexperienced operators. They might have been effective if given proper sea room, but their performance was spoiled by side echoes from land, with the ships deployed to fill the approach channels to Savo Sound and the American beachhead on Guadalcanal. Warning was entrusted to two destroyers, one watching the approach to the south channel and one to the north, each with radar. Though of limited range, this should have been sufficient.

Just after midnight, Japanese seaplanes correctly reported the Allied dispositions. The Japanese ships approached Savo Island, sighted the two American picket destroyers, and passed between them undetected. Some of the Japanese ships crossed the wake of the southernmost destroyer at a distance of only 500 yards.

The fox was in the henhouse, and there was a great slaughter. Japanese floatplanes illuminated the Allied ships with parachute flares, and their ships opened fire first on the southern force (minus the *Australia*, away at a command conference), mortally damaging the *Canberra* by torpedo. Next they turned on the northern patrol, sinking the *Quincy* and *Vincennes* almost at once and crippling the *Astoria*, so that she sank next day. All of this was at the expense of one hit on the flagship *Chokai*. The Americans had just one consolation. On 10 August the seventeen-year-old submarine *S44*, with time-expired machinery and obsolete fire control but carrying the more dependable old Mark 10 torpedoes, sighted the four heavy cruisers of Carrier Division Six, which had taken part in the Savo Island battle, and sank the *Kako* with four torpedoes.

The Savo holocaust was only the opening round in four months of "meat-grinding" struggle by sea and air for Guadalcanal. On 21 August the Japanese landed a force of under 2,000 men from destroyers at night, which was easily repulsed. On 24 August four destroyers packed with troops, protected by cruisers and destroyers, made another attempt. Nagumo provided deep cover with the *Shokaku* and *Zuikaku*, two battleships, and three heavy cruisers. Scouting ahead was an advance force of six cruisers and the seaplane carrier *Chitose.* Six submarines were also pushed out as pickets ahead of the fleet, with others prowling the Coral Sea. The light carrier *Ryujo,* a cruiser, and two destroyers were sent out as sacrificial goats, to try to reproduce the accidental diversion by the *Shoho* in the Coral Sea battle.

In the forenoon of 23 August, two of the submarines were sighted and forced down by *Enterprise* planes. In the afternoon a Guadalcanal-based search plane sighted the Japanese transports. Rear Adm. Raizo Tanaka saw the aircraft, and as soon as it had disappeared, the whole Japanese fleet reversed course northward with the idea that the inevitable American striking force would run out of fuel on a fruitless search. When the *Saratoga,* whose fighters had earlier shot down a reconnaissance flying boat detected by her SC radar, sent thirty-one Dauntlesses and six Avengers to attack, they found an empty ocean. Past the point of no return to their carriers, they were able to make the new Henderson Field on Guadalcanal in order to refuel before rejoining the *Saratoga* next forenoon. Meanwhile Fletcher, considering their sortie to have been a wild-goose chase, felt able to detach the *Wasp* 240 miles to the south to refuel. He did not know that the Japanese fleet had turned south again and was making straight for him.

Early in the forenoon of 24 August, a search plane from Henderson Field sighted a Japanese carrier force 300 miles to the north, steaming south. Fletcher at once headed for the contact at flank speed and launched an armed search by twenty-nine Dauntlesses and Avengers. Soon after they had disappeared, his SC radar picked up an aircraft formation coming in from the west. At 1345 he launched an unescorted striking force of thirty Dauntlesses and eight Avenger torpedo bombers from the *Saratoga,* retaining all his fighters to repel the expected Japanese attack. The enemy force picked up by his radar, however, was actually a small strike force from the *Ryujo* flying to join up with a force of Betty bombers from Rabaul to attack Henderson Field. They ran off his SC screens and, over Henderson, found marine Wildcats ready for them, losing twenty-one planes for a score of only three.

Meanwhile the *Saratoga*'s strike force had found the *Ryujo*'s diversionary force, while the *Enterprise*'s search planes had sighted the main Japanese carrier force. Fletcher tried to divert the *Saratoga* group to attack Nagumo, but heavy static garbled his signals. Several 1,000-pounders and one torpedo disabled the *Ryujo,* which sank that evening.

As this attack was under way, Nagumo launched a first wave of thirty Vals and a second of eighteen Vals and nine Kate torpedo planes from the *Shokaku* and *Zuikaku,* with a strong Zero escort. Fletcher's radars picked up the first wave at 1602. All planes in the *Enterprise* and

Saratoga were launched, fifty-three Wildcats for CAP and a strike of thirteen Dauntlesses and twelve torpedo Avengers to attack the Japanese carriers.

The two American carriers had separated and were steaming 10 miles apart when the Japanese planes arrived. With only one radio channel, available for every chattering fighter pilot as well as the two fighter-direction officers, the latter were unable to vector separate groups of Wildcats to deal with the Vals as well as the Zeros. The prestige of bagging a Zero drew most of the Wildcats. The Zeros sacrificed many of their number in drawing down the Wildcats to sea level so that the Vals had a clear sky. The Vals, however, were unwisely attracted by the twinning of the *Enterprise* with the new *North Carolina*, equipped with an awesome arsenal comprising twenty 5-inch and sixteen 1.1-inch guns; forty 20-mm cannons; and twenty-six .50-inch machine guns. Few of the Vals returned to their carriers, but three of them hit the *Enterprise*, damaging her badly and starting fires, but not cutting her power. In just over an hour her deck was patched and she was recovering aircraft. Ten miles away the *Saratoga* remained completely unmolested. Later a small force of her Dauntlesses and Avengers attacked the enemy advance force but only managed to damage the seaplane carrier *Chitose*.

The USS *Enterprise*. (U.S. National Archives)

In the forenoon of 25 August, Tanaka's transports were attacked by Dauntlesses from Henderson and B-17s from Espiritu Santo. The sinking of a transport and a destroyer and heavy damage to Tanaka's flagship *Jintsu* caused him to turn back. The Japanese carriers returned to base having lost some ninety aircraft to the Americans' twenty.

The Japanese gave up trying to land troops on Guadalcanal by daylight. Their planes from Rabaul bombed Henderson Field by day, engaged by fighters flown in from the American carriers, which also contributed their own planes. From Bougainville and Faisi Islands in the northern Solomons, Japanese destroyers steamed down "the Slot" and landed troops nightly on Guadalcanal, then bombarded Henderson Field.

The Americans were not ready to supply or reinforce their garrison significantly until mid-September, when the *Hornet* and *Wasp* covered a convoy carrying 4,000 marines up from Espiritu Santo. This was the dangerous Torpedo Junction run, on which the *Saratoga* had been crippled by the *I-26*'s torpedo on 31 August. On 15 September a combined attack by the *I-15* and *I-19* sank the destroyer *O'Brien* and fatally damaged the *Wasp*, which was dispatched by B-17s the next day. But the troops were landed safety. With the *Hornet* the only carrier now available, the Americans could not halt an increased flow of Japanese troops into Guadalcanal from New Guinea by day and night.

On the night of 11–12 October, Rear Admiral Goto was steaming down the Slot with three cruisers and two destroyers to bombard Henderson Field when off Cape Esperance, the northwestern point of Guadalcanal, he ran into Rear Adm. Norman Scott's two heavy and two light cruisers covering American reinforcements. The cruiser *Helena*'s sharp radar watch first picked up the enemy, but her message to Scott did not get through. He was reversing course when the destroyer *Duncan* made contact with Goto. Making good use of his FC radar, Scott sank the cruiser *Furutaka* and a destroyer and badly damaged the *Aoba* and *Kinugasa*, for the loss of the *Duncan* and serious damage to the cruiser *Boise*. Admiral Goto lost his life.

The next day a convoy from Noumea was able to land 3,000 U.S. troops on Guadalcanal. Marine aircraft strength at Henderson Field rose to ninety, but lacking radar they were unable to prevent Japanese bombers from damaging planes and airstrip that afternoon, and that night they lost half their number and their fuel dump to the 14-inch shells of the battleships *Haruna* and *Kongo*. Cruiser bombardments followed for three nights running, under cover of which 4,500 more Japanese troops were landed.

This enabled the Japanese to make a major assault on Henderson Field, supported by bombarding warships. They were confident that they would be in possession by 22 October, as scheduled. In position to the northwest was a Japanese fleet under Adm. Nobutake Kondo comprising a vanguard force of two battleships, four cruisers and seven destroyers; Nagumo with the *Shokaku, Zuikaku,* and light carrier *Zuiho*; in the rear two battleships, five cruisers, twelve destroyers, and the carrier *Junyo,* a recently completed conversion from a luxury liner design. As soon as the airfield was captured, Kondo was to transfer most of his aircraft there, with Yamamoto hoping, as ever, for a showdown with the American fleet.

The U.S. Pacific Fleet, now commanded by Rear Adm. Thomas C. Kinkaid, comprised three task forces: 61, the patched-up *Enterprise,* the new battleship *South Dakota,* two cruisers, and eight destroyers; 17, the *Hornet,* four cruisers, and six destroyers; and Rear Adm. Willis A. Lee's 64, the battleship *Washington,* three cruisers, and six destroyers.

Vice Admiral Halsey had relieved Vice Adm. R. L. Ghormley as commander, South Pacific, and the effect of the new regime was swiftly felt. While, just occasionally, the word *caution* went missing from Halsey's vocabulary, *defeat* was a permanent stranger. Those of his staff who suggested preparing plans for evacuating Guadalcanal were swiftly reprimanded. His specific order to Kinkaid was to sweep north around the Santa Cruz Islands, east-southeast of the southern Solomons toward the Coral Sea, to intercept any enemy force heading for Guadalcanal. Lee was to look for trouble off Savo.

At noon on 25 October, with the marines still holding their line on Guadalcanal, a PBY sighted Kondo. PBYs with torpedoes and B-17s attacked him without effect, and Kondo turned north for the night. Kinkaid's search planes found nothing. Kondo reversed again and was sighted again on the morning of the twenty-sixth, about 300 miles from Kinkaid. Torpedo PBYs that attacked at 0300 failed to score but caused Kondo to double back once more, though the distance between the two forces was now 200 miles, and Kinkaid was overhauling Kondo.

Halsey signaled "Attack—repeat—attack!"[1] and, at 0512, sixteen Dauntless scout bombers were launched from the *Enterprise.* Kinkaid feared a surprise attack and held back his first striking force until 0730, when fifteen Dauntlesses, eight torpedo Avengers, and eight Wildcats left the *Hornet,* followed later by a smaller force from the *Enterprise.* By this time Nagumo's sixty-five-plane strike had been airborne almost an hour. At 0740 two of the *Enterprise's* scout bombers from her first sortie jumped the *Zuiho* from cloud cover and put her out of action with two 500-pound bombs. At 0822, however, Nagumo launched a second strike of forty-four aircraft.

On their way to their targets, Nagumo's and Kinkaid's groups clashed. The stronger Zero contingent shot down four Wildcats and four Avengers for the loss of three. The two American carriers, though operating 10 miles apart to split the enemy attack, relied on the *Enterprise's* more reliable radars to pinpoint enemy aircraft, and on her fighter-direction officer to control all the Wildcats. But jammed airwaves and confusing clutter on the screens made it impossible.

Then a rain squall hit the *Enterprise*, and twenty Kates and fifteen Vals fell upon the *Hornet*. They lost twelve Vals and as many Kates, but one Val pilot, hit before dropping his bomb, deliberately crashed into the flight deck. Serious fires started. Then two torpedoes struck home, flooding two boiler rooms and the forward engine room. The *Hornet* was left dead in the water and listing, whereupon she was hit by two 500-pound bombs, and a blazing Kate crashed her bow and blew up.

The second Japanese wave, picked up by the *South Dakota's* radar at 55 miles, did not bother with the sorely stricken *Hornet* but concentrated on the *Enterprise*, her presence having been detected by eavesdropping on ship-to-ship telephone chatter. Mutilated fighter direction again spoiled Wildcat defense, but they and the fierce antiaircraft fire from the *Enterprise* and particularly the *South Dakota* shot down fifteen Kates and twenty-one Vals—two of whose bombs temporarily wrecked the forward elevator. Repair was under way when twenty bombers from the *Junyo* dived out of the overcast on the *Enterprise*, causing more damage.

When eleven *Hornet* Dauntless crews returned in high spirits, having disabled the *Shokaku* with four 1,000-pounders, they found no ship to go to, but had to crowd aboard the damaged *Enterprise*. To preserve his depleted fleet, Kinkaid reluctantly withdrew to the southeast, abandoning the doomed *Hornet*. In a tribute to her builders, she resisted four further attacks by Japanese carrier planes, 8 torpedoes from U.S. destroyers (a further 8 rogue torpeckers ran wild), and 500 of their shells before more efficient Japanese torpedoes gave her the coup de grâce.

Kondo's battleships prowled the night of 26–27 October looking for Kinkaid's fleet, but without radar they failed to find it. With the *Zuiho* disabled, the *Shokaku* crippled, his aircraft and aircrews decimated, and the *Zuikaku* off to find and train a new air group, he could no longer reinforce Guadalcanal. The only Japanese carriers now operational in the South Pacific were the slow converted liners *Junyo* and *Hiyo*, and the Combined Fleet was down to its last 100 planes, of all types. These were the sort of losses the Americans could far more easily replace.

Unharried by Kondo's aircraft and supported by Lee's battleship force, the Guadalcanal marines routed the spendthrift *banzai* charges of the Japanese 17th Army, which left nearly 3,000 dead on the field. The Japanese resumed their night supply runs, while Halsey kept the marines supplied by day under cover of planes from Henderson.

On 11 November American transports reached Guadalcanal under cruiser escort, unloaded, and withdrew. Next day more transports arrived and offloaded, with a fierce air battle in progress overhead. American air reconnaissance detected a large Japanese force, with transports and two battleships, advancing down the Slot. Rear Adm. Dan Callaghan escorted the transports clear of land, then took his five cruisers and eight destroyers back to face the Japanese in a night battle.

His flagship *San Francisco's* reliable radar had been knocked out by a suicide plane the day before. Other ships picked up the enemy fleet but the usual radio-telephone babble blocked their signals to Callaghan. The Japanese sighted him first and illuminated his ships with searchlights. The *San Francisco* was hit by the battleship *Kirishima* and Callaghan was killed, the *Portland* was battered to a standstill, the *Juneau* crippled by torpedoes, the cruiser *Atlanta* badly hit, and Rear Adm. Norman Scott killed. The cruiser was scuttled the next day. Three American destroyers sank; one was wrecked. The damage might have been even worse if the Japanese battleships had not been fighting with the thin-walled shells intended for Henderson Field. American armor-piercing shells hit the *Hiei* and slowed her down, and the rest of the Japanese force withdrew up the Slot.

Next morning, 13 November, the *Juneau*, limping back to Espiritu Santo, was sunk by the submarine *I-26*. But nine Avengers from the *Enterprise* found the *Hiei*, jammed her rudder with one torpedo, refueled at Henderson Field, and returned to finish her off. Lee's Task Force 64 was too far south to prevent a night bombardment of Henderson Field by three cruisers, but seventeen Dauntlesses from the *Enterprise* hit the cruisers the next morning, sank the *Kinugasa*, and damaged the *Chokai* and *Maya*. A second Japanese supply convoy of eleven transports, under "Tenacious Tanaka," was detected, escorted by eleven destroyers and covered by fighters from the *Hiyo* and *Junyo*. In conjunction with planes from Henderson and B-17s from Noumea, *Enterprise* planes battered the Japanese all day, sinking eleven transports. Tanaka transferred some of their troops to destroyers and pressed on.

Meanwhile Kondo was approaching to make a second attempt at the bombardment thwarted by Callaghan, bringing up the *Kirishima*, four cruisers, and nine destroyers. He was sighted in the afternoon by the submarine *Trout*. Lee's Task Force 64, with the *Washington* and *South Dakota*, was sent to intercept him.

Lee came up from the south and passed outside Savo Island into the north channel to turn west into Savo Sound. He did not detect Kondo's bombardment force coming in from the northeast, nor Tanaka's remaining transports heading for the sound from the northwest. But at 2210 Kondo sighted him and detached the light cruiser *Sendai* and two destroyers to shadow him. At 2300 the *Washington*'s radar detected the *Sendai*, and at 2316 the American battleships opened fire, driving her off.

Kondo's force was on the other side of Savo Island, screened from Lee's radar detection. But destroyers he sent ahead ran into their American counterparts, also "in the van" (lead), and sank two of them. They drove off the other two, one of which later sank. The American battleships emerged from the shelter of the Guadalcanal shore, Kondo's ships slid out from behind Savo Island, and the battlewagons opened fire, with the Americans confident in their gunnery-control radar.

Then blast from a 5-inch gun firing starshell to illuminate the Japanese ships knocked out the *South Dakota*'s main electrical system. This shut off vital services, including both search and gunnery radars. The ship was thrown into confusion so that she blundered to within 5,000 yards of the Japanese battle line and took heavy punishment from the *Kirishima*, including the loss of one 16-inch turret.

The *Washington*, however, kept her fireworks in the box and her searchlights dark. Her guns returned the fire, blasting the *Kirishima* into a sinking condition. Kondo turned back, but the stubborn Tanaka beached his transports to make sure that his troops, some 2,000, got ashore.

This was a mere fraction of the force he had started out with, and Japanese losses now meant that they could no longer oppose daylight landings by the Americans. In contrast, the latter put a whole army infantry division and two new marine regiments ashore. Air strength at Henderson was raised to 127, including eight B-17s.

On the night of 30 November–1 December, Tanaka led eight destroyers to unload supplies in buoyant containers. An American force of five cruisers and six destroyers made radar contact at 2306. The four van destroyers made a torpedo attack but only succeeded in sinking one Japanese destroyer, which had betrayed her position with gunfire. Her consorts used their Long Lance oxygen-driven torpedoes to devastating effect, hitting the *Minneapolis, New Orleans, Northampton,* and *Pensacola*. Good damage control saved three of them, but the *Northampton* was abandoned.

In itself the Battle of Tassafaronga was a humiliating defeat for a materially superior radar-equipped force against destroyers with no radar, encumbered with troops and drums of stores for floating on to the beaches. Japanese leadership and night tactical training were, as always, superb, and the Americans' initial indecision had thrown away the big advantage offered by radar. They were overconfident in their gunnery-control radar, which gave accurate ranges and could spot the fall of shot at medium ranges but was of little use for laying and training guns. Even if the correct range was set, the spread of salvos meant few hits. The Americans put their hopes in the more general fitting of SG radar and the new FC centimetric fire-control set. Later in 1943, the idea of the radar-controlled barrage was successfully introduced. The Americans' use of a long, snaking column formation at night made their task forces ideal torpedo targets, and the reliability and hitting power of the Japanese 24-inch oxygen-propelled torpedoes was still not fully appreciated.

In three more runs in December 1942, however, the Tokyo Express was able to put only a dribble of supplies and reinforcements ashore. By New Year's Day 1943, the *Saratoga* had returned to the South Pacific Fleet along with four of the battleships knocked out at Pearl Harbor. Three of the new *Essex*-class carriers had been launched but would not be ready until late in the year. On 4 March 1943, the British fleet carrier *Victorious* reached Pearl Harbor, and on 8 May, after training in U.S. Navy signaling and aircraft-operating drill, she relieved the *Enterprise*, which was badly in need of major repair and refit.

In the first week of February 1943, the Tokyo Express went into reverse, lifting off all surviving Japanese troops, with the loss of three destroyers. In April the Japanese suffered another serious blow when Admiral Yamamoto, commander in chief of the Combined Fleet (and its inspiration) was shot down and killed by U.S. Army P-38 fighters near Bougainville Island in the Solomons, as the result of an intercepted radio message. He had been there on a tour of inspection.

Yamamoto had been the architect of the modern Japanese navy, though he had had grave doubts about the advisability of provoking the American "sleeping tiger." He believed above all in naval air power and had built up the expert and aggressive Japanese naval air fleet. Where American general Billy Mitchell's forecasting of the end of the battleship as the foremost naval fighting vessel was rewarded by court-martial and suspension from duty, Yamamoto's views had been accepted.

With the airfield on Guadalcanal and another constructed in the Russell Islands 60 miles away, Admiral Halsey extended the Allied line in the South Pacific further to the northwest by landing in New Georgia and on Kolombangara Island in the Solomons to secure their airfields. The Japanese resisted strongly and attempted to reinforce their garrisons by night through Kula Gulf, which precipitated two actions in early July 1943.

By this time all U.S. cruisers and destroyers had SG radar and combat information centers, and the cruisers had the new FC fire-control radar with which complete blind fire was possible. This technology made little difference in Kula Gulf, however. In the first encounter, three American cruisers and four destroyers made the initial contact with ten Japanese destroyers. One of these, the *Niizuki*, had been fitted with the Mark II Model 2 14-cm set, an early type of Japanese radar using only a half-kilowatt's power, which could not pick up ships as far away as lookouts, with their good binoculars, could see them. Adm. W. L. Ainsworth's SG found the Japanese ships at 24,700 yards, but by the time the American ships had assumed battle formation the range was down to 12,000 yards, and the *Niizuki* had picked them up. Ainsworth engaged with full radar control but he was closing so fast that the range was down to 6,800 yards before he could open fire. The *Niizuki* was destroyed but two other destroyers fired sixteen torpedoes, three of which hit and sank the cruiser *Helena*, and the Japanese landed most of their troops.

HMS *Leander* replaced the *Helena*, and with ten destroyers Ainsworth made radar contact with a light cruiser and four destroyers soon after midnight on 13 July. A Catalina had reported them, but this time the Japanese had a search receiver that picked up the SG impulses at 100 miles. Unsuspecting, Ainsworth came on and ordered a destroyer torpedo attack. Both sides launched torpedoes almost simultaneously, but whereas the fifty U.S. tin fish all malfunctioned or missed, the *Leander* and U.S. cruisers *Honolulu* and *St. Louis* were hit. Both groups opened fire, the Americans in radar control, the Japanese using searchlights, and the Japanese cruiser *Jintsu* was sunk.

The Americans were determined to improve radio telephony discipline, communications between ships, and radar plotting. On the night of 6–7 August, six U.S. destroyers made full use of their radar to pick up four Japanese troop-carrying destroyers before they were sighted. They launched torpedoes, turned away, then attacked with gunfire. Three Japanese destroyers were sunk. In a final destroyer action in the Solomons in which each side lost one ship, the Japanese managed to evacuate 600 remaining troops from Vella Lavella.

On 1 November 1943 Halsey, with the *Saratoga*, the new light carrier *Princeton*, cruisers, and destroyers; a force of four light cruisers and eight destroyers under Rear Adm. A. S. "Tip" Merrill; and an amphibious force under Rear Admiral Wilkinson, embarked on the taking of the last Japanese stronghold in the Solomons. The big island of Bougainville in the north was the site of several airfields within bombing range of Rabaul.

Marines were landed, and the same night a Japanese force of four cruisers and six destroyers attempted to cut them off. Tip Merrill, who understood radar, kept the enemy at long range to avoid the Long Lances and controlled his fire entirely by his SGs, with frequent alterations of course. These tactics made control of his own gunnery more difficult, and only twenty hits were scored out of more than 4,500 rounds fired at 19,000 yards. At this range the primitive radar of the Japanese could not pick up the Americans at all, and they lost one cruiser and one destroyer.

This American victory was the first battle fought entirely by radar, with the Americans seeing the enemy only on their screens. American transports were unmolested. Withdrawing slowly to protect a damaged destroyer, Merrill suffered a heavy air attack, but using the new proximity (TV) fuzes actuated by radar, which exploded a shell as it neared its target, he shot down more than a quarter of the attackers and sustained no losses.

Kaisers and Kamikazes

"'Multitudes, multitudes in the valley of decision,'" quotes Herman Wouk's Lt. Tom Keefer, seeking a title for his novel of the carrier war in the Pacific.[1]

In the gritty actuality of January 1943, the multitudes—ships and planes—were still to come. The old *Lexington, Yorktown, Hornet,* and *Wasp* were gone. Only three of the eleven new *Essex*-class fleet carriers had been launched to replace them, with delivery months ahead in the fall.

To take up some of the slack, the hull of the USS *Amsterdam,* one of a new class of light cruisers still in a stage of construction at which a category change was practicable, was taken over for experimental conversion into a light fleet carrier. The slender, knifelike hull was not ideal, but to prevent the hangar and flight deck causing top heaviness, underwater blisters were added, with concrete in the port-side bulge to counteract the weight of the bridge island. To save more weight on the starboard side of the ship and to create more space for aircraft, four small funnels were fitted instead of a fleet carrier's bulky single-funnel trunking. Space was also saved by confining the antiaircraft battery to 40-mm cannons, twenty-six of which were carried. From forty to sixty aircraft could then be accommodated, compared with an *Essex*'s ninety-seven—depending, in each case, on the proportion of fighters to bombers and torpedo planes. So promising was the experiment that eight more such conversions were ordered, and four of them had been launched when the Japanese evacuated Guadalcanal in February 1943.

Twenty small auxiliary carriers of the *Long Island* and *Bogue* type had been ordered for conversion from C-3 merchant-ship hulls after Pearl

Harbor, as well as four larger oiler conversions of the *Sangamon* class. To add to these, in the summer of 1942, twenty-four of the *Prince William* class, improved *Long Islands*, were ordered.

These immensely useful small carriers had been thought of as ferry carriers or convoy escorts, but they had given sound support to the North African and Salerno landings. Still more of them were needed, but Allied shipyards were full. Then "Hurry Up Henry" stepped in.

Henry J. Kaiser's specialty was carrying out big industrial jobs in half the time taken by other companies. When war demanded a vast increase in shipbuilding, he had rapidly built seven shipyards on the Pacific Coast, a steel mill, an engine plant, and Vanport City, a whole community for his work force on swampland between Portland and Vancouver, Oregon. Unskilled workers, mostly female, were used. Each worker was taught to become expert at just one simple job. "Rosie the Riveter" worked three shifts, twenty-four hours a day, one shift in fierce competition with the next, using new techniques like prefabrication and all-welding to turn out utility merchant Liberty Ships at the rate of one every eight days.

When Henry J. heard of the dire need for more "jeep" escort carriers he talked briefly with his designers and hurried along to the Bureau of Ships with drawings of a very basic aircraft carrier prepared by the naval architects Gibbs and Cox, based on one of his merchant hulls. He offered to build thirty or more ships in six months, provided the Navy gave him a free hand in design and construction. BuShips turned him down. Liberty Ships were one thing, carriers quite another—more complex, and subject to many more stresses.

Undeterred, Henry hurried along to the White House and showed a sketch, making his pitch to his old patron FDR. The president looked briefly at the drawing and Henry got a contract to build fifty-five small carriers on Maritime Commission PL fast transport hulls, with BuShips and the Bureau of Aeronautics to supervise development and construction. Four ships were promised for delivery in February 1943, the rest by the end of the year. George Sharp, Kaiser's design agent, went ahead with the help of BuShips' James Bates, and the Navy gave special advice on the design of the flight deck.

There was a problem with engines. With the number of U.S. shipyards increased from 12 to 300, there was fierce competition for all materials and equipment. The *Bogue* and *Prince William* classes had cornered all the available steam engines, and the forthcoming twenty-three carriers of the BuShips-designed *Commencement Bay* class, copies of the *Sangamon*s, had accounted for all available standard geared turbines.

But Kaiser quickly found the Skinner Uniflow reciprocating steam engine, developed in 1912. Among mercantile engineers the Skinner

Escort carriers fitting out at the Western Pipe and Steel yard, San Francisco, in mid-1942. Foreground HMS *Stalker*, background HMS *Striker*. (D. Mawdsley)

was a bit of a joke. It was hard to control, expensive to operate, unable to maintain a proper supply of clear boiler feed water, and expanding steam tended to carry lubricating oil into the condenser. But for Henry J., problems were just opportunities wearing their working clothes.

He built a plant to turn out the rogue engines and put his engineers to work righting the faults. They put loofah sponges in the hot wells and diatomaceous earth filters in the condensate lines. The Skinner became a working proposition, driving twin screws for greater safety and easier maneuvering in the crowded spaces of a wartime harbor or when facing fast Long Lances.

In contrast to these huge programs of carrier construction, Japanese industry could manage only one new custom-built fleet carrier, the *Taiho*, built with an armored flight deck after the disasters of Midway, and she could not be completed until March 1944. The rest of Japan's replacement carrier fleet consisted of various conversions: the *Chitose* and *Chiyoda* from seaplane carriers; the *Chuyo, Kaiyo, Ryujo, Shinyo,* and *Taiyo* from liner hulls. None could raise more than 29 knots (three of them only 21 knots) or carry more than thirty-three aircraft.

By October 1943 the new *Essex, Yorktown, Lexington,* and *Bunker Hill* fleet carriers, and the light fleet carriers *Independence, Princeton, Belleau*

The USS *Nehenta Bay*, typical Kaiser-built escort carrier. Her standard composite squadron of twelve to sixteen Wildcat FM-2s and nine to twelve Avenger TBMs flew at Tinian, Guam, Saipan, and Okinawa. (U.S. National Archives)

Wood, Cowpens, and *Monterey* were ready for service with Vice Admiral Spruance's Fifth Fleet as the Fast Carrier Force, or Task Force 50, commanded by Rear Adm. Charles A. Pownall. Joining them were all six of the *Washington*-class 16-inch battleships and the larger and faster *Iowa* and *New Jersey.*

Aboard the carriers of Task Force 50 were some new aircraft. The Curtiss SB2C Helldiver was 42 MPH faster than the Dauntless, which it had been designed to replace, could carry a torpedo internally like the Avenger as well as bombs, and had two 20-mm cannons for strafing. The Helldiver was suffering from teething troubles, however, and veteran pilots missed their reliable SBDs.

Another new promising machine with problems was the Chance-Vought Corsair F4U-1. This big new fighter had a maximum speed of 357 MPH at 2,500 feet and 405 MPH at 19,500 feet, being the first single-engine fighter to exceed 400 MPH in level flight. Its combat endurance was four and a half hours, range 1,562 miles with a 142-gallon drop tank. It had a battery of six .50-inch machine guns with 400 rounds per gun, and capacity for two 1,000-pound bombs. The main self-sealing fuel tank was armored, as were windscreen, seat, and cockpit sides. For a six-ton machine, two tons heavier than the Wildcat, the Corsair had a remarkable turning circle, could match the supremely aerobatic Zero in the first half of a turn, and could turn inside a Seafire with ease. The machine was easily identifiable by its

Chance-Vought Corsair F4U-1. (U.S. Navy)

inverted gull wing, which served to raise the fuselage so that the powerful 2,250-horsepower Pratt and Whitney engine had room to swing the big 13-foot Hamilton propeller; it also reduced drag considerably by its 90-degree interception with the fuselage. Also incorporated was a hydraulic system by which the pilot could fold the wings, open and shut the engine cowlings and air cooler ventilators, operate the undercarriage and deck hook, and load the guns.

But there were serious faults. To give the machine its great range, big self-sealing fuel tanks were added to the prototype fuselage forward of the cockpit, which was moved 3 feet farther back, lengthening the nose to 20 feet and giving a very poor view of the deck. The sophisticated hydraulic system also held a trap for the careless pilot.

He could put the selector level into the Spread, Stop, or Fold position. For takeoff he would choose Spread. For choice he could then move the lever to Stop, which blanked off the hydraulic system in the wings from the rest of the system, or leave it in Spread. In the latter case it was essential to select a manual locking device as well to secure the wings. Otherwise the hydraulic jacks in the wings remained dangerously open to the whole hydraulic system. Attempting to retract the undercarriage on takeoff would then drain the fluid out of the wing jacks, and the wings would fold, with fatal results.

The most uncontrollable weakness, however, was the Corsair's built-in bounce. The compression of air inside the olio-pneumatic struts of the undercarriage did not absorb the shock of a carrier landing sufficiently, and the machine often jumped all the arrester wires, with the large wing area adding a floating effect.

When the Royal Navy's Number 1830 Squadron, the first British unit to equip with the Corsair F4U-1, tried to fly aboard HMS *Illustrious* in the fall of 1943, it turned her unyielding armored flight deck into an aircraft scrapyard, and its commanding officer was lost overboard. Corsair pilots of Task Force 50 had similar experiences with their machine prior to their first action with the Fifth Fleet, which came in November 1943 with the invasion of the Gilbert Islands.

The *Saratoga* and *Princeton* made two heavy raids on Rabaul, where the remaining planes from the roughly handled Japanese carriers had collected. The Allies virtually destroyed them for the loss of only eight American aircraft, besides seriously damaging cruisers, destroyers, and other ships. At Pearl Harbor, Vice Admiral Spruance was preparing his drive to the Philippines via the Gilberts and Marshalls.

In parallel, Gen. Douglas MacArthur advanced on the Philippines northwest from New Guinea, flanked by Navy carriers. He drove northward from Port Moresby and established airfields on the northeast coast from which Rabaul, still the main source of opposition, was bombed heavily. On 24 March 1944 he captured Marcus Island at the head of the Bismarck Sea, which gave the Americans a good advanced fleet base for the attack on the Philippines. MacArthur was supported by a squadron of escort carriers and occasionally by the new Fast Carrier Force, formed from veteran ships and the new fleet, light fleet, and escort carriers that U.S. shipyards were producing at an accelerating rate. The fiercely contested capture of Biak Island on 21 June 1944 signaled the end of the preliminaries to the invasion of the Philippines.

Meanwhile the central Pacific campaign was on course, with the carriers facilitating the capture of only important island bases, leaving the rest to wither on the vine. This route could swiftly bring the Americans to the threshold of the Philippines via the Marianas Islands. It also kept the enemy guessing as to the direction of the vital strike, it confused his strategy and stretched his resources, while the Allies brought land-based heavy bombers within striking distance of Japan.

Though opposed fanatically by the Japanese every step of the way, this strategy succeeded brilliantly. First objectives were Makin and Tarawa Islands in the Gilberts, the only bases within effective bombing range of American-held airfields in the Ellice Islands.

Their efforts were combined with those of the Fifth Fleet carriers. The Northern Attack Force, which was to support the landing on Makin Island, known to be comparatively poorly defended, included the first three Kaiser-built escort carriers, the *Casablanca, Liscome Bay*, and *Coral Sea*. "Kaiser's Coffins" were commonly said to be shoddy goods whose welds would crack in bad weather or in the blast from a near miss, and they were on trial here. Supporting the landing on heavily defended Tarawa were three tried and trusted *Sangamon*s. The three Kaisers each carried sixteen FM Wildcats, improved versions of the F4F, and twelve Avenger TBFs.[2] The larger *Sangamons* were equipped with nine TBFs and twelve Grumman F6F Hellcats, successors to the Wildcat and designed to stop the Zero scourge, which it was to achieve spectacularly.[3] Between them the six CVEs added nearly 200 planes to the 700 put up by the eleven CVs and CVLs of the Fast Carrier Force.

Off Makin, the three Kaisers of Carrier Division 24 had formed part of the Task Group 52.13 with the battleships *New Mexico* and *Mississippi*, the cruiser *Baltimore*, and seven destroyers. At 0500 on 24 November the group was steaming in the Circular Cruising Disposition 73. The *Liscome Bay* was acting as guide in the center, and there was a gap on the formation's starboard left by the departure of the destroyer *Hull* at 0400.

The rose of dawn was tinting a black, moonless night when three bells struck, summoning the carriers to flight quarters. The *Liscome Bay* was scheduled to fly off a dawn patrol, and there were thirteen armed and fueled aircraft spotted on the flight deck. In the hangar, planes kept degassed during the night by standing order were being fueled. At 0510 the *Liscome Bay* began a 60-degree turn to starboard to face east in anticipation of daybreak, and the formation followed. At 0513 the "talker" of a gun's crew on the starboard gallery just forward of the carrier's bridge island reported a torpedo wake off the starboard bow heading for ship.

The *I-175* had set herself up for a good shot through the gap left by the *Hull*. The Long Lance hit the *Liscome Bay* on her starboard side between the forward and after engine rooms. Both elevators were blown skyward, breaking the power systems. Fire raced along the open fuel lines through which the volatile avgas surged at pressure, and through the fractured points to engulf the whole hangar. The bow section caught fire, then the entire hull. The ship stopped, listing to starboard, and there was a second, cataclysmic explosion aft, where at least nine 2,000-pound, seventy-eight 1,000-pound, ninety-six 500-pound bombs, and a large number of torpedo warheads were stored. Some 100 feet of the after flight deck were blown off, and the whole side of the ship opened up along the starboard gun gallery. Men jumped off the side into a lake of flaming oil. At 0535 the *Liscome Bay* sank, leaving 204 survivors from a crew of 846.

The *Liscome Bay* was the fourth escort carrier to be destroyed by internal explosion associated with the igniting of fuel and ammunition, in three cases (the *Audacity, Avenger,* and *Liscome Bay*) initiated by torpedo hits. It revived all the criticism of the type with respect to structure (particularly the CVEs' thin unarmored sides and insufficient internal bulkheads), speed, and fuel systems.

With the support of the carriers, the islands were taken, after much bloody fighting at Tarawa. Airfields were promptly occupied, ready for attacks on the next targets—the atolls of Kwajalein and Eniwetok in the Marshall Islands, 200 miles to the northwest and on the latitude of the Philippines.

The rogue Corsair F4U-1s were temporarily banned from carrier use and confined to marine service from island bases for ground support. In this role, with carrier-aggravated faults absent, they were an outstanding success. Chance-Vought's emergency Program Dog solved the problem of the bouncing undercarriage, and the machine's fierce touchdown swing was reduced. The hydraulically operated cowl flaps and the valve push-rod mechanism were modified to prevent oil escaping and covering windscreen and cockpit, and the cockpit was raised and provided with a bubble canopy to improve the forward view. The cockpit controls were rationalized.

The Corsair was returned to carrier service in 1944 and became the "Whistling Death" feared by the Japanese. Later optional armament included eight rocket projectiles, and other developments introduced four-cannon armament in the F4U-1C; radar and an autopilot in the night fighter F4U-2; and a supercharger in the F4U-3, a high-altitude fighter. The last wartime model was the F4U-4, with uprated engine and four-blade propeller. FG versions were built by Goodyear, and the F3A by Brewster. Production and development continued after the war until 1953, and the Corsair saw service in Korea and with the French in Indochina. Meanwhile, for the central Pacific campaign of 1943–44, the American fleet carriers standardized on the Hellcat, a better-behaved, though highly potent, aircraft.

On 1 February 1944 the assault on Kwajalein began, and by the fifth all resistance was at an end, with comparatively light American casualties. Some valuable lessons had been learned at bloody Tarawa, where the marines had been initially pinned down on the invasion beaches. Kwajalein, less heavily defended, had been pounded by twice the weight of bombardment inflicted on Tarawa, and the shells from the 16-inch guns of the eight battleships taking part were controlled at a steep angle of descent, as opposed to the close-range flat-trajectory fire of the earlier operation. Artillery landed on nearby islands also proved its value. The result was that more than half the defenders had been killed before the assault troops landed, and most of the rest were in no state to fight properly. This time, too, the invaders came with amphibious tanks and armored troop carriers that did not get stranded on the reef.

The Fast Carrier Force, redesignated Task Force 58, was growing all the time and at this point comprised six large and five light carriers, with eight fast battleships, six or eight cruisers, and thirty or forty destroyers, commanded by aviator Vice Adm. Marc Mitscher. Captain of the *Hornet* at Midway, he continued until May 1945 in command within the main Pacific force, designated either the Third or Fifth Fleet according to whether Halsey or Spruance was in command.[4]

Eniwetok was captured on 18 February 1944, all Japanese air opposition on Truk Island having been destroyed by Mitscher. Assault on Saipan in the Marianas, 600 miles to the northwest, was prepared, while Task Force 58 destroyed enemy aircraft and shipping in the Palau Islands.

Saipan when captured would provide an air base from which to bomb Japan, 1,300 miles away, and the operation would also create a diversion, while the main thrust was to be made at the Philippines. The capture of Saipan would also prevent the Japanese from staging aircraft along the chain Japan–Iwo Jima–Marianas–Palaus–Moluccas.

Of vital importance would be the U.S. "Fleet Train," formed when the rapid progress of the fleet across the Pacific had made return to Pearl Harbor for supplies impracticable. The Train worked from the advanced forward bases—it was now at Majuro—with ships either returning there for supplies of fuel, food, ammunition, or aircraft, or being serviced at sea by mobile squadrons of supply ships, tankers, and escort carriers with fresh planes and aircrews.

A mobile service squadron moved up to Eniwetok from Majuro, and the Marianas operation got under way. En route, Task Force 58 aircraft hit airfields on Guam, Rota, Tinian, and Saipan itself, until the assault force was in the Philippine Sea off the western beaches of Saipan. On 14 June the assault went in and made steady progress, though once again the Japanese fought for every inch of ground.

Meanwhile, the newly formed Japanese First Mobile Fleet, with nine carriers, six battleships (including the 18-inch sisters *Yamato* and *Musashi*), thirteen cruisers, and thirteen destroyers under Vice Adm. Jisaburo Ozawa, had left Tawi-Tawi in the East Indies. They penetrated the central Philippines through the San Bernadino Straits into the Philippine Sea, stretching between the Philippines and Saipan.

With Guam or Rota convenient for refueling, Ozawa's plan was to send his planes (some 450) in conjunction with 500 aircraft in the Marianas to attack Spruance at long range, leaving his own carriers out of range of the U.S. carrier planes. Meanwhile the Japanese surface ships would fall upon Adm. Richmond Kelly Turner's amphibious assault force at Saipan. Ozawa was not told that Japanese fighters in the Marianas had been decimated by Mitscher's planes.

Spruance's best move would almost certainly have been to steam west and meet the Japanese fleet as far from the Marianas as possible, but all he knew (through the constant vigilance of American submarines) was that Ozawa had left Tawi-Tawi and that some of these

ships had passed through the San Bernardino Straits. On the afternoon of 18 June 1944, the U.S. submarine *Cavalla* reported the Japanese fleet, which by sunset would be some 300 miles west of Spruance.
Now he had to decide whether he should close on Ozawa during the
night, ready for a dawn attack on the latter well away from the Marianas airfields that Ozawa was counting on. Another commander
might have been tempted, but Spruance knew that his main duty was
to protect Turner's force at Saipan and ensure the success of the landings. To stretch Ozawa's reach he steamed east during the night, a
sighting signal from a patrolling Catalina being lost en route to him.

Ozawa was kept informed of the U.S. fleet's position by superior
reconnaissance, and he waited to send in a strike at dawn, out of
range of a counterstrike. At first light he launched his planes, but at
0900 the U.S. submarine *Albacore* torpedoed his flagship, the new carrier *Taiho*, which blew up after Ozawa had transferred his flag. At
noon the untiring *Cavalla* torpedoed the *Shokaku*, starting fires and
explosions that sank the veteran carrier three hours later.

Meanwhile Spruance, handicapped by constantly having to turn
into the east wind to launch planes, had steamed west again and sent
his aircraft ahead to find the Japanese fleet. At 300 miles they had not
found it, but at 1000 Ozawa's strike planes began to appear on American radar screens.

They were met by massed Hellcat fighters and nearly all shot down.
Hellcats and Avengers kept Guam from refueling the Japanese planes,
and a great air battle raged all day. Four U.S. ships were slightly damaged, and in the Marianas Turkey Shoot some 400 out of 545 Japanese
aircraft (carrier borne and shore based), were destroyed, with more
going down in the *Taiho* and *Shokaku*. Once again the Japanese naval
air squadrons had been virtually annihilated. In the whole fleet there
remained only forty of them, in the *Zuikaku*. The Americans had lost
17 fighters out of 300.

Next day Mitscher's aircraft located Ozawa at the extremity of their
range, sank the *Hiyo*, and badly damaged the *Junyo*. In their return
eighty U.S. planes ran out of fuel and ditched, but many of their crews
were rescued. Others crashed on their flight decks. Unlike the Japanese, who had suffered proportionately far heavier losses than the
Americans, there were plenty more planes—and men. After more savage fighting ashore, Saipan fell, then Guam and Tinian, and by 8
August 1944 the Marianas were in American hands.

The organization for controlling the large number of U.S. fighters
had advanced greatly since the carrier battles of 1942. The latest ships
were fitted with a new air warning SR radar set that could find echoes
at 150 miles. Most other ships had at least SC (air and surface warn-

ing) radar. New very-high frequency (VHF) radios were in the process of being fitted in the U.S. fleet, and many channels were available. Overall control was in the hands of the task-force fighter-direction officer (FDO) in the *Lexington*, who was in touch with all group and individual ship FDOs. The force FDO allocated raids to groups and kept back enough reserves for emergencies; group FDOs allocated individual interceptions to ships. In the Philippine Sea conditions were good, the sky clear, and vapor trails easily seen.

The Japanese attacked piecemeal, the first raids being detected at 150 miles. The whole U.S. task force turned into the trade wind so that fighters could be operated continuously. Most raids were intercepted by fighters before they could reach the task force. The new Hellcat fighters and the fine training of their pilots achieved much of the American success, as did the fleet radars and the greatly improved voice communication.

The increased warning distance by radars did not cater to low-flying planes. Centimetric radars could detect them low above the horizon but were defeated by the curvature of the earth. In 1944 the U.S. Navy began to use destroyer pickets with air warning stationed from 10 to 50 miles in the direction of the enemy to report low fliers, the *Stockham* and *Yarnall* being used in this way in the Philippine Sea. These ships were very vulnerable, and the *Stockham* was attacked several times, though not hit.

By the autumn of 1944 the two great pincers of Allied attack in the Pacific were poised and ready to converge on the Philippines. MacArthur's Sixth Army was under the protection of Admiral Kinkaid's Seventh Fleet, supported by the U.S. Far East Air Force. Halsey's Third Fleet was in the Philippine Sea to beat off any Combined Fleet attacks from the north, or west out of the Sulu Sea. At 1000 on 20 October 1944, MacArthur made good his promised "I will return" and landed at Leyte Gulf.

To attack Kinkaid's transports and support ships off Leyte, Adm. Takeo Kurita, with the *Yamato, Musashi*, and two other battleships, ten heavy cruisers (the *Atago* flying his flag), two light cruisers, and destroyers, was to head north from Brunei in Borneo, east through the Sibuyan Sea, through the San Bernardino Straits into the Philippine Sea and south to Leyte Gulf. A second force under Rear Adm. Shoji Nishimura, with two battleships, a cruiser, and four destroyers, would reach Leyte from the south via Surigao Straits. A third force, Ozawa with the *Zuikaku* and three light carriers, would steam off Cape Engano, the northernmost tip of the Philippines. Ozawa had only twenty aircraft with half-trained pilots, but he hoped to draw off Halsey while Kurita went south for Leyte Gulf.

Radar in the submarines *Darter* and *Dace* picked up Kurita. They crippled the *Takao* and sank the *Atago* and *Mayo*. Kurita had to swim for his life; he was picked up and taken to the *Yamato*. His force was sighted in the Sibuyan Sea and heavily attacked by Halsey's planes. The *Musashi* was sunk, with Halsey losing the light carrier *Princeton* in a counterattack from Luzon. Then Ozawa's carriers were reported to the north-northeast. Estimating from pilots' reports that Kurita had been hobbled, Halsey took Ozawa's bait and raced north with his whole fleet. He informed Kinkaid, who assumed that he had left a guard on San Bernardino Straits just in case the apparently crippled Kurita should chance his arm. Meanwhile Nishimura and another group under Shima had been reported to him, both heading for Surigao Straits, which they would reach in the darkness.

Rear Adm. Jesse B. Oldendorf's bombardment force of six battleships, four heavy and four light cruisers, twenty-eight destroyers, and forty-five PT boats was ordered to greet them. Oldendorf was short on armor-piercing shells but had centrimetric radar for surface warning and fire control. The Japanese had only a few of the sixty puny 2-kilowatt Mark II Model 2 10-cm sets in the fleet.

Oldendorf's first line of PT (patrol torpedo) boats attacked Nishimura with torpedoes but all missed. The destroyers detected the enemy at 36,000 yards and fired forty-seven torpedoes entirely by radar control. They hit both battleships, one of which sank, along with two destroyers. The U.S. battleships fired by radar at 22,800 yards with the latest Mark 8 control system, sank the second battleship, and sent one heavy cruiser reeling away fatally damaged, to collide with a cruiser of Shima's force. The latter also lost a cruiser, fired sixteen Long Lances by radar and missed, then retired. This battle was fought entirely by radar, and the Japanese obligingly helped by a display of searchlights and star shell. The results were devastating.

In the Philippine Sea, however, the situation looked critical for the Americans. Kurita, his force far less damaged than Halsey thought, had pushed on for San Bernardino Strait, passed through into the Philippine Sea, and headed south. The only ships between him and the American invasion force at Leyte Gulf was Task Group 77.4 of sixteen escort carriers in three units steaming off the island of Samar, their planes supporting the troops ashore and their commanders believing themselves to be covered by Halsey.

The task group was commanded by Rear Adm. Tommy Sprague. To the south steamed Taffy One (the *Sangamon, Suwannee, Santee*, and *Petrof Bay*) under the group commander himself. Next in order, to the north, was Taffy Two (the *Manila Bay, Natoma Bay, Kadastan Bay, Marcus Island, Ommaney Bay*, and *Savo Island*) under Rear Adm. Felix Stump.

Two FM-2 Wildcats from the escort carrier *White Plains* on patrol in the Pacific. (U.S. National Archives)

Further north, in the immediate path of Kurita's battle fleet, was Taffy Three (the *Fanshaw Bay, Kalinin Bay, Saint Lo, White Plains, Gambier Bay*, and *Kitkun Bay*) under Rear Adm. Clifton A. F. Sprague, known by his Annapolis nickname of Ziggy to distinguish him from Tommy Sprague. With the exception of the three veteran *Sangamons*, all the CVEs were Kaisers, each with a composite squadron of eleven to eighteen Wildcat FM-2s[5] or Hellcat F6F fighters and eleven or twelve Avenger TBM-1Cs.[6] The *Sangamons'* air groups were larger and with a different mix, with seventeen to twenty-six F6F-3s or -5s and six to nine TBM-1Cs or TBF-1s.

Some of the FM-2s attacked Japanese artillery with the new weapon napalm, a form of gasoline thickened with aluminum soap of naphthenic[7] and palmitic[8] acids into a sticky gel that burned more slowly than gasoline but at a much higher temperature (1,800 degrees Fahrenheit). The results were awesome. An explosive charge scattered the goo, which stuck to whatever it hit until burned out. Other aircraft supported ground forces fighting on Leyte, provided fighter sweeps against the western Vinayan Islands and northern Mindanao, and launched strikes against enemy airfields in those areas. Antishipping sweeps sank coasters, luggers, and PT boats. Enemy troops and installations were attacked.

Escort carriers were also useful for ferrying replacement aircraft. (U.S. National Archives)

At 0640 one of Taffy Three's antisubmarine patrol planes reported a Japanese task force 20 miles on the unit's starboard beam. Radar PPI repeaters showed the force heading 269 degrees from them. At 0647 Ensign Jensen from *Kadashan Bay* reported four Japanese battleships and eight cruisers with destroyers. Ziggy Sprague turned Taffy Three around southeast to 130 degrees to put as much distance as possible between his frail "Woolworth carriers" and the enemy, who could make 30 knots to his 18. Geysers of red, green, and yellow foam began to rise among the escort carriers. Only the Japanese, their radar crude and unreliable, used this old-fashioned method of checking the fall of shot from individual ships. Then, dim but unmistakable through the mist and drizzle, the pagodas of the emperor's battle fleet rose up from the horizon astern.

Smoke pouring from the vents, the ships of Taffy Three sought flank speed, calling on Taffys One and Two for help as they looked down the 18-inch barrels of the *Yamato*. But the other units also had many planes away on various support or supply missions for Kinkaid and the troops ashore. Meanwhile Taffy Three had to take the weight. Sprague's one advantage was that, steering 090 degrees, with the wind coming from 070 degrees, he could run and launch at the same time, then make smoke and take it with him like a friendly cloud, using his destroyers and destroyer-escorts as well. Meanwhile Kurita pressed on with his intention first to cripple the carriers, then to destroy Task Force 38—not crediting that the American commander would expose his auxiliary carriers to such a risk.

Soon the two Japanese cruiser columns were closing on Taffy Three's circular formation, with the battleships close behind. The *White Plains* and the flagship *Fanshaw Bay* were surrounded by colored fountains. Water from a straddle splashed across the bridge of the *White Plains*, as the Japanese used their salvoes like calipers. Captain Sullivan threw the helm hard over. The movement opened the general circuit breaker, and all electrical power and steering control was momentarily lost. The *Fanshaw Bay*'s remaining fighters and her eleven TBMs were already airborne. The *Gambier Bay* got off three planes with torpedoes, one with only five minutes' gas. Another was catapulted with no pilot. At 0715 a heavy rain squall got between Taffy Three and the enemy, giving Ziggy Sprague's ships temporary respite.

In Taffy One, Tommy Sprague thought of Kinkaid's 16-inch guns and asked permission to seek their shelter. Kinkaid refused. The *Yamato* had a flank speed of 34 knots and would not take long to reach the invasion beaches. At 0740 Taffy One was rearming and refueling the striking force that had finished off the blazing cruiser *Mogami* in the Surigao Straits when the unit was attacked by nine enemy planes.

These aircraft were units of the Shimpu Special Attack Corps. Vice Adm. Takajiro Onishi, commander of First Air Fleet in the defense of the Philippines, desperately short of aircraft, had activated these kamikaze units, which embodied Nison Seishin, the spirit of Japan. Kamikaze (divine wind, or tempest) was the name traditionally given to the typhoon of August 1281 sent, according to Japanese mythology, by divine providence. It destroyed two fleets sent by Kublai Khan from Korea and South China to conquer Japan. There had been cases of self-immolating sacrifices by wounded pilots and crippled aircraft, but the first formal kamikaze attack on an American carrier had been carried out on 15 October 1944, off Luzon. Rear Admiral Arima, commander of the 26th Air Flotilla, dived his Yokosuka D47 Susei (Judy) bomber and one 500-pound bomb into the fleet carrier *Franklin*, killing three men and wounding twelve but causing little damage to the ship.

After the ritual drinking of sake, wearing their divinely inscribed white headbands, ceremonial swords at their waists, five young knights of the samurai climbed into their Zeros on the airfield at Mabalacat on Luzon. They took off for the American fleet off Samar, escorted by four ordinary mortals in A6Ms.

The *Santee* had just completed launching five Avengers and eight FM-2s for Taffy Three relief when an enemy plane dived on her out of cloud and hit the flight deck on the port side forward, boring a hole through to the hangar deck where it exploded, starting fires next to a pile of eight 1,000-pound bombs. A second kamikaze A6M circled the *Suwannee*, was hit by an antiaircraft shell, spun, recovered, and dived straight for the *Sangamon*. About 500 feet up it was hit by another shell and deflected into the sea, and a third was brushed off in the same way by the *Petrof Bay*.

Five minutes after the *Santee* had extinguished her fires, she was hit by a torpedo from the submarine *I-56*. The sturdy ex-tanker survived the blow, reduced to 16.5 knots. Meanwhile another Zero dived from cloud on the *Suwannee*. The carrier's Oerlikons hit the plane, which rolled over smoking, straightened out, and penetrated the *Suwannee's* flight deck forward of the after elevator, starting fires on the hangar deck. The elevator was inoperative for two hours, after which flying resumed. The *Santee* had also extinguished her fires.

If necessary, Task Group 77.4 would be sacrificed to delay Kurita from reaching the invasion area in the south, but Rear Admiral Olden-dorf was ordered to take three battleships, five cruisers, and two destroyers from the Seventh Fleet and go the aid of the escort carriers, which were desperately fighting time.

They were also fighting back. Under heavy fire, the destroyers attacked with torpedoes. The heavy cruiser *Kumano* was hit and turned away. The *Yamato* and *Nagato* were also hit, and even they had to break off for a time. The rest of the Japanese line raced to outflank the carriers. The destroyers *Johnston, Hoel*, and *Samuel B. Roberts* harassed them until they sank. The ground support planes of Taffy Three had few torpedoes or armor-piercing bombs, but they threw RPs and depth charges, then bullets, then made dummy runs to keep the Japanese gunners busy. Ensign Shroyer's 500-pounder hit the fantail of a cruiser, and she slowed and stopped. Ensign Ostercorn dropped two bombs on a cruiser. Lt. Leonard Waldrop exploded a torpedo from the *Yahagi* by strafing it. The *St. Lo's* solitary 5-inch gun deflected another Long Lance. "Open fire!" Sprague had ordered.

He was being herded south, with the enemy on both quarters. To alter to the east meant a suicide charge down the muzzles of thirty-two 8-inch rifles. With its sixth round the *Gambier Bay's* 5-inch hit a cruiser, then another. At 0750 the *Kalinin Bay*, on the exposed port flank, was hit by several 14-inch and 16-inch shells, and by thirteen 8-inch. Badly damaged and flooding, she managed to hold her course, peashooter firing. At 0815 the *Gambier Bay* was hit, and fires started. She slowed down, and the magazines were ordered flooded. The 5-inch jammed. The *Kalinin Bay, Kitkun Bay, St. Lo, White Plains*, and *Fan-shaw Bay* were all damaged by near misses. The Japanese, believing they were facing Halsey's big carriers, fired armor-piercing shells, and one passed right through the flagship. The *St. Lo* hid in her own smoke.

Away to the north, a 186-strong strike from the Third Fleet carriers had been unleashed on Ozawa's skeleton force, when, at 0822, Halsey, racing with his fast battleships to be in at the death, received Kinkaid's signal reporting Kurita's attack on Taffy Three. Grudgingly, Halsey ordered Vice Adm. John S. McCain's carrier group to divert to Samar.

Off Samar, the *Gambier Bay* was in extremis, taking salvo after salvo from the *Chikuma*. Bodies strewed the flight deck, which literally ran with blood. The ship no longer answered her helm. The stench of burning diesel oil, cordite, and incinerating flesh was all pervading. At 0850 came the order to abandon ship. At 0907 the *Gambier Bay* rolled over and sank into the Cape Johnson Deep, 3,500 fathoms down, after the last shell to hit her had knocked off the threshing starboard propeller.

The *White Plains* exchanged shells with the *Chokai*, hit her at least twice, knocked out a forward turret, and damaged her engines. Planes from the *Kitkun Bay* hit the cruiser, which blew up and sank. At 0841 Taffy Two came under 14-inch fire. Stump launched two more strikes to add to the four that had already bombed and rocketed Kurita's ships, and hit the *Chikuma*.

Before and after the kamikaze attack, Taffy One's planes attacked Kurita. Hellcats from the *Suwannee* bombed and hit the *Tone*, slowing her down, and destroyed thirty Japanese planes in the air. Her Avengers hit two battleships. Two reconnaissance floatplanes launched from the *Yamato* were promptly shot down. The cruiser *Suzuya* sank.

Taffy Three's Ziggy Sprague, incredulous that only the *Gambier Bay* had been lost thus far, wondered how long his other battered and burning carriers could hold out. The *St. Lo* and *Kitkun Bay* were damaged and barely able to launch planes. The *Kalinin Bay* was held together by damage control, her flight deck hopelessly torn up. His own "Fanny Bee" was under fire from two cruisers and several destroyers. Then suddenly, unbelievably, the Japanese were seen to be retiring.

Hauled off when they had the enemy carriers reeling, Kurita's captains were as amazed as Sprague. Suffering from earlier experiences that day, Kurita had taken council of his fears. His ships were now dangerously spread out, and intercepted American signals suggested the formation of a strong carrier force to the south and the presence of enemy aircraft newly based on Leyte. For two and a half hours, apparently inexhaustible groups of enemy fighters and bombers had come at him. By this time American troops must surely be too strongly entrenched to be dislodged. At 0811 he signaled, "Cease action. Come north with me."

"Oh hell," said a signalman aboard the *Fanshaw Bay*, "they got away!"[9]

The CVEs' aircraft continued to attack Kurita. Avenger torpedo-bombers and Wildcat FM-2 fighters from Taffy Two hit his cruisers. Air attacks finished off the already damaged *Chokai* and *Chikuma*.

Taffy Three sailors and fliers were watching the pagodas shrink to mastheads on the horizon when six suiciders jumped the force. For a kamikaze pilot the almost vertical high-level plunge in the enemy radar's overhead blind spot was the most difficult, as the high terminal velocity gave him less time to make a last-second correction to allow for evasive action by the target ship. Alternatives were either a climb to 10,000 feet and a steep dive, or to less than 500 feet for a shallow-angle attack. The latter was generally preferred, as a steep dive needed good weather and high skill, whereas even a green pilot could make corrections in a slower attack at an angle that could be steepened or flattened easily. Aiming point was a carrier's flight deck abreast the island, or with other ships the base of the bridge structure. The four Zeros that had attacked the *Santee, Suwannee*, and *Petrof Bay* of Taffy One had eluded radar, as these six banzai self-immolators had done, by flying very low, under the beams, then climbing into cloud near the targets to prepare attack.

The Zeros plunged out of the overcast before CAP could deflect them, while most of the carriers were recovering aircraft. One bounced off the *Kitkun Bay*'s port catwalk into the sea. Two were shot down by the *Fanshaw Bay* and *White Plains*.

Lt. Yuko Sehi's Zero smashed through the *St. Lo*'s flight deck and burst into flames, its two bombs and bombs in the hangar exploding. More huge explosions tossed planes and great sections of the flight deck high into the air. In minutes the whole ship was ablaze. She sank at 1115.

Fifteen Judys approached from astern. One struck and seriously damaged the *Kitkun Bay*'s forecastle; another hit the badly holed *Kalinin Bay*, but she continued steaming.

Halsey was still smarting from Nimitz's curt "Where is the Third Fleet?" received in Halsey's *New Jersey* at 0925. At 1115, with desperate reluctance, he reversed course to 180 degrees. He took with him six fast battleships, two heavy cruisers, and eighteen destroyers of Task Force 34 and Rear Adm. Gerald F. Bogan's carriers of 38.2 to try to intercept Kurita. The carriers of Rear Adm. Frederick Sherman's 38.3 and Rear Adm. Ralph E. Davison's 38.4 were left to continue the attack on Ozawa's remnant. This reduced force made heavy weather of the job but reduced the *Chitose* to a sinking condition, crippled the *Chiyoda*, damaged the *Zuiho*, sank a destroyer, and sent the light cruiser *Tama* and Ozawa's flagship the *Zuikaku* crawling home with torpedo holes. Then a massive strike by 200 planes from both task groups sank the *Zuikaku* and *Zuiho*, and the *Chiyoda* was finished off by cruisers.

At 1145, following Halsey's previous order, a ninety-eight plane strike was launched from McCain's *Hancock* and the new *Hornet* and *Wasp*, for a 340-mile haul to Samar. It was more than extreme range for the planes, and there was no time to fit disposable wing tanks, so the thirty-three Helldivers and nineteen TBMs carried only a light bomb load and no torpedoes. Even so, a safe return was doubtful.

Planes from all the Taffys were also dispatched with anything lethal left in the armories. Homeless FM-2s from the *Gambier Bay* used captured Tacloban airfield on Leyte to refuel and rearm, then found a better home aboard the *Manila Bay*. About 1115 they joined her fighters and ten TBMs in an attack on a cruiser, later combining with some of the *Kitkun Bay*'s VC-5 Squadron in bombing a battleship before landing on the *Manila Bay* or *Fanshaw Bay*.

Just after noon, Taffy Two's Stump gave McCain's fliers, tired after a three-hour flight, the enemy's position, and at 1310 they attacked Kurita's ships. Though their fighters held off defending Zeros, three bombers were lost to very fierce flak and others damaged, without significantly harming the enemy. Of the twelve *Hancock* Helldivers, only three returned before dark. One was lost to flak; two ran out of fuel some 40 miles short of the ship; two landed at Tacloban, one of them crashing; four found a home aboard Stump's CVEs. Nine McCain planes landed on rough strips on Leyte, and eleven were reported missing. A second, fifty-three plane strike had left the *Hornet* and *Hancock* at 1245, two hours closer to the target. Four hits were claimed on the *Yamato*, one on the *Nagato*, nine on other battleships, and others on cruisers and destroyers.

At 1700 Tommy Sprague's Taffy One launched all remaining planes to attack Kurita, then continued a northeasterly course to join Taffy Three. Taffy Two patrolled the area of the landing beaches and in the morning sighted, in the channel between Leyte and Cebu Islands, a Japanese force. Four transports were escorted by the light cruiser *Kinu* and the destroyer *Uranami*, which had just landed 20,000 troops at Ormoc Bay on the west coast of Leyte under cover of darkness. Taffy Two had no heavy bombs or torpedoes left, but light bombs and rocket projectiles sank both escorts.

Halsey missed Kurita at San Bernardino by three hours. He sent air strikes from Task Groups 38.1 and 38.2 but only managed to sink the light cruiser *Noshiro*. Kurita had returned through the straits and had reached Brunei with the *Yamato, Kongo,* and *Nagato*.

There was a coda to the great battle. On the afternoon of 27 October Taffy One was approaching the Admiralty Islands en route southeast for Espiritu Santo when it came under attack by a force of Judys and A6M5s. CAP shot down twelve of the enemy, who narrowly missed the *Santee, Sangamon,* and *Petrof Bay,* but one Zero crashed into a manned Avenger on the *Suwannee's* forward elevator, damaged previously by a kamikaze. Both planes exploded, and seconds later another plane dropped a 500-pound bomb in the midst of nine planes parked forward, starting fires that raged for several hours. Thanks to efficient damage control, the blaze did not imperil the ship by spreading to the lower decks.

The *Suwannee* was now in a sorry state, however, with gaping holes in the flight deck, shrapnel-torn superstructure, and a tangle of wreckage that had once been the forward elevator and catapult. To expedite the ship's return to the fight, her first lieutenant was flown across the Pacific, direct to the Puget Sound Navy Yard, Washington state, with photographs of all the damage. Marine architects, engineers, and technicians studied the pictures and Lieutenant Dobson's reports, preparing blueprints in advance of the ship's arrival for repair. Shipfitters, under the supervision of the master shipfitter, began construction of a new elevator; welders started the prefabrications of large stretches of

A kamikaze aims for the USS *Sangamon.* (U.S. National Archives)

new deck plating; machinists commenced building a new accelerator, to await the carrier's docking.

To give longer warning of future kamikaze attacks, some destroyers were to be fitted with radar and stationed as pickets up to 60 miles from the carriers, in the direction of likely attacks. Tomcat Pickets were to be used as delousing stations, past which all aircraft returning from a mission were to pass for a check that they had not picked up a Japanese tail. If so, it would be dealt with by attached CAP fighters. Jack Patrols of fighters at low level, controlled by screen destroyers, would provide fast-reaction, last-ditch defense of the big ships. Group fighter-direction officers in headquarters ships were to hand over control to any ships in a better position to handle the fighters, which were to be increased in numbers at the expense of SB2C dive-bombers.

The CVEs met kamikazes again en route to the landing at Lingayen Gulf, Luzon, in January 1945. Constant attacks by the suiciders began on the afternoon of the fourth in the Sulu Sea off Panay Gulf. The American radar was partially blanked off by nearby land masses, and two kamikazes got through the screen and the Jack patrols. One was shot down near Makin Island, but the other dived on the *Ommaney Bay*, nicked the bridge island, and crashed into the starboard side of the flight deck, releasing its two bombs. One bomb penetrated the deck and exploded in the hangar, setting off a series of explosions among the fully gassed planes. The second bomb went through the hangar deck, ruptured the fire main on the second deck, and penetrated to the engine room, where it exploded and started oil fires. All power and bridge communications were cut off, and fires soon spread everywhere. At 1750 stored torpedo warheads blew up, and the order to abandon ship was given. The ship sank two hours later. Three minesweepers were sunk, three other CVEs were hit and forced to withdraw, and battleships and cruisers were damaged.

The subsequent capture of Iwo Jima and Okinawa enabled heavy bombers with fighter escort to attack Japan itself. Even with heavy bombardment from sea and air, the taking of both islands was long and bloody. One of twelve CVEs supporting the Iwo Jima landings, the *Bismarck Sea* was hit by two kamikazes. Devastated by fire, she finally blew up in one huge explosion and sank.

For the Okinawa assault—Operation Iceberg—on 1 April 1945, the newly arrived British Pacific Fleet, with four fleet carriers, two battleships, cruisers, and destroyers, was ordered to bomb and shell airfields on the Sakishima Islands. The idea was to prevent the Japanese from staging aircraft through to attack the invasion forces. Designated Task Force 57, the British fleet created its own Fleet Train, the amenities of

The escort carrier USS *Bismarck Sea* explodes after hits by two kamikazes. (U.S. National Archives)

which almost rivaled those of the U.S. Navy. The steel closed hangars of the British fleet carriers were ovens in the tropics, but in the desperate wave of kamikazes thrown against the supporting ships at Okinawa, the suiciders tended to bounce off them. Great damage was done to American carriers, with their open hangars and wood-planked flight decks. Almost 5,000 American sailors were killed, the greatest loss ever suffered by the U.S. Navy in a single battle. If kamikazes had been introduced earlier in greater numbers, the great carrier strikes of the Fast Carrier Force could have been rendered impossible and the war protracted infinitely longer. At it was, the suiciders came too late.

Air power, key to modern sea warfare, had passed from the hands of the pioneering Japanese firmly into the grip of their opponents. The switch of roles was definitely symbolized on 7 April 1945, when American aircraft sighted a fast Japanese task force of one battleship, two light cruisers, and nine destroyers steaming southwest from their home waters in the Inland Sea of Japan.

The battleship was the *Yamato*, pride of the Imperial Japanese Navy—sent out with insufficient fuel to return. Like the *Prince of Wales* and *Repulse*, sunk by unopposed Japanese air strikes early in the east-

The *Yamato*. (U.S. National Archives)

ern war, the great battlewagon was now wholly naked of air support. She was sunk by at least eight torpedoes and eight bombs. The two cruisers and three of the destroyers also went down before Mitscher's massed might, with three more destroyers left burning.

The Hit Parade

The contribution that U.S. submarines made to the Battle of the Philippine Sea reflected the magnitude of their achievements in the Pacific, which was as important as the great work of British boats in the East Indies.

When the war in the east began, the U.S. Navy had 111 submarines in commission. Some were small coastal types and two were huge minelayers with 6-inch guns, but most were the standard large fleet boats of 1,450–2,200 tons, with four diesel engines and electric drive giving a high surface speed of 20 knots. New construction was modeled on these.

During the first year of operations, when the U.S. submarines and the carriers held the line for the Allies in the Pacific, they were handicapped by faulty new magnetic torpedoes, though boats like the *Pollock* and *Plunger* sank ships off Tokyo Bay. The *Thresher* signaled the weather report, which was important to Doolittle for his epic B-25 attack on Tokyo from the *Hornet*. Other submarines gave warnings of the Midway armada.

From then on submarines formed the spearhead of the growing American offensive. The old *S-44* took on four cruisers and sank one, the *Seadragon* sank four marus in the South China Sea, and the *Gudgeon* two tankers and a freighter west of Truk. In August 1942 the *Nautilus* and *Argonaut* took the famous Carlson's Raiders to Makin and, firing blind, the *Argonaut* lobbed 6-inch shells over the island to sink two enemy ships in the lagoon. The *Guardfish* braved the fog and the Black Current off northeastern Japan, used her radar to feel out the land, and, in spite of malfunctioning torpedoes, sank eight ships (70,000 tons). This was one-tenth of the shipping sunk by U.S. submarines in

The USS *Argonaut*. (U.S. National Archives)

the Pacific in 1942, which considerably exceeded the very slow rate of Japanese construction.

Some U.S. submarines had been fitted with the unpopular SD warning radar, which gave range but not bearing, had a poor performance in rough seas, and tended to alert Japanese search receivers. But in the autumn of 1942, the superior Type SJ began to reach the flotillas. The SJ could pick up a merchantman at 10,000 yards, sometimes farther. It was ideal for night surface attacks as it could find ships over a wide area, targets being detected before they were seen so that a submarine could use her fast surface speed to reach her attacking position without being sighted. The target's course and speed could then be plotted, with more chance of a hit.

The first submarine to take SJ on patrol was the USS *Haddock* in August 1942, and she promptly sank two ships in a night attack. From then on Japanese losses increased dramatically.

In January 1943 Lt. Comdr. Dudley "Mush" Morton navigated his *Wahoo* down the twisting, reef-strewn 9-mile channel leading to Wewak harbor on the north coast of New Guinea. Inside, he sank the Japanese destroyer *Harusame* with a Down the Throat salvo straight at the enemy's oncoming bows. Two days later the *Wahoo* was in her billet south of the Carolines when she intercepted a troop convoy. Morton sank two freighters with torpedoes, a tanker and a troopship, and shot up troops in barges lowered by the troopship.

U.S. losses were not small—an oil slick and pieces of wood and cork were all that was left of many boats, but the pigboats sank twenty-one marus in March 1943, ships bringing essential materials from the Indies and Manchuria or supplying Japanese Pacific outposts. In 1942 submarines of both Pacific Ocean Areas and South-West Pacific Commands had sunk 134 ships (580,000 tons), including four carriers and five cruisers, rising to 284 ships in 1943 (1,342,000 tons). By 30 June 1944 they had sunk twenty-eight destroyers, the submarine's worst enemy, many with Down the Throat attacks.

In September 1943 they took up wolf-pack tactics, with variations. Packs of two to four boats patrolled together with free use of VHF voice radio, which could not be picked up far beyond the horizon. They spread out at night to look for targets, and if a convoy was located, the pack closed in. One boat (a flanker) attacked from the beam, then dropped astern to shadow. This boat, now the trailer, would pick off any damaged ships, sometimes using radar, and then use high surface speed to get into a favorable position from which to make a submerged attack at first light.

The destruction of Japan's merchant marine became the priority target for the Pacific boats, under the commander of submarines, Pacific, Adm. Charles "Uncle Charlie" Lockwood. He set up a troubleshooting campaign to cure whatever ailed the dud magnetic torpedoes. Lt. Comdr. E. A. Johnson from Command Services Force duplicated a torpedo hitting the steel side of a ship by dropping Mark 14s with concrete heads but real detonators, from 90 feet on a steel plate. Seven of the first ten that were dropped failed to detonate, thus confirming what had previously been thought—that the main defect was in the action of the detonator's firing pin. Weakened by the deceleration effect of contact, this would often strike the primer cap with insufficient force for the detonator to function. By September 1943 the first torpedoes with a successfully modified firing pin were ready.

By the end of 1943 U.S. submarines had sunk 2 million tons' worth of Japanese merchant shipping. In January 1944 they added fifty marus, another 240,840 tons. In February Metcalf's *Pögy* sank four merchantmen loaded with rice and sugar from Formosa for the Japanese troops, contributing 20,152 tons to the month's total. On 17 February Tommy Dykers's *Jack* sighted a convoy of four tankers in the light of a quarter-moon and dodged attacking destroyers, to sink four of the tankers and their 30 million gallons of gasoline, a record for one patrol up to that time.

In their quest to destroy Japan's mercantile fleet, the U.S. Pacific submarines found convoy escorts dangerous enemies. On 13 April

1944 Admiral Lockwood signaled all his boats on patrol to make them equal first choice of targets.

Sam Dealey's USS *Harder* followed these orders with spectacular success. In her first patrol in June 1943, the *Harder* had sunk seven ships from one convoy, including a big transport and a tanker, winning the boat the amended name of Hit 'em *Harder*. Early in April 1944, she sank the destroyer *Ikazuchi* with two torpedoes in four minutes. At dusk on the evening of 6 June, the *Harder*, on her fifth patrol, was threading the reefs of the Sibutu Passage between the Sulu Archipelago and North Borneo, heading north to rescue Australian intelligence agents from a beach on the Borneo coast. She picked up a convoy of three tankers heading south for the Borneo oil port of Tarakan. The escorting destroyer *Minazuki* sighted and attacked the *Harder*, and at 1,100 yards Dealey fired a four-torpedo spread. Two of them hit, and the destroyer sank in minutes. Next morning a floatplane forced the *Harder* down and called in the destroyer *Hayanari*. Dealey let the range close to 650 yards, then fired three tin fish down the throat. The destroyer threw the helm hard-over, but the first torpedo hit amidships and the second one aft. She sank swiftly.

The *Harder* carried on north through the Sibutu Passage into the Sulu Sea, struggling against the current and with destroyers always close. She picked up the six Australians and returned down the Sibutu Passage for her main mission, a reconnaissance of the anchorage at Tawi-Tawi, an island in the Sulu Archipelago chain dividing the Sulu from the Celebes Sea. Admiral Ozawa's fleet was moored there. In the passage, the *Harder* met and sank the destroyer *Tanikaze* and her consort.

As the *Harder* approached Tawi-Tawi, on 10 June, she saw and reported the *Yamato* and *Musashi* and their squadron of cruisers and destroyers leaving the anchorage to attack MacArthur's forces off New Guinea. A keen destroyer sighted the *Harder*'s periscope feather and raced in for the kill at 35 knots. Dealey fired three torpedoes down the throat and she blew up. He then closed the anchorage to count the ships. When he had reported his findings, he was ordered to a quieter area.

The *Harder*'s place was taken by Lt. Cdr. Marshall H. Austin's *Redfin*. On 11 June Austin sank the tanker *Asanagi Maru* when she approached with oil for Ozawa's ships. He watched the Japanese fleet leave the harbor and maneuvered to get a shot in, but Ozawa was steaming too fast for him. At dusk he came up and made the signal that sent Spruance into the Philippine Sea, where nine U.S. submarines were stationed. The *Flying Fish*, *Cavalla*, and *Albacore* reported Ozawa and sank the big new carrier *Taiho*, his flagship, and the veteran *Shokaku*. In June 1944 Richard O'Kane's *Tang* sank ten ships, the *Sealion* four, and the *Tinosa* two, all in the Japanese "safe" area of the Yellow Sea.

In the South China Sea, known as Convoy College, Lt. Cdr. Lawson
P. Ramage's *Perch* and Lt. Cdr. David L. Whelchel's *Steelhead* got into a
convoy at night on 31 July. Between them they sank five freighters
and three tankers. The *Croaker* and *Hardhead* sank two cruisers there,
but the *Harder* was lost with all hands.

On 11 October 1944, Lt. Cdr. David H. McClintock's *Darter* and Lt.
Cdr. Bladen D. Claggett's *Dace* were patrolling the west coast of Borneo
when they were ordered northeast to cover the Balabac Strait, off
northern Borneo, and the Palawan Passage. They were to watch for
Admiral Kurita's battleship force heading for the Philippines, where
General MacArthur was due to land on 20 October, protected by
Kinkaid's Seventh Fleet and Halsey's Third Fleet.

On 14 October the *Dace* sank two of Kurita's tankers. On 20 October
the *Darter* picked up the news that MacArthur had landed. At 0016 on
the twenty-third, both boats were cruising in the Pelawan Passage on
the surface when the *Darter* made radar contact with Kurita's force of
eleven warships. McClintock informed Claggett by bullhorn, and they
headed to the enemy force. Kurita was not hurrying, and the two
boats were able to stay with him on the surface. By 0532 McClintock
could see well enough to fire his bow tubes at the leading cruiser. As
he swung hard to port to bring his stern tubes to bear on the second
cruiser, he heard his torpedoes make five hits on the first cruiser. He
fired his after tin fish, and, as he went deep to avoid the destroyers, he
heard these hit their target as well. His sonar registered his first target
breaking up, and he heard the four explosions of the *Dace*'s torpedoes.
At 0820 he raised his periscope and saw his second target listing and
dead in the water. His first target, Kurita's flagship the *Atago*, had
sunk, forcing the admiral to swim for his life. The *Dace* sank the cruiser
Mayo, and the *Jallao* another cruiser.

"The American subs in the Pacific were getting all the good targets,"
recalled ex-leading torpedoman Iain Nethercott, late of HM submarine
Tactician, fifty years after the underwater war had reached its climax in
the east.[1] He spoke for all the British submariners who sweated on the
equator in 1943, confined, Nethercott said, "like orphans outside a
cake shop" to the Sunda side of the street, with a patrol in the mouth
of the Malacca Straits as a special treat. Unlike the big American boats,
the early British T-class boats like the *Tactician* had no air-conditioning
and became sweatboxes in the tropical heat. But they carried on sinking marus, junks, and sampans in the Straits.

Gun action was the norm. On the approach to the target, submerged,
the captain and gun captain examined it in the periscope and decided
on the form of attack. The magazine was opened and a mix of high
explosive (HE) and semi-armor-piercing (SAP) readied. The gun's crew
opened the lower hatch of the gun tower beneath the gun hatch and

climbed up into it. The boat closed on the target, blowing ballast tanks, hydroplanes holding her at 32 feet. At about 1,000 yards the planes were put hard-to-rise and the first lieutenant blew a whistle. The gun captain knocked the clips off the gun hatch and got a bath (the hatch was still underwater), tumbled up and out, knocked off the training stops on the gun, pulled the tampion out of the gun muzzle, and swung the gun on to the correct bearing, still partially underwater.

Gun telescopes were passed and shipped, and the first round got away, all in about thirty seconds. A submarine chaser off Singapore, after a mine-laying sortie, was very persistent, and the *Tactician*'s 4-inch fought a hard bout, finally destroying the enemy even though the rifling of the gun had worn smooth with heavy use. Batteries and engines were also time-expired and prone to overheating. Men collapsed from heatstroke, especially with ventilation shut off when submerged.

By the autumn of 1944, however, British submarines, some of them new, were arriving at the Allied submarine base at Fremantle in southwestern Australia. HMS *Sturdy*'s second patrol took her into the Java Sea, where she arrived on 25 November 1944. That evening she sank a coaster by gunfire and demolition charges, then a schooner and a junk.

In these older boats, gun action was a more complicated process, the shells having to follow a long and devious route from the magazine up the conning tower, through the gun shield and out to the gun. On 29 November the *Sturdy* surfaced and sank two armed luggers after a gun battle, and destroyed a prau's cargo of lubricating oil. On 1 December a coaster was sunk, and next day the *Sturdy* outgunned a Japanese auxiliary vessel.

While the *Sturdy* was catching some of the lesser fish, around the corner in the South China Sea a three-boat U.S. wolf pack known as Loughlin's Loopers (after their senior officer Comdr. C. E. Loughlin, in the *Queenfish*) was lucky enough to be offered bigger targets. On 8 January 1945 the Loopers were in the Formosa Strait when they picked up a big convoy heading for Takao. Comdr. Eugene E. Fluckey in the *Barb* got between the convoy and the coast to try to drive it into deeper water. He torpedoed an ammunition ship, which blew up like a volcano. The *Barb* hid in the mud for a while, then rose to destroy a second ammunition vessel.

The aggressive U.S. boats in the South and East China Seas and Mitscher's Fast Carrier Force, which pounded Formosa and the Ryukus, forced Japanese supply ships to steer inshore along the China coast, though the latter moved only in daylight, as the rocky shore was unlit. In 1944 492 marus had been sunk, nearly 2,400,000 tons'

The USS *Barb*. (U.S. National Archives)

worth, and targets were getting scarce. So when Looper intelligence placed a big convoy anchored off Wenchow, the *Barb* headed that way.

On 22 January 1945 the *Barb* picked up two ships steaming inshore in eight fathoms, but she lost them in the darkness. Fluckey went after them, finding the scores of scattered, darkened junks good cover even though they demanded alert ship handling. At 0300 he rounded Incog Island and was confronted with the convoy, his original target, anchored in the lower reaches of Namkwan harbor. Visibility was almost nil, three escorts guarded the best entrances to the harbor, patrol boats prowled, and searchlights swept the water. But Fluckey saw a stretch of unguarded rocky shore. With lookouts forward, the *Barb* crept past the jagged teeth of the rocks on either hand into six fathoms, and there was a dream target of thirty sitting ducks.

He fired five tin fish. With five fathoms of water beneath the boat, two more torpedoes left the tubes. He steered for the next column of ships and fired three more. A big tanker exploded and settled in the water, then another in the second column, and another, and a freighter, and another freighter . . . An ammunition ship's whole side blew out and another blew up in a cataclysmic blast. Then it was time to run, jinking through the junks at 22 knots, some of them hit by following fire. Two hours later the false sun of a convoy on fire was still glaring over the Ryukus.

By the beginning of February 1945, the Allies were closing in on Japan via Iwo Jima and Okinawa. The Japanese navy was now perilously weak. The marus still plied, but Allied submarines decimated them, none more decisively than Lt. Comdr. George Street's USS *Tirante* on her first patrol in the Yellow Sea.

Street left Pearl on 3 March. In the waters called the Hit Parade off the coast of Japan, he sank three tankers. Then he passed into the Yellow Sea, where the marus were hugging the coastal shallows. Penetrating strong escort screens, he launched four devastating torpedo attacks. He sank a big transport and was pounded by depth charges, then inched his way into a small, closely guarded, dangerously shallow harbor on the north shore of Quelport, negotiating patrol boats, mine fields, and radar stations. These failed to pick up the *Tirante*'s periscope among the assortment of vessels in the harbor.

With gun crew standing by below in case he was forced to surface and fight his way out, Street checked the current, fed the relevant data into his attack computer for a 10,000-ton tanker target, and fired two torpedoes. A huge mushroom of white, blinding flame rose 2,000 feet in the air, followed by a thunderous roar. The light revealed the *Tirante* to two new *Mikura*-class frigates, which steamed in for the kill. Swinging the *Tirante* around toward the leading frigate, Street fired two torpedoes down the throat, then swung toward the other vessel and gave her his last tin fish, confident that he had bagged them both, as the pursuit stopped.

The only Japanese major warships left in the southwest Pacific area were four heavy cruisers based at Singapore, two of them already damaged by U.S. submarines. Two Royal Navy submarines, Lt. R. G. P. Bulkeley's *Statesman* and Lt. B. J. B. Andrew's *Subtle*, were patrolling the Malacca Straits in early May when they sighted the heavy cruiser *Haguro*, which was making for Burma with supplies for the Japanese army. The submarines' reports brought up ships from Ceylon. The *Haguro* was sighted again and attacked by British Fleet Air Arm Avengers from the Lend-Lease escort carrier *Emperor* on 16 May. She was finished off by four British destroyers that night.

The *Trenchant*, under Comdr. A. R. Hezlet, RN, was patrolling the Java Sea in early June when she was ordered to the Malayan coast. On her way there she intercepted contact reports from the U.S. submarines *Blueback* and *Chub* that the heavy cruiser *Ashigara* had put into Batavia from Singapore. Hezlet received permission to follow his hunch and head for the Bangka Strait between the southeast coast of Sumatra and Bangka Island, through which he was sure the *Ashigara* would pass when she returned to Singapore. The *Trenchant*, having negotiated the mine field in the northern entrance to Bangka, took the inside of the Strait, the British submarine *Stygian* the other. On 8 June the *Blueback* reported that the *Ashigara* had left Batavia northbound.

A Japanese destroyer steamed up the Strait, fired at the *Trenchant*, and was missed by the *Stygian's* torpedo. Depth charges were exploding all around the *Trenchant* as Hezlet sighted the *Ashigara* heading north, hugging the Sumatran coast. He fired eight torpedoes from his bow tubes at a range of just over 2.5 miles. The *Ashigara* saw them coming but was so close inshore that she had only limited movement to seaward. Five hits reduced her to a shambles, though she moved ahead slowly to avoid Hezlet's stern torpedoes and opened fire briefly on the *Trenchant's* periscope before she sank.

Lying at Singapore, with her engines still inoperative after *Darter's* torpedo attack on the previous 23 October, was the heavy cruiser *Takao*. She lay behind dense and dangerous harbor defenses, but there was the possibility of a crash repair program, and the Royal Navy had some midget submarines available that might reach the crippled cruiser. These XE-craft were a development of the X-craft used against the *Tirpitz* in Norway. They had been specially designed for operations in the Far East, with longer range, better sea-keeping features, and air-conditioning. Soon after the sinking of the *Ashigara*, the *XE3* got through to the *Takao* and sank her at her moorings in the Straits of Jahore, then returned safely.

On 1 April 1945 the U.S. Marines had landed at Okinawa, and the battles on and around the island had drained Japanese traffic out of the East China Sea. Now the only "safe" approach to the Asian mainland for Japanese ships lay across the Sea of Japan. The *Wahoo* had been sunk there in the autumn of 1943, and since then these waters had been "no go" for U.S. submarines. Mines and patrol vessels blocked the La Perouse Strait to the north, which "Mush" Morton's *Wahoo* had used, and the Tsugaru Strait between Honshu and Kyushu, but the defenses in the Tsushima Strait in the southwest were not quite so dense.

Boffins and technicians in the University of California Division of War Research had developed a sophisticated type of sonar they claimed would detect a mine at 700 yards and permit a submarine to pass through a mine field, provided it was not unusually dense. Lockwood decided to trust this device to send a super–wolf pack into the Sea of Japan.

Nine boats assembled at Guam under Comdr. E. T. Hydeman for training with the new hardware and were christened Hydeman's Hellcats. The Hellcats were divided into three groups: Hydeman's Hellcats, with the *Sea Dog* (under Commander Hydeman), the *Crevalle* (Comdr. E. H. Steinmetz), and the *Spadefish* (Comdr. W. J. Germerhausen);

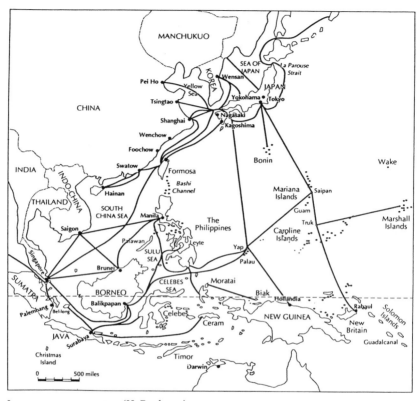

Japanese convoy routes. (K. Poolman)

Pierce's Polecats, with the *Tunny* (Comdr. G. E. Pierce), the *Skate* (Comdr. R. B. Lynch), and the *Bonefish* (Comdr. L. L. Edge); and Risser's Bobcats, with the *Flying Fish* (Comdr. R. D. Risser), the *Bowfin* (Comdr. A. K. Tyree), and the *Tinosa* (Comdr. R. C. Latham).

The Hellcats left Guam on 27 May for Tsushima. On passage the Bobcats acted as a lifeguard unit, and the *Tinosa* rescued ten men of a splashed B-29. On learning the boat's destination, one pilot said, "Hell, Commander, throw us back!"[2]

Reaching Tsushima Strait on 3 June, they divided into the three groups for the passage through. That night the *Sea Dog* dived and led her group into the Strait. The new device was named Hell's Bells, from the ringing tone of a mine in the operator's ears. By this time they were confident of differentiating between the real thing and the unwanted echoes reflected by fish, kelp, and thermal layers. Hydeman's own three boats surfaced in the Sea of Japan eighteen hours later. That night the Polecats went in. The *Skate* scraped a mine cable but they all made it, and the Bobcats steered safely through next day. By that time Hydeman's *Sea Dog*, *Crevalle*, and *Spadefish* had gone to their stations off northwest Honshu, the Polecats to the southeastern sector. Risser took his three boats to watch western waters off Korea.

On the evening of 9 June, the *Sea Dog* sank a freighter just north of Sado Shima Island with one torpedo, added another maru before midnight, and four more while her torpedoes lasted. Steinmetz's *Crevalle* bagged three, and Germerhausen's *Spadefish* sank five off Hokkaido.

The Polecats too scored well, off western Honshu. The *Tunny* had a running gunfight with two destroyers; Lynch in the *Skate* sank the submarine *I-122* when she crossed his bows at a range of 800 yards, and he surprised and sank three marus at anchor in Matugushita Cove. Edge's *Bonefish* sank a 6,892-ton freighter on 13 June and a 5,488-ton cargo liner a week later.

To the west, Risser's *Flying Fish* sank two marus and Tyree's *Bowfin* two more farther north. Off foggy Korea, Latham's *Tinosa* sent four freighters to the bottom after she had freed her screws from a fisherman's net.

Hydeman assembled eight Hellcats in yellow fog on the night of 24 June for departure through La Perouse Strait, confident by now in his Hell's Bells. In twelve days they had sunk twenty-seven marus and one submarine, a total of 57,000 tons. They entered Pearl Harbor on the Fourth of July, their jubilation tempered by the absence of the *Bonefish*.

At a second rendezvous with Pierce in the *Tunny*, Edge had asked permission to make a reconnaissance of the bay of Toyama Wan, farther up the Honshu coast. Pierce had agreed, the *Bonefish* had departed and was never heard from again. A Japanese antisubmarine hunting group reported an attack on a submarine in Toyama Wan that produced a lake of oil and the usual flotsam of a shattered submarine. The *Bonefish* was the last U.S. submarine sunk in World War II.

While the *Spadefish* was sinking marus off Hokkaido, not far away Fluckey in the *Barb* was bombarding the port of Shari and seal-fishery buildings. A moored fleet of sampans fired back without scoring. On 5 July the *Barb* sank a 2,820-ton freighter, moving on to plant a 55-pound demolition charge on the railway track, which blew up the last train from Sapporo. Then the *Barb* shot up canneries in the town of Chiri. At Shibertoro on the island of Kunashiri, the sub cruised along the waterfront in broad daylight, picking out a lumber mill, a sampan-building yard, and oil tanks with the 5-inch.

Other U.S. submarines entered the Sea of Japan in July, though targets were few. They bagged only eight marus and two escorts in two months. Sennett's *Chub* sank four small marus. When the war ended, there were five U.S. submarines in these waters.

On 5 August 1945, Admiral Lockwood ordered all his boats at sea to retire at least 100 miles from the coastline of Kyushu, and a big carrier strike on the island scheduled for the seventh was canceled. On 6 August the first atomic bomb was dropped on Hiroshima, and three days later the second fell on Nagasaki. On 14 August the *Torsk* sank two coastal vessels, the last Japanese ships to be sunk by a U.S. submarine. This was the day when Emperor Hirohito ordered his forces to lay down their arms, informing the Japanese people, in his first-ever broadcast to the nation, that "the war situation has developed not necessarily to Japan's advantage."[3]

The U.S. Navy had commissioned 288 new submarines for war service. More than 250 had served in the eastern theaters, and at least 185 had each sunk one or more enemy ships (some of them many more), a total of over 1,000 merchantmen and more than 200 warships. The prewar Japanese merchant marine of some 8,000,000 tons had been reduced to well under 2,500,000 tons. Japanese admirals asserted after the war that the American submarines, more than any other weapon, had brought about the fall of their empire, even allowing for the great destruction wrought by carrier planes. Of fifty-two U.S. submarines lost, thirty-seven were sunk with all hands.

Japanese destroyers and escort vessels were no match for the American underwater offensive, in spite of U.S. submarine losses. Japanese submarine hunters had an echo-ranging set similar to asdic and sonar, but at the end of 1943 they still lacked radar search receivers. Some sixty low-power (2-kilowatt) 10-cm sets were produced. The Japanese HF/DF network, though, with twelve stations from the Aleutians to Rabaul, was able to tell roughly how many U.S. submarines were at sea and in which areas.

Japanese intelligence failed to break any U.S. codes and believed, wrongly, that their own were secure. On 29 January 1943 in the Japanese submarine *I-7*, sunk off Guadalcanal, were found the new code books. They yielded up to U.S. Navy crytographers the key to an immense amount of information on ship movements. Admiral Lockwood estimated that this coup led to 30 percent of Japanese losses.

In six years of war, sea fighting had been of vital importance and had demanded enormous national effort by the belligerents—even by Germany, which had made the land and air war its priorities. In the Atlantic their U-boats had almost severed the link upon which victory in Europe depended. In the Pacific the United States Navy had not only recovered from early crippling losses, but had conveyed the United States Army, plus its air force, step by step forward to positions from which Japan could have been invaded. Never before had sea power been used so decisively so far from home bases.

Changes in equipment and technique had fundamentally altered traditional views of naval strategy. A principal change had been in the effect of aircraft. Hostilities had proved that in normal weather and daylight, the airplane and its new weapons had replaced the big gun. The new technology of radar had revolutionized sea warfare. With radar, carriers were able to use their fighters and antiaircraft guns effectively to defend themselves and their fleet despite efforts by enemy aircraft, shipborne or shore-based. With radar, an enemy surface vessel or aircraft could be found as easily at night or in bad visibility as in clear daylight. Ships' gunners could engage enemy vessels without ever seeing them. Asdic/sonar had not achieved the degree of success anticipated, but its faults had been countered by inventive tactics. The sonar buoy was a brilliant development. Improvements in guidance systems and explosives had made the torpedo a more decisive weapon, despite the improvement in ship construction.

The replenishment of ships—even whole fleets—at sea, without the need to return to a shore base, made possible the extended operations of the United States Navy in the Pacific. Even in the more restricted North Atlantic, German raiders, including submarines, were resupplied.

Disastrous failure of underprepared landings on enemy beaches in World War I led to the special landing craft and equipment and the improved cooperation between land, sea, and air forces that made amphibious warfare so successful in World War II. Seaborne assaults became not merely a standard form of warfare, but operations upon which final victory depended.

Notes

1 Secret Fleet

1. Padfield, *Dönitz, The Last Führer,* 141.

2 Soundings

1. Churchill, Winston, *The Second World War,* vol. 1, *The Gathering Storm,* 146–47.

4 Covered Wagons

1. The Short seaplane was designated 184 after the number allocated to the first machine. Later it was renumbered 225 from the horsepower of the first engine fitted. It first saw service in 1915. Engines: 240-horsepower Sunbeam or Renault; 250, 260, 275-horsepower Sunbeams. Performance with 260-horsepower Sunbeam: maximum speed 88.5 MPH at 2,000 feet, 84 MPH at 6,500 feet; endurance 2 hours; service ceiling 9,000 feet. Nine hundred 184s were built, the last being retained until May 1921.
2. William Mitchell, born 1879 of Scottish descent, enlisted in 1898 and in one week became the U.S. Army's youngest officer. In 1903, as a captain, he set up the first field radio station, at Fort Leavenworth, Kansas, and received a message from Puerto Rico, 1,900 miles away. The 10,000-foot antenna was carried aloft by a kite. At the age of thirty-six, he took flight training at the Curtiss school in Newport News, Virginia. On 17 March 1917 he was sent to Europe to observe the manufacture and development of aircraft. About this time he began open criticism of the outdated theories of warfare among army and navy brass. On 15 July 1918 his air reconnaissance of the Marne battlefield facilitated an Allied counterattack, but his idea for a parachute drop behind enemy lines by 1,200 Handley Page heavy bombers was rubbished by the General Staff. In 1919 he predicted a Japanese air attack on Pearl Harbor, with a probable time of attack as 0730 on a Sunday morning. He insisted loudly and publicly, to Congress and in the press, that the airplane and the submarine would be the

major weapons in the next war, that the battleship would succumb to the bomber. The successes by his army bombers against moored warships in the early 1920s appeared to support him. In 1925, however, he was court-martialed for insubordination. With practically his sole support coming from Douglas MacArthur, he was found guilty. Reduced to colonel and sent to Fort Sam Houston, Texas, away from contact with the Air Corps, he resigned from the service. Afterward he toured the States, speaking publicly of the urgent need for a strong air arm, carriers, fast fighters, and long-range bombers. He died in 1936, with his far-sighted theories as yet unproven.

3. Creswell, *Sea Warfare, 1939–1945*, 14.
4. Author's interview with Comdr. Anthony Oliver, RN, London, 12 November 1954.

5 Wolf at the Door

1. Padfield, *Dönitz, the Last Führer*, 181.
2. Cargo and passenger liners of 8,000–20,000 tons with twin screws; top speed of at least 15 knots; range of at least 4,500 miles (6,000 miles preferred); space for naval crew with boarding parties and prize crews; suitable locations, not less than 14 feet above the waterline, for at least eight 6-inch guns. Peacetime modifications: stiffening of scantlings near gun locations; fitting of gun-pedestal packing rings; shoring-up of gun decks with steel plate. Early conversions in 1939 were armed with guns made in 1909, 1901, even 1895, previously used in action.
3. Author's interview with Capt. B. S. McEwan, RN, 1955.

6 Panzer Ship

1. Arado Ar 196A-1 twin-float monoplane. Delivery of the first twenty began in June 1939, and the *Graf Spee*'s was one of the first to go to sea. Wings and tail were of metal stressed-skin, fuselage light alloy over welded steel tubes forward, fabric-covered aft. Fuel was carried in two 66-gallon tanks, one in each float. A BMW 132K 960-horsepower engine driving a Schwarz three-bladed propeller produced a maximum speed of 194 MPH at 3,280 feet and a range of 497 miles. Armament: one aft-mounted 7.92-mm MG 15 machine gun with seven 75-round saddle-type magazines, and a container on each wing for one SC50 110-pound bomb. Handling was outstanding, both on water and airborne.
2. HMS *Cumberland*, 10,000-ton heavy cruiser of the New County class, built 1926–29, with eight 8-inch guns, top speed 32 knots. Poorly armored and expensive to run, they were called, partly from their tropical paint scheme of white hulls and yellow funnels, Whited Sepulchres.
3. Dudley Pope, *The Battle of the River Plate*, 98.
4. Ibid., 103.
5. Ibid., 139.
6. Ibid., 147.
7. Ibid., 146.
8. In addition to the armed merchant cruisers, ten small British merchantmen were fitted out as decoy ships. They had false funnels and bulwarks; dummy deckhouses; deck cargoes and derricks; and covered-in welldecks. These disguised an armament of three to five 4-inch guns and various mixes of two 12-pounder or 20-mm antiaircraft guns, as well as torpedo tubes. HMS *Fidelity* also carried two aircraft and a motor torpedo boat. They had little success.

7 Air Power, Norway

1. Quisling was executed as a traitor in 1945.
2. Designated A-36 or Apache, the Mustang's original name.
3. Letter to the author from Lt. Comdr. H. A. Monk, DSC and Bar, RN (Ret.), 22 February 1988.
4. Ibid.
5. Ibid.
6. Ibid.
7. U-boat Type IXB, a large fleet boat of 1,000 tons.
8. Letter to the author from Lieutenant Commander Monk.
9. Author's interview with Vice Adm. St. G. Lumley Lyster, RN, 16 October 1954.

8 *Bismarck* and the 284

1. HMS *Malaya*, battleship of the *Queen Elizabeth* class of five ships, built 1913–15, 27,500 tons, eight 15-inch guns, top speed 26 knots.
2. HMS *Rodney*, battleship of the *Nelson* class of two ships. Built in 1925, they were to have been super-battleships of 50,000 tons, but the Washington Naval Treaty of 1922 limited battleship size to 35,000 tons. As a result, the *Nelson* and *Rodney* lost their two after turrets, emerging with three triple 16-inch turrets, all forward. Their lack of astern fire was criticized, but armor protection could thus be concentrated over a much-shorter stretch of hull.
3. Letter to the author from William Earp, 15 January 1988.

9 Wolf Pack

1. Allied convoy code letters were:
   Flight Convoy ferrying aircraft
   GU   Gibraltar to USA
   HG   Gibraltar to Britain
   HX   Halifax to Britain
   JW   Britain to Russia
   KM   Britain to Gibraltar
   MK   Gibraltar to Britain
   OB   Liverpool to Halifax
   OG   Britain to Gibraltar
   ON   Britain to Halifax
   OS   Britain to West Africa
   PQ   Britain to Russia
   QP   Russia to Britain
   SC   Britain to USA
   SL   West Africa to Britain
   SLF   West Africa to Britain (fast)
   SLS   West Africa to Britain (slow)
   UG   USA to Gibraltar
2. In World War I the British Grand Fleet's base at Scapa Flow, the wide anchorage in the Orkney Islands north of Scotland, had proved impregnable, but by 1939 northern weather had eroded the Kirk Sound entrance. A Dornier Do 215B-1 reconnaissance

plane reported this, and on the moonless night of 13–14 October Kapitänleutnant Gunther Prien's *U-47* got through at high tide into the Flow and sank the old battleship *Royal Oak* after expending seven torpedoes. Prien was awarded the Iron Cross, and shortly afterward Dönitz was promoted to Befehlshaber der U-boote (BdU).

3. The Short Sunderland flying boat was widely used by RAF Coastal Command for maritime reconnaissance, convoy escort, and search-and-rescue work. Eight 0.303-inch machine guns were carried, four of them in a power-operated tail turret. Four Bristol Pegasus XXII engines produced a top speed of 210 MPH at 6,500 feet and a range of at least 1,250 miles. The large hull was double decked, with a workshop and a well-stocked galley that won the Sunderland an unsurpassed reputation for hospitality.

10 Mother of Invention

1. Letter to the author from Mr. Ron Spencer, 10 January 1988.
2. Sea Hurricanes from CAM ships *Empire Darwin, Empire Lawrence, Empire Moon, Empire Morn,* and *Empire Tide* destroyed Condors and Heinkel He 111s.
3. MAC ships made 170 round trips with Atlantic convoys, a total of 4,447 days at sea, including 3,057 spent in convoy. Flying took place on 1,183 of these days, with the merchant Swordfish putting in 9,016 flying hours on 4,177 sorties. MACs were quickly and inexpensively convertible. Attacks by their Swordfish often prevented U-boats from attacking. Out of 207 convoys in which a MAC was included, only one was successfully attacked by U-boats. If there was a MAC in the convoy, everyone slept better.
4. RAF Hurricanes were converted to Sea Hurricane Mark IAs, with catapult spools for operation from fighter-catapult and CAM ships, and Mark IBs with arrester hooks for carrier work.
5. After early failures of gyro compass, steering gear, and radar in December 1941, the *Archer,* typically of her class, suffered from persistent engine breakdowns, mostly due to the continual failure of the magnetic clutch connecting her Busche-Sultzer diesels to the propeller shaft. As she berthed in June 1943 for a thorough refit in Hoboken next to her sister the *Dasher,* the latter's Sun-Droxford diesels backfired explosively, her exhaust vents excreting shards of sharp metal.
6. Giles Elza Short, born in Lohrville, Iowa. U.S. Naval Academy, Annapolis, 1915–18; qualified naval aviator Pensacola, Florida; Scouting Squadron 1; Bombing Squadron 5, USS *Langley;* command of Patrol Squadron 5, June 1943; fitted out, commissioned and commanded Bombing Squadron 7, USS *Yorktown;* air-group commander, USS *Enterprise,* 1939; staff, Naval War College, 1941; joined USS *Bogue* at Seattle Tacoma yard, June 1942.
7. Many of the *Bogue's* ship's company were survivors from the USS *Lexington,* sunk on 8 May 1942 in the Battle of the Coral Sea.

11 Firepower, Arctic

1. U.S.-converted auxiliary carriers were first designated AVG, the first six, allocated to the Royal Navy, being BAVG (for British). The AVGs were reclassified ACV on 20 August 1942, and reclassified again on 15 July 1943 as CVE. E was for escort, as distinct from CVL for light carrier and CV for fleet carrier. To many crew members, CVE stood for Combustible Vulnerable Expendable.

12 Battle of the Boffins

1. In simple terms, the basic Schlusselmascine E (cipher machine E), or Enigma, resembling a cross between a portable typewriter and an old-style cash register, contained five adjustable rotors or drums on a shaft, allowing a choice of any three for use. Each rotor was marked with an alphabet around the outside and wired so that a letter selected by a typewriter-type key could be passed from one rotor to the others in succession or back again, producing sixty different transpositions. Then they were transposed once more through a plugboard's electrically interconnected letter display. The final result appeared in an illuminated aperture for the encoding operator to use. Tables of settings, changed daily and known as keys, enciphered the signal even further. The Kriegsmarine version of Enigma captured aboard the *U-110* could select any four rotors from a total of eight, making the permutations almost limitless.
2. In May 1954 the *U-505* was towed to a floating dock on Lake Michigan from Portsmouth, New Hampshire, via the Atlantic, the St. Lawrence River, the Welland Canal, and Lakes Ontario, Erie, and Huron, preparatory to installation at the Chicago Museum of Science and Industry. To beach her there the U-boat was jacked up inside the dock above the level of the lake in a special cradle on rollers above a rail track. Dock and contents were towed across the lake despite a high water surge, and the busy Outer Drive highway was closed with the note Drive Carefully: Submarine Crossing, so that the *U-505* could be hauled to her site at the museum.

13 Torpedoes at Taranto

1. Hansard daily record of proceedings, House of Commons, London. Speech on the Navy Estimates, March 1939.
2. Four Sea Gladiators had been left in crates by HMS *Glorious* when she had departed in a hurry for Norway. Three were made operational and nicknamed Faith, Hope, and Charity by the Maltese. Two of these obsolete fighters deflected the first bombing raid.
3. These machines had flown from Hyères in southern France, where they had been training and practicing touchdowns with the old carrier *Argus*.
4. A term coined by the American admiral Alfred T. Mahan (1840–1914), naval historian and strategist (*The Influence of Sea Power Upon History, 1660–1783*, published 1890, and *The Influence of Sea Power Upon the French Revolution, 1793–1812*, published 1892). A fleet in being is a fleet possessing great potential power that is held back in harbor to influence an enemy's conduct of the war, in particular to force him into a wasteful deployment of sea power to guard against a breakout. The fleet in being rarely puts to sea. Two fleets that did were the Italian Fleet in World War II and the German High Seas Fleet in World War I.

14 Stuka Strada

1. Quoted in obituary notice on Captain Phillips, *Sunday Telegraph*, 5 October 1995.
2. These torpedoes would also explode if they made contact with a ship's hull. Hence Duplex, meaning double.
3. From *My Dear and Only Love* by James Graham, 1st Marquis of Montrose, Scottish general, poet, and supporter of King Charles I against Parliament in the English civil war of 1642–48.

4. Single-engine, three-seater British Fairey Albacore biplane naval bomber with enclosed cockpit and all-metal monocoque fuselage, powered by sleeve-valve 1,065-horsepower Bristol Taurus II or 1,130-horsepower XII to give a maximum speed of 161 MPH at 4,000 feet, a very rapid takeoff, and excellent fuel economy in cruise. Hydraulic flaps formed air brakes for dive-bombing. The Albacore supplemented the Swordfish, which it was intended to replace, in attacks on European ports and carrier operations in the Arctic, Atlantic, Mediterranean, and Indian Ocean. It also covered the Sicily and Salerno invasions from HMS *Formidable*.
5. David Brown, *The Seafire*, 19.

15 The New Dreadnoughts

1. Stanley Goodall, British director of Naval Aviation, on a visit to the United States Navy's Bureau of Construction and Repair, Washington, 1918. See Humble, *United States Fleet Carriers of World War II*, 14.
2. Signatories to the Nine Power Treaty were the United States, Canada, Britain, France, Japan, China, the Netherlands, Belgium, and Portugal, all nations with Pacific interests.
3. After the Washington Naval Treaty of 1922, the United States faithfully limited new construction. But the figures for new ships from 1922 to 1927 were: United States 120,000 tons, Britain 285,000 tons, Japan 339,000 tons. The Geneva Convention of 1927 was wrecked by Britain's insistence on an unacceptably large number of cruisers and their limitation to 7,500 tons apiece, with 6-inch guns, whereas the United States voted for 10,000 tons and 8-inch guns. At the London Conference of 1930, however, each nation was allowed a majority of its choice, with a common global limit of 330,000 tons.
4. These ships were old but had been refitted and fully stored with shells, torpedoes, and depth charges; binoculars for officers and lookouts; sextants and chronometers for the navigating officer; paint and cordage; silver cutlery and china crockery; typewriter and stationery in the ship's office; canned hams, fruit, corn, and a refrigerator packed with T-bone steaks.
5. Admiral Isoroku Yamamoto (1884–1943), Japan's leading naval strategist, principal architect of its air-based modern navy and inspiration of its naval effort. Formerly a Harvard student and naval attaché in Washington, he forced through the Pearl Harbor plan as the only way to preempt U.S. industrial power in war. With the U.S. carriers untouched, he promoted the Midway offensive. As head of his navy's technical branch, he sponsored the Zero fighter.
6. Vice Adm. Chichi Nagumo (1887–1944), an expert in torpedo warfare and outstanding destroyer-squadron commander. Once an energetic advocate of breaking the Washington Naval Treaty, by 1942 "his once-vigorous fighting spirit seemed to have gone" (Fuchida and Okumiya, *Midway*, 130), and he lacked confidence in commanding an air fleet. Failures at Midway and Guadalcanal lost him this command and he was posted to Saipan, where he later committed hara-kiri rather than surrender.

16 "Hit 'Em When You Can"

1. Comdr. Mitsuo Fuchida (1902–76), veteran naval aviator, led the Pearl Harbor attack but was in sick bay for the Midway battle and lost a leg in the bombing of the *Akagi*. After the war he converted to Christianity and became a Protestant minister, frequently preaching to Japanese immigrants in North America. He became a U.S. citizen in 1966.
2. Richard Humble, *United States Fleet Carriers of World War II*, 40.

3. President Franklin Delano Roosevelt's radio address to the American nation, 8 December 1941.
4. Frank and Harrington, *Rendezvous at Midway*, 21.
5. Brewster Buffalo single-seat fighter, maximum speed 313 MPH at 13,500 feet, range 650 miles with one 1,200-horsepower Wright Cyclone engine.
6. Humble, *U.S. Fleet Carriers*, 40.
7. Frank and Harrington, *Rendezvous at Midway*, 21.

17 The Carrier Weapon: Midway

1. In Japan's huge expansion from an enclosed feudal society to a world military power, the officer class was dominated by a revival, after a long decline, of the ethics of the medieval samurai caste. This had emerged in the twelfth century from clans of provincial warriors (*bushi*) to establish the Bushido ("way of the warrior") code of behavior. Bushido was based on pride in military and athletic skills, fearlessness in battle, honor, filial piety, honesty, and above all unquestioning loyalty to a feudal lord (daimyo or shogun, later emperor). Ritual suicide by disembowelment (seppuku or hara-kiri) was established to avoid or follow dishonor or defeat. Samurai members were entitled to wear two special swords.
2. Divine Wind (kamikaze) after the typhoon that destroyed a Mongol invasion fleet in 1281.
3. Fuchida and Okumiya, *Midway*, 154.
4. Ibid., 161.
5. Ibid., 164.
6. Ibid., 171.
7. Ibid., 174.
8. Ibid., 175.
9. The old *Nautilus* had risen in the midst of the Japanese striking force. Lt. Comdr. William H. Brockman was ranging on a battleship when he was attacked from the air and hunted by escorts. Later he rose and sighted a Japanese carrier, which he thought was the *Soryu* but was more likely the *Kaga*, bigger but similar in appearance.
10. Fuchida and Okumiya, *Midway*, 181.
11. Some five hours before this, Brockman in the *Nautilus* had sighted what he assumed to be the enemy carrier he had seen previously. This time a thick pall of smoke lay over the flight deck, and the ship moved at a cripple's pace. On the forecastle men appeared to be preparing a towing hawser. At 1359 Brockman fired three torpedoes and later reported three explosions, with men lowering boats. Damage-control officer Lieutenant Commander Kurisada in the *Kaga* saw two torpedoes miss the ship and the other hit but fail to explode. The latter broke in two, the warhead sinking. The buoyant after section was grabbed by sailors in the water.
12. Fuchida and Okumiya, *Midway*, 194.
13. Ibid., 215.
14. The *Ryujo* and *Sanyo* accompanied the Aleutian attack force.

18 Microwaves and Long Lances: Guadalcanal

1. Richard Humble, *United States Fleet Carriers of World War II*, 88.

19 Kaisers and Kamikazes

1. Herman Wouk, *The Caine Mutiny*, 111. Keefer is quoting from the Bible, Joel 3:14: "Multitudes, multitudes in the valley of decision! For the day of the Lord is near in

the valley of decision, The sun and the moon are darkened, and the stars withdraw their shining."

2. The Wildcat FM-1 was a version of the F4F-4, with the outer pair of guns eliminated but the number of rounds increased from 1,440 to 1,720. It was built by the Eastern Aircraft Division of General Motors at Linden, New Jersey.

3. The rugged Grumman F6F Hellcat, successor to the Wildcat, proved more than a match for the Zero beginning with the Gilbert Islands operation. It had greater speed, acceleration, and firepower. Power plant of the F6F-5 was a 2,000-horsepower Pratt and Whitney R-2800-10W Double Wasp 18-cylinder engine; maximum speed 386 MPH at medium altitude; climb 3,410 feet per minute; range on internal fuel 1,040 miles; armament six .5-inch Browning machine guns, each with 400 rounds. It had provision for 2,000 pounds of bombs and six 5-inch HVAR rocket projectiles. A total of 12,274 Hellcats were built, 1,262 of them for the British Fleet Air Arm.

4. On 15 March 1943 the ships of the United States Navy's Central Pacific Force, commanded at the time by Vice Admiral Spruance, were designated the Fifth Fleet. Thereafter command of this fleet alternated between Admirals Spruance and Halsey. Under Spruance's command it was the Fifth Fleet, under Halsey's it was the Third Fleet. Its constituent parts followed the procedure. The Fast Carrier Force was alternately Task Force 58 and Task Force 38.

5. The Wildcat FM-2, built by General Motors, was a version of the FM-1 specially designed for the short decks of escort carriers. Its Pratt and Whitney R-1820-56 engine contributed to a 500-pound reduction in weight and gave an improved output of 1,350 horsepower at 2,700 RPM, compared with the 1,200 horsepower at 2,900 RPM of the F4F's R-1830-86.

6. Prototype Grumman Avenger XTBF-1 first flew in August 1941. From November 1942 General Motors' subsidiary Eastern Aircraft built the near-identical model TBM. In early 1944 Grumman stopped production of the TBF, after delivering 2,290 of them. All subsequent Avengers were built by Eastern, 7,546 in all. The TBMs were fitted with the 1,900-horsepower Wright R-2600-20, most powerful of the wartime R-2600 series. Maximum speed of TBF and TBM was 275 MPH, range on internal fuel 1,100 miles. Bomb and torpedo load was 2,000 pounds.

7. Derived from naphthalene, a liquid hydrocarbon contained in naphtha, a flammable oil distilled from petroleum.

8. A fatty acid ($C_{16}H_3O_2$), colorless, odorless, and tasteless, lighter than water, and solid at ordinary temperatures. Contained in palm oil and in vegetable and animal fats, generally.

9. C. Vann Woodward. *The Battle for Leyte Gulf*, 159.

20 The Hit Parade

1. Letter from Mr. Iain Nethercott to the author, 2 October 1988.
2. Interview by the author of Rear Adm. Richard O'Kane, U.S. Navy. London, 11 February 1988.
3. The Reader's Digest, *The World at Arms*, 443.

Select Bibliography

Interviews and Correspondence

Earp, William. Letter to author, 15 January 1988.
Lyster, Vice Adm. St. G. Lumley, RN. Interview with author, London, 12 November 1954.
McEwan, Capt. B. S., RN. Interview with author, 1955.
Monk, Lt. Comdr. H. A., RN (Ret.). Letter to author, 22 January 1988.
Nethercott, Iain. Letter to author, 2 October 1988.
O'Kane, Rear Adm. Richard, U.S. Navy (Ret.). Interview with author, London, 11 February 1988.
Oliver, Comdr. Anthony, RN. Interview with author, London, 12 November 1954.
Spencer, Ronald. Letter to author, 10 January 1988.

Printed U.S. Government Documents

King, Admiral Ernest J., commander in chief, United States Fleet, and chief of naval operations. Reports to the secretary of the United States Navy, 1 March to 8 December 1945, covering combat operations.

Autobiographies, Memoirs, and Firsthand Accounts

Anscombe, Charles. *Submariner.* London: Kimber, 1957.
Beach, Edward. *Submarine!* London: Heinemann, 1953.
Brown, Eric. *Wings on My Sleeve.* London: Barker, 1976.
———. *Wings of the Navy.* London: Airlife, 1989.
Churchill, Winston S. *The Second World War.* London: Penguin Books, 1988.
Clark, Joseph J. *Carrier Admiral.* New York: McKay, 1967.
Gallery, Daniel V. *We Captured a U-boat.* London: Sidgwick, 1957.
Hill, Roger. *Destroyer Captain.* London: Kimber, 1975.
Jubelin, André. *The Flying Sailor.* London: Hurst and Blackett, 1953.
Lamb, Charles. *War in a Stringbag.* London: Cassell, 1977.
Lloyd, Sir Hugh. *Briefed to Attack.* London: Hodder, 1949.
MacIntyre, Donald. *U-boat Killer.* London: Weidenfeld, 1956.
———. *Battle of The Atlantic.* London: Batsford, 1961.

———. *Fighting Under the Sea.* London: Evans, 1965.

Mars, Alastair. *Unbroken.* London: Muller, 1953.

———. *British Submarines at War.* London: Kimber, 1959.

O'Kane, Richard. *Clear the Bridge.* London: Jane's, 1977.

Raeder, Erich. *Struggle for the Sea.* London: Kimber, 1959.

Tameichi, Hara. *Japanese Destroyer Captain.* New York: Ballantine, 1969.

Other Books

Alden, C. S., and A. Westcott. *The United States Navy.* London: Robert Hale, 1946.

Alden, John D. *The Fleet Submarine in the U.S. Navy.* Annapolis, Md.: Naval Institute Press, 1979.

Archibald, E. H. H. *The Fighting Ship in the Royal Navy.* Poole, Dorset, U.K.: Blandford Press, 1989.

Bagnasco, Erminio. *Submarines of World War Two.* London: Arms and Armour Press, 1977.

Baxter, Charles. *Stand By to Surface.* London: Cassell, 1944.

Bekker, Cajus. *The Luftwaffe War Diaries.* London: Jane's, 1966.

Belote, James H., and William M. Belote. *Titans of the Seas.* New York: Harper, 1975.

Blair, Clay, Jr. *Silent Victory.* New York: Lippincott, 1975.

Brennecke, Jochen. *The Hunters and the Hunted.* London: Burke, 1958.

Brown, David. *The Seafire.* Shepperton, Middlesex, U.K.: Ian Allan, 1973.

———. *The Spitfire That Went to Sea.* Annapolis, Md.: Naval Institute Press, 1989.

Bryan, J., III. *Mission Beyond Darkness.* New York: Duell, 1945.

———. *Aircraft Carrier.* New York: Ballantine, 1954.

Carse, Robert. *Blockade.* New York: Rinehart, 1958.

Cave Brown, Anthony. *Bodyguard of Lies.* New York: Harper and Row, 1975.

Compton-Hall, Richard. *The Underwater War.* Poole, Dorset, U.K.: Blandford Press, 1969.

Costello, John, and Terry Hughes. *Battle of the Atlantic.* London: Collins, 1977.

Creswell, John. *Sea Warfare, 1939–1945.* London: Longmans, 1950.

Davis, Burke. *The Billy Mitchell Affair.* New York: Random House, 1967.

Frank, Wolfgang. *The Sea Wolves.* London: Weidenfeld, 1955.

Frank, Pat, and Joseph D. Harrington. *Rendezvous at Midway.* New York: Paper Library, 1968.

Friedman, Norman. *USS Yorktown.* Annapolis, Md.: Leeward, 1977.

———. *Submarine Design Developments.* London: Conway Maritime, 1984.

Fuchida, Mitsuo, and Masatake Okumiya. *Midway.* London: Hutchinson, 1961.

Grant, Robert M. *U-boats Destroyed.* New York: Putnam, 1964.

Green, William. *Warplanes of the Third Reich.* London: Jane's, 1970.

Halpern, Paul G. *A Naval History of World War I.* Annapolis, Md.: Naval Institute Press, 1994.

Harrison, W. A. *Swordfish Special.* Shepperton, Middlesex, U.K.: Ian Allan, 1977.

Hart, Sydney. *Submarine Upholder.* London: Oldbourne, 1960.

Herzog, Bodo. *U-boats in Action 1939–45.* Shepperton, Middlesex, U.K.: Ian Allan, 1970.

Holmes, W. J. *Undersea Victory.* New York: Doubleday, 1966.

Humble, Richard. *United States Fleet Carriers of World War II.* Poole, Dorset, U.K.: Blandford Press, 1984.

Jameson, Sir William. *The Most Formidable Thing.* London: Hart-Davies, 1965.

Jensen, Oliver. *Carrier War.* New York: Simon and Schuster, 1945.

Johnson, Brian. *The Secret War.* London: British Broadcasting Corporation, 1978.

Jones, Geoffrey. *The Month of the Lost U-boats.* London: Kimber, 1977.

Kemp, Paul J. *British Submarines in World War II.* London: Arms and Armour Press, 1987.

Kemp, P. K. *Victory at Sea, 1939–1945.* London: Muller, 1952.

Lewis, David D. *The Fight for the Sea*. New York: New World, 1961.

Leyland, Eric. *Crash Dive*. London: Edmund Ward, 1961.

Lockwood, Charles A. *Battles of the Phillipine Sea*. New York: Crowell, 1967.

Lord, Walter. *Incredible Victory*. London: Hamish Hamilton, 1968.

Lund, Paul, and Harry Ludlam. *Night of the U-boats*. London: Foulsham, 1973.

Masters, David I. D. *New Tales of the Submarine War*. London: Eyre and Spottiswood, 1975.

———. *Up Periscope*. London: Eyre and Spottiswood, 1976.

Miller, Max. *Daybreak for our Carrier*. New York: Whittlesey, 1944.

Natkiel, Richard, and Anthony Preston. *Atlas of Maritime History*. London: Weidenfeld, 1986.

Newhafer, Richard L. *The Last Tallyho*. New York: Putnam, 1964.

Padfield, Peter. *Dönitz, the Last Führer*. London: Gollancz, 1984.

Poolman, Kenneth. *Faith Hope and Charity*. London: Kimber, 1954.

———. *Night Strike from Malta*. London: Macdonald and Jane's, 1978.

———. *Scourge of the Atlantic*. London: Jane's, 1978.

———. *The Sea Hunters*. London: Arms and Armour Press, 1982.

———. *Allied Escort Carriers of World War II in Action*. Poole, Dorset, U.K.: Blandford Press, 1988.

———. *Allied Submarines of World War II in Action*. London: Arms and Armour Press, 1989.

Potter, E. B., and Chester W. Nimitz. *The Great Sea War*. London: Harrap, 1960.

Pratt, Fletcher. *The Compact History of The United States Navy*. New York: Harper, 1942.

———. *Fleet Against Japan*. New York: Harper and Row, 1944.

———. *The Navy's War*. New York: Harper, 1944.

Preston, Anthony. *U-boats*. London: Arms and Armour Press, 1978.

Reynolds, Clark G. *The Fast Carriers*. New York: McGraw-Hill, 1968.

———. *Command of the Sea*. New York: Morrow, 1974.

———. *The Carrier War*. New York: Time-Life, 1981.

———. *The Fighting Lady*. Missoula, Mont.: Pictorial Publishing Company, 1986.

Rohwer, Jürgen. *The Critical Convoy Battles of March 1943*. Shepperton, Middlesex, U.K.: Ian Allan, 1970.

Rohwer, Jürgen, and G. Hummelchen. *Chronology of the War at Sea*. Shepperton, Middlesex, U.K.: Ian Allan, 1972–74.

Roskill, S. W. *Poems 1942–67*. London: Eyre and Spottiswoode, 1967.

Ross, Alan. *Poems 1942–67*. London: Eyre and Spottiswoode, 1967.

Ruge, F. *Sea Warfare 1939–1945*. London: Cassell, 1957.

Rush, C. W. *The Complete Book of Submarines*. New York: World, 1955.

Showell, J. P. *U-boats Under the Swastika*. Shepperton, Middlesex, U.K.: Ian Allan, 1973.

Smith, Peter C. *The Story of the Torpedo Bomber*. London: Almark, 1974.

———. *Dive Bombers in Action*. Poole, Dorset, U.K.: Blandford Press, 1988.

Spurr, Russell. *A Glorious Way to Die*. New York: Newmarket, 1981.

Steichen, Edward. *The Blue Ghost*. New York: Harcourt Brace, 1947.

Thetford, Owen. *British Naval Aircraft Since 1912*. London: Putnam, 1991.

Thomas, David A. *Submarine Victory*. London: Kimber, 1961.

Tillman, Barrett A. *Hellcat*. Annapolis, Md.: Naval Institute Press, 1979.

Turner, J. F. *Periscope Patrol*. London: Harrap, 1957.

Warren, C. E. T., and James Benson. *The Admiralty Regrets*. London: Harrap, 1958.

Wemyss, D. E. G. *Relentless Pursuit*. London: New English Library, 1974.

Werner, Herbert J. *Iron Coffins*. London: Barker, 1969.

Winterbotham, F. W. *The Ultra Secret*. London: Weidenfelt, 1974.

Winton, John. *The Victoria Cross at Sea*. London: Michael Joseph, 1987.

Woodward, C. Vann. *The Battle for Leyte Gulf*. London: Four Square, 1958.

Wouk, Herman. *The Caine Mutiny.* London: Fontana/Collins, 1989.
Y'Blood, William T. *Red Sun Setting.* Annapolis, Md.: Naval Institute Press, 1981.

Other Published Sources

U.S. Navy Department, Naval History Division. *Dictionary of American Naval Fighting Ships.* Washington, D.C., 1959–81.
————. *U.S. Submarine Losses World War II.* Washington, D.C., 1963.
The World at Arms. London: The Reader's Digest Association, 1989.

Index

About the Author

Kenneth Poolman, whose father served in submarines in World War I and cruisers in World War II, himself spent 1943–46 in minesweepers, destroyers, and aircraft carriers. When he returned to civilian life he attended Cambridge University and eventually worked for the BBC as a writer/producer of documentaries for radio and as a script editor for television.

He has twenty-three books published, mostly on air-sea warfare in World War II. He is also the author of radio and television scripts and many articles on maritime and air warfare. His first book, *The Kelly* (a history of Early Mountbatten's wartime destroyer command), was commissioned after a radio feature program for the BBC.